Tolerance

TOLERANCE

A Sensorial Orientation to Politics

Lars Tønder

OXFORD
UNIVERSITY PRESS

OXFORD
UNIVERSITY PRESS

Oxford University Press is a department of the University of Oxford.
It furthers the University's objective of excellence in research, scholarship,
and education by publishing worldwide.

Oxford   New York
Auckland   Cape Town   Dar es Salaam   Hong Kong   Karachi
Kuala Lumpur   Madrid   Melbourne   Mexico City   Nairobi
New Delhi   Shanghai   Taipei   Toronto

With offices in
Argentina   Austria   Brazil   Chile   Czech Republic   France   Greece
Guatemala   Hungary   Italy   Japan   Poland   Portugal   Singapore
South Korea   Switzerland   Thailand   Turkey   Ukraine   Vietnam

Oxford is a registered trademark of Oxford University Press
in the UK and certain other countries.

Published in the United States of America by
Oxford University Press
198 Madison Avenue, New York, NY 10016

© Oxford University Press 2013

Library of Congress Cataloging-in-Publication Data
Tønder, Lars, 1972–
Tolerance : a sensorial orientation to politics/Lars Tønder.
pages cm
Includes bibliographical references and index.
ISBN 978–0–19–931581–9 (pbk.:alk. paper)—ISBN 978–0–19–931580–2 (hardcover:alk. paper)
1. Toleration.   2. Pluralism.   3. Democracy.   I. Title.
HM1271.T668 2013
179'.9—dc23
2013002346

9 8 7 6 5 4 3 2 1
Printed in the United States of America
on acid-free paper

For Sacra

CONTENTS

ACKNOWLEDGMENTS

This book is the result of a long journey that began in earnest at the University of Copenhagen, where I first encountered the study of political theory. Although I had no clear idea about the itinerary, let alone the final destination, it is hard to imagine a better experience. I am pleased to acknowledge the many institutions that supported me while I was writing this book, and to express my deep gratitude to an even greater number of people whom I had the good fortune to learn from along the way.

It has been a pleasure to complete this book in the Department of Political Science at Northwestern University. The department in general, and the political theory group in particular, has been a steadfast fixture, never failing to offer the support and encouragement needed to make the solitude of book writing tolerable. Equally important is my colleagues' commitment to interdisciplinary research and conversations across subfields, something to which I have grown happily accustomed. While at Northwestern, I have also benefited from several other groups and programs, including the French Interdisciplinary Group, the Rhetoric and Public Culture Cluster, the Critical Theory Cluster, the Phenomenology Workshop, the Center for Global Culture and Communication, and the Alice Kaplan Institute for the Humanities. I thank students and faculty in all of these places for lending me an ear, for sharing their impressions, and for making critical theory, broadly understood, such a worthwhile enterprise. I also thank the Humanities Council for granting me a 2009–10 Alice Kaplan Institute for the Humanities fellowship, and the Dean's Office in the Weinberg College of Arts and Sciences for its generosity with leave time and research funds.

My time as a graduate student in political theory at Johns Hopkins University was crucial to the development of the ideas, readings, and arguments presented in this book. I owe thanks to the Department of Political Science at Johns Hopkins for inviting me into its family of students and faculty, and to the Danish Social Research Council for financial support during my first three years of graduate studies. My biggest debt—one I cannot overstate—is to my two dissertation advisors at Hopkins, William Connolly and Jane Bennett. Ever since we met at the University of Essex on a rainy November day back in 1999, I have benefited from their astute insights and ongoing support. Bill introduced me to the image of thought underpinning Spinoza's philosophy of immanence, and Jane taught me the importance of linking political theory to the wondrous remainders of lived experience. Without the encouragement each of them offered, the journey might never have started; and the book itself would certainly not have turned out the way it did without their unwavering willingness to discuss and explore its various parts.

During the time of writing the book, I have benefited from help on three occasions in particular. The first was a book manuscript workshop generously supported with funds from the John D. and Catherine T. MacArthur Foundation. The workshop brought John Seery, Patchen Markell, Diana Coole, and Hasana Sharp to Evanston for two days of intense discussion, which opened up new lines of inquiry and forced me to rethink issues I thought I had settled. I thank John, Patchen, Diana, and Hasana for taking time out of their busy schedules, for sharing their unparalleled wealth of knowledge, and for bringing their individual perspectives and contagious sense of humor to bear on the texts and topics discussed in this book. Needless to say, neither they nor anyone else other than myself is responsible for whatever mistakes or weaknesses remain in the final product.

The two other occasions that helped me finish the book were a pair of month-long visits to Centre d'Études en Rhétorique, Philosophie et Histoire des Idées (CERPHI) at École Normale Supérieure Lettres et Sciences Humaines in Lyon, France. The visits to CERPHI offered a break from my daily routine and gave me the tranquility needed to think and write. I would like to thank Pierre-François Moreau for inviting me, and Delphine Kolesnik-Antoine for being the best of all hosts during both of my visits.

Almost all the parts of the manuscript have been presented at various conferences and workshops: at University of California-Riverside, Johns Hopkins University, University of Chicago, University of Essex, University of Copenhagen, Aarhus University, École Normale Supérieure Lettres et Sciences Humaines-Lyon, École Normale Supérieure-Paris, University of Exeter, Northwestern University, Trent University, University of Amsterdam, and various meetings organized by the American Political Science Association, the Western Political Science Association, and the Midwest Polical Science Association. I thank the hosts and organizers at these places for inviting me, and all the audiences for their incisive responses.

Bonnie Honig helped me sharpen the argument and commented on innumerable drafts, including the penultimate one. In addition to thanking Bonnie for her exemplary commitment to the study of political theory, I would like to thank the following people, who have either commented on a part of the manuscript or shared important conversations with me about issues pertinent to it: Elizabeth Anker, Anders Berg-Sørensen, Wendy Brown, Randall Bush, Ross Carroll, Terrell Carver, Samuel Chambers, Theodore Christov, Marc Crèpon, Jennifer Culbert, Hent de Vries, Jodi Dean, Penelope Deutscher, Mary Dietz, Thomas Donahue, James Farr, Kathy Ferguson, Richard Flathman, Jason Frank, Daniel Galvin, Dilip Gaonkar, Jessica Greenberg, Jairus Grove, Robert Hariman, David Howarth, Elizabeth Hurd, Steven Johnston, Sharon Krause, John Christian Laursen, Daniel Levine, Paula Duarte Lopes, Michael Loriaux, Andrew March, Michelle Molina, Sara Monoson, Per Mouritsen, Aletta Norval, Brett O'Bannon, Paulina Ochoa Espejo, Didier Ottaviani, Davide Panagia, Paul Passavant, Smita Rahman, Sacramento Roselló Martínez, Andrew Ross, Diego Rossello, Christian Rostbøll, Andrew Schaap, Matthew Scherer, Morton Schoolman, Regina Schwartz, Kenneth Seeskin, Kam Shapiro, Michael Shapiro, Christopher Skeaff, Jacqueline Stevens, Bruce Stinebrickner, Mina Suk, Nicholas Tampio, Christina Tarnopolsky, Lasse Thomassen, Douglas Thompson, Samuel Weber, Mary Weismantel, Stephen White, Geoffrey Whitehall, Nathan Widder, Mabel Wong, and two anonymous readers who reviewed the manuscript for Oxford University Press and provided helpful guidance for the last stages of revision.

At Oxford University Press, I am much obliged to Angela Chnapko, who acquired the manuscript and embraced it as if it were her own. Thomas Finnegan copyedited the manuscript with good cheer and succinct care. Peter Woger and Sreejith Viswanathan oversaw the production process with courtesy and professionalism for which I thank them. Thanks to Rebecca Cain who preparred the index. Thanks also to Arda Gucler, who provided crucial research assistance and helped in preparing the manuscript for final submission. I owe a special debt to Miguel Amat, who took the photograph on the cover of this book. The cover photo is a detail of one of seven stainless steel sculptures titled "Tolerance" by the Barcelona-based artist Jaume Plensa. The sculptures are located along the Buffalo Bayou in Houston, Texas, and were commissioned by the city's Arts Alliance in response to a vicious 2006 hate crime attack against then sixteen-year-old David Ritcheson, who one year later committed suicide. The work of expanding the commitment to democracy and tolerance is not finished until the day when the memory of David Ritcheson is honored and society has embraced the conditions of empowerment and pluralization that he did not enjoy.

Parts of Chapter 2 were previously published as "Remember Tolerance Differently: Kant and the Politics of Becoming Tolerant," in *Teoria: Revista filosofia*, vol 32, no. 1 (2012), pp. 93–108. Parts of Chapter 4 were previously published as "Freedom of Expression in an Age of Cartoon Wars," in *Contemporary Political Theory*, vol. 10, no. 2 (2011), pp. 255–272. Both pieces have been significantly revised for the purposes of this publication.

This book is dedicated to my most important travel companion, Sacramento Roselló Martínez. No matter how many twists and turns this journey took, she never failed to see through the fog of confusion and frustration, setting the right course for more than a decade. No words can express my gratitude for the privilege of becoming part of her enchanted world of beauty and creativity. I thank her for her wisdom, perspective, companionship, love, and everything in between.

Introduction

Diogenes, one terrible frosty Morning, came into the *Market place*, and stood Naked, shaking, to show his *Tolerance*.

Francis Bacon (1625)[1]

I. TOLERANCE IN QUESTION

Long at the heart of democratic politics, questions about tolerance have resurfaced with great intensity in the past fifteen years because changes provoked by globalization and new information technologies have heighten our attention to differences within all significant domains of human experience. Due in large part to the success of the Internet, the circulation of preferences and interests is now so fast that the encounter with alternative life forms, which in the past was mostly periodic, prolonged only by religious wars and cultural struggles, has become a daily occurrence that demands ongoing attention. Whether it is the news of a video on YouTube or a demonstration in the Middle East or the imprisonment of an activist in China, the underlying conditions of our contemporary world suggest it is no longer possible to live in relative isolation, free from the risk of offending others or being offended by them. Tolerance is no longer above the fray of disagreement; rather, in a pluralistic and interconnected world like ours, tolerance has once again become a subject of contestation because, as with most other approaches to democratic politics, it is perceived as favoring a certain regime of experience and engagement. The questions run deep, indeed: What motivates citizens to become tolerant of each other? Are some circumstances—cultural, social, religious, economical, or political— more conducive to tolerance than others? What limits, if any, are there to what a society should tolerate?

Answers to these questions typically depend on the ontological and epistemological assumptions that inform our judgments about political issues derived from a condition of pluralism and interconnectedness. This is especially evident within contemporary democratic theory, where the questioning of tolerance has generated a bifurcation of sorts. To one group of theorists, the changed conditions of our contemporary world emphasize the importance of neo-Kantian procedures of reason, which define tolerance as a practice of self-restraint that must be followed, so long as our respect for others is reciprocated by those whom we tolerate. To another group, however, the changes provoked by globalization and new information technologies highlight what latently has been the case since early modernity: that tolerance is a limited virtue that defies true justice because it assumes a fundamental inequality between the tolerator (the privileged) and the tolerated (the underprivileged). Which of these two viewpoints is the more accepted one is an open question to which I shall return later in this book.[2] For now it suffices to say that the steadfastness of both viewpoints has become so pronounced that contemporary democratic theory has split into two camps giving significantly different answers to the questions outlined above: whereas one camp sees tolerance as a practice of restraint, necessary for the existence of a just and fair society, the other sees it as a practice of repressive benevolence needed to reinforce the norms set by the powerful.

The bifurcation of contemporary democratic theory raises the stakes of the discussion and adds another important layer to the already difficult questions about tolerance. In order to address questions about tolerance, it is not sufficient to focus on tolerance as a concept in its own right; rather, in addition to different conceptual analyses of tolerance, we must also examine the many vocabularies that mobilize tolerance and make the practice of tolerance seem more or less reasonable, more or less emancipatory. What historical narratives do present-day vocabularies invoke as the precondition for different claims about tolerance, and in what ways—and with what implications—do these vocabularies privilege some futures at the expense of others? An important motivation for addressing this question is the desire to break the stalemate that occurs when two camps such as the ones just outlined are locked into a mirrorlike negation of each other. Another motivation, which might be more pressing, is the continued relevance of tolerance to a vibrant democracy. At a moment in time where tolerance has become the universal "solution" to problems of free speech, multiculturalism, and religious conflict, the tendency to bifurcate the discussion into two opposing camps may not be the most productive way to disclose tolerance's potential in a world challenged by globalization and other societal changes. Not only does the bifurcation overlook how tolerance continues to resonate across vocabularies and registers of lived experience, it may also prevent us from grasping how tolerance can be mobilized to both deflect the anxieties about living in a world of pluralism and interconnectedness and invigorate one of democracy's noblest aims: to empower a pluralization of society through creative modes of endurance and resilience.

Motivated by uneasiness with the lack of attention to this side of tolerance, this book is an experiment in reorientation. The book is based on the wager that tolerance can be theorized, in all its richness and diversity, in terms that are quite different from the ones responsible for the bifurcation outlined above. Tolerance exceeds self-restraint and repressive benevolence, I argue, because neither precludes the possibility of a more "active tolerance" in which tolerators are motivated by the desire to experiment and to become otherwise.[3] The main task of the ensuing chapters is to call attention to this tolerance as an active force in a world of deep pluralism. The objective is to discuss what gets lost, conceptually as well as politically, when we neglect the subsistence of active tolerance within other practices of tolerance, and to develop a theory of active tolerance in which the relative absence of tolerance's mobilizing character is replaced with an interest in exploring how its affirmative potential might be delimited by a set of circumstances other than the ones suggested by existing models in contemporary democratic theory. Reorienting the discussion of tolerance, my aim is to disclose new possibilities within our given context of theory and practice. Once contemporary democratic theory moves away from the current models of restraint and benevolence, other ways of understanding the politics of democratic pluralism might be developed, which in turn will enable us to conceive of tolerance's future in terms distinct from those currently on offer.

How, then, to commence a reorientation of this kind? From the perspective advocated here, the answer is not to distance oneself from a given context of theory and practice, but rather to put it to work differently.[4] Consider Francis Bacon's aphorism cited above regarding the Ancient cynic Diogenes of Sinope (c. 412–323 BC): "*Diogenes, one terrible frosty Morning, came into the Market place, and stood Naked, shaking, to show his Tolerance.*"[5] Invoked as an exemplar of the true meaning of tolerance, this aphorism is typically taken to represent a "passive tolerance," one that curbs Diogenes' desire to act on his conviction that the majority's beliefs and practices are false, if not evil.[6] Diogenes, it is said, personifies tolerance because he substitutes "forbearance" for "vengeance," and because he thereby resists the temptation of making everyone else feel, think, and act the way he does. Diogenes, of course, does not end up empty-handed because of this: by avoiding the temptation to act on his own conception of the good, Diogenes receives in return the feeling of righteousness and superiority that comes from being benevolent vis-à-vis one's opponents.

Although this reading of Bacon's aphorism seems to capture parts of what tolerance can mean, it would be inaccurate to say that it represents everything Bacon wanted to teach his early modern audience. Most striking is how Bacon uses tolerance's etymological meaning as "the endurance of pain" in order to illustrate how Diogenes challenges the Athenian world of pretense and wealth.[7] Bacon's Diogenes stands forth "naked," without any protection, and he endures the pain of risking his own body in the face of a society he wants to criticize for its failure to secure the kind of ascetic wisdom that not even Plato could muster in his Socratic dialogues. Add to this that Diogenes neither laments his tolerance nor sees it as a virtue of benevolence; rather, he "shows" tolerance because he wishes to express a viewpoint—or manifest a difference, you might say—engaging the world with which he so profoundly disagrees. The combination of these two characteristics captures elements of the active tolerance to which contemporary democratic theory has become mostly inattentive. Recognizing that tolerance sometimes can be more passive than active, Bacon enlists Diogenes on behalf of another tolerance, one that does not require the tolerator or the tolerated to shrink his or her presence to make room for the other, but instead aims to expand the connections between citizens so as to proactively engage with the anxieties that characterize a society in which disagreement and conflict is front and center. For Bacon's Diogenes, tolerance represents a precondition, not a hindrance, for mobilizing disagreement and conflict as an enabling resource in a political society in which there are no clearly defined (let alone universally shared) standards for thought and action.

Pursuing readings such as this one in connection with other exemplars in the history of political thought, this book attends to the various sides of tolerance in order to develop a theory of active tolerance relevant to contemporary democracy. The wager is that all the facets of tolerance, all the constitutive components of tolerance and their possible outcomes, can be as adequately theorized by using the link between pain and tolerance as a theoretical framework as it would be by using reason or some related concept in contemporary democratic theory. Furthermore, by focusing on the endurance of pain, the wager is also that we can better grasp the difficulties that someone who wishes to become tolerant is likely to encounter, and that, by virtue of this perspective, we may be in a better position to identify the range of circumstances that must be mobilized to overcome the drive to indifference or intolerance. Although the reasoning behind both of these wagers will be substantiated later in this introductory chapter, it should already now be noted that the turn to pain does not entail abandoning appeals to reason in contemporary democratic theory. Like the active tolerance it seeks to cultivate, this book is not "against" reason. What I am arguing is that contemporary democratic theory as well as politics more generally can be remapped according to exemplars and theories that conceive of collective action and social existence more in terms of the endurance of pain than in terms of principles and procedures of reason, and that this reorientation generates a sense of possibility centered on what, in Chapter 4, I call "sensorial reasoning"—a reasoning that does not detach itself from the circumstances in which it is invoked but instead emphasizes the enabling power embedded in various lived experiences. It is with this sensorial reasoning in mind that I seek out philosophers, historians, scientists, novelists, painters, and cartoonists who are critical of the terms that define contemporary democratic politics, and who experiment with the interplay between mind and body as well as with the role that active tolerance can play in transforming this interplay. Bringing these intuitions to bear on a variety of issues in contemporary democratic politics, my aim is to show how attention to the many sides of tolerance can model an alternative, and indeed much-needed, way of both reading and doing political theory.

The stakes of reorienting the discussion of tolerance are high, of course. As tolerance has become the hallmark of contemporary democracy, and as modern liberalism has crowded out alternative approaches to democratic politics, tolerance itself has come to mean everything and nothing, serving causes that range from respect for minorities, defined in religious, racial, or sexual terms, over the fight against economic inequality in third world countries, to the justification of military wars waged at home and abroad. Mirroring the idea that tolerance is a practice of *either* restraint *or* repression, the majority of contemporary democratic theorists have responded to these uses by paralleling the bifurcation introduced above: that is, contemporary democratic theorists have either called for practices that "go beyond" tolerance, insisting that tolerance's link to modern liberalism prevents it from being anything but a form of repression, or tried to salvage tolerance's appeal, subjecting it to allegedly stabler concepts such as reason, justice, and autonomy. Neither response is adequate, I argue. Although the move to reason, justice, and autonomy seems morally attractive, and although liberalism has played a significant role in shaping the history of tolerance, reducing the practice of tolerance to only two options leaves both contemporary democratic theory and democrats more generally without the resources needed to develop a valuable third option latent in tolerance's own history. This book is an attempt at bringing these resources back into view. At the same time this book seeks to reorient contemporary democratic theory so as to offer fresh insights into the character, circumstances, and limits of tolerance, it also aims to show how renewed interest in the endurance of pain can change how we, as political theorists and members of various democratic regimes, have come to think about the embodied subject position that underpins most, if not all, aspects of politics as it is experienced and practiced in a condition of pluralism and interconnectedness. The latter, I submit, is crucial if we want to ensure that tolerance once again becomes what it once was: a progressive practice of empowerment and pluralization.

The aim of the Introduction is to outline the approach and main arguments underlying this claim. Section II shows why the discussion of contemporary tolerance should be reconnected with the study of pain. Section III elaborates on the idea of "a sensorial orientation to politics." Section IV concludes with an overview of the theory of active tolerance, describing how each of the book's four chapters contributes to the articulation of this theory.

II. BRINGING PAIN BACK IN

Let us begin by noting how the ambition of bringing pain back in resonates with the phenomenology of tolerance as well as with everyday uses of tolerance as a response to something or someone of which or whom one disapproves.[8] When we say that x tolerates y, we don't simply mean to say that x is bound by a norm to treat others with respect; rather, what we say is that x perceives y to have caused a feeling of distress, and furthermore that x is struggling to keep this feeling in check on a number of levels, which can range from moral imperatives, or institutional structures, to how a body endures what is objectionable by "looking away," "growing accustomed to it," or "fighting back." What counts as endurance of pain on all these levels will most surely differ from case to case.[9] In some instances, the endurance of pain may seem mostly physical, and in that sense be closer to the endurance of torture characteristic of Stoic and early Christian discourses on how to become tolerant.[10] In other cases, the pain can have a mental quality, which resembles the anxiety and vulnerability we find in contemporary conflicts in which a religious tradition or sexual orientation feels threatened by another.[11] Attention to differences between bodily and mental pain is important if we want to make sense of how citizens can become tolerant in a pluralistic world troubled by various societal changes, including those associated with globalization, immigration, inequality, and war. But the differences rarely, if ever, express themselves independently of each other, and indeed in many cases of tolerance we see that the physical and the mental mix in ways that make it hard to separate them from one another. Given this, it might be better to say that the connection between pain and tolerance is physical *and* mental, and that this connection is indicative of the many difficulties involved in becoming tolerant. To become tolerant is not only to endure the pain of something or someone of which or whom we disapprove; it is also to endure the anxieties and hardship that arise from resisting the desire to eliminate the tolerated's presence in a situation of difference and disagreement.

In the extant literature devoted to the conceptualization of tolerance, the relationship between these difficulties is mitigated through two of the five components that are said to define the concept of tolerance: the "objection component" and the "acceptance component."[12] Associated with disgust and repugnance, the objection component tracks tolerance's etymology as the endurance of pain and it is balanced out by a consideration of the various consequences and reasons that decide whether something or someone "objectionable" can become "acceptable." According to the dominant neo-Kantian model, this balancing entails rephrasing the objection component, which ensures that the component is conceptualized not by a consideration of pain or other sensorially inflected experiences, but by principles and procedures of reason that separate frivolous objections from those that are said to be "normatively substantive."[13] The idea, in other words, is to establish a normative threshold for the objectionable, and then to use this threshold as a way to delimit the moral space in which some objections but not others can be deemed acceptable regardless of how they are experienced by those affected by them. As Rainer Forst puts it, "Tolerant citizens are 'reasonable' in accepting that the 'context of justification' for ethical beliefs and general norms are different: they see that an *ethical objection* does not amount to a *moral rejection*."[14]

When I suggest that contemporary democratic theory reorients the discussion of tolerance by bringing pain back in, it is primarily in relation to arguments such as this one. As we shall see, the attempt to separate ethics from morality is part of an intellectualist orientation to politics, which tends to disavow the sensorial forces that motivate and empower the endurance of pain and that subsist within all practices of tolerance, including the ones advocated by contemporary theorists who privilege reason in their analyses of democratic politics.[15] The result has been a problematic detachment of the discussion of tolerance from the circumstances in which tolerators live and act, a detachment that has empowered what I call, borrowing from Bernard Williams, "impossible tolerance."[16] Impossible tolerance serves here as an attempt to capture some of the problems that occur when we don't attend to the connections between pain and tolerance. Once contemporary democratic theory moves our attention away from sensorially inflected experiences, what we face is a turning point, which limits our ability to theorize the experiences of those who either already are tolerant or seek to become tolerant. Once principles and procedures of reason are naturalized—once they are detached from their location in space and time—any alternative to the neo-Kantian way of theorizing tolerance is cast as a step toward either subjectivism or, worse, nihilism. Once conceptions of tolerance are classified as "reasonable" or "unreasonable"—once these intellectualist terms do service for more complex distinctions concerning the objectionable and the acceptable—questions about who should bear the brunt of suffering no longer call us to attend to pain itself. Once all of this has been achieved—once pain and tolerance have been severed from each other, and contemporary democratic theory no longer entails an account of what the endurance of pain has meant, does mean, or could mean—tolerance itself loses its sense of difficulty and no longer signifies an engagement with a world so complex that morality's demands defy any single definition or form.

Among the many conflicts that illustrate the difficulties associated with the severing of pain and tolerance, the publication of twelve cartoons of the Prophet Muhammad in the Danish newspaper *Jyllands-Posten* is one of the most recent and best known. In Chapter 4, I examine the publication of the twelve cartoons to show how some of the most prevalent conceptions of democratic politics helped to frame the conflict in binary terms, which in turn restricted the two sides in their ability to articulate and contest one another's experiences of pain. Although the Danes and the Muslims obviously disagreed on who should carry the burdens of restraint and suffering, and although neither side was completely homogeneous, their shared appeal to pain as an impenetrable absence, as something either too sacred or too private to be contested and criticized, generated a zero-sum game in which no one was moved to engage in a transformation of their divergent beliefs, identities, and claims to recognition. The ensuing stalemate reflects the impasse that troubles the discussion of tolerance in contemporary democratic theory. As the Danish cartoon war suggests, the societal changes associated with globalization and new information technologies mean we now must attend not just to the norms and principles regulating the contexts in which political conflicts arise, but also to the sensorium enabling tolerators to endure feelings of pain in more than a passive manner. Attention to the latter is crucial because it enables us to theorize the kinds of desires that pluralize the span of acceptable differences in society, and because it reduces the risk of accepting rather than reversing the tendency to see tolerance as a second-best option, as a "need" rather than a "want."[17] As I argue in this book, the price paid for leaving experiences of pain untouched is that we lose sight of how tolerance can also be an active practice of empowerment and pluralization, one that underpins the resiliency needed to engage the feelings of anxiety associated with contestation and disagreement.

An important reason for bringing pain back in, then, is that it can reignite interest in democracy's sensorially inflected life-world, and thus make it easier to identify as well as counter the challenges that trouble the politics of tolerance as it is practiced today. But what does it mean to speak of pain in the manner suggested here? As I am using the term, *pain* evokes, in the first instance, the sensed experience of an obstacle to unhindered movement and effortless creation—a sense of being limited, stopped in one's tracks, for reasons that may seem more or less than just, more or less given. Contained within this experience are (1) a sensory-somatic expression of being hurt or injured caused by the encounter with some obstacle, and (2) a more psychological-discursive state of being displaced, expressed through various moods and sentiments, ranging from negative ones such as anger, anxiety, and fear to more positive ones such as excitation, resistance, and surprise. Common to these expressions is an effect akin to what Heidegger calls *Unheimlichkeit*, a feeling of "not-being-at-home"—a feeling that emerges in registers of alienation, distress, exposure, harm, suffering, and vulnerability, and that for Heidegger signifies the difficulties of "becoming home in not being at home (*das Heimishwerden in Unheimischsein*)."[18]

An important task of the ensuing chapters is to locate the feeling of pain as "not-being-at-home" within historical and contemporary discourses on tolerance, and furthermore, to discuss how a critical engagement with this feeling can shed new light on the commitment to empowerment and pluralization, which is so central to the politics of active tolerance. To be sure, this task may seem inherently impossible because the very experience of displacement transports pain beyond established categories of meaning and sense, and thus prevents pain from being captured by any kind of discourse (meaningful or not). For Emily Dickinson, pain "has an Element of Blank," which means that even the most eloquent writer will find himself or herself doomed to communicate the feeling of pain, not through proper words, but through howling, lamentation, or simply silence.[19] True in one sense, there is nonetheless reason to caution against this view because the discursive displacement caused by pain generates a stronger-than-usual desire for language, something that may be especially evident in discourses on tolerance broadly understood. The endurance of pain, you might say, tears one out of the world, but it also generates a heightened desire to develop an account of why the world is occurring in the way it is, as well as to explain how this development can be managed, endured, or eliminated.[20] Given this, it is important not to draw the conclusion that twentieth-century theorists such as Hannah Arendt and Elaine Scarry have drawn, and insist too strongly on the idea that pain is "private," and that whatever it achieves, "it achieves in part through its unsharability."[21] Although pain may not be expressed perfectly, although it may not be fully shared and can appear only to the extent that it invokes a screen of partiality and secrecy—although it is something about which, in our culture, many of us are silent—pain is always occupied with communicating "something" to "someone"—be it through words and discourses or through moods and sensibilities that range from anger and hatred to surprise, enticement, and affirmation.

These comments suggest that an interest in pain changes the terms by which we conceptualize tolerance in conditions of pluralism and interconnectedness. Most basic is the suggestion that we see tolerance as a world-making process subject to framing and redefinition. Why world-making? Because the encounter with pain embodies *both* a transition from a state of more power to a state of less power (hence the feeling of an obstacle, of something objectionable), *and* a creative, perhaps even affirmative, power defined in its own right. Rarely evident in contemporary democratic theory, this way of theorizing pain is inspired by Talal Asad, Rosi Braidotti, David Biro, and others who treat pain as a world-making process, not because it can be perfectly communicated and shared (it can't), but because our desire to express it perpetuates the creation of new relations among self, other, and world, which in turn appear through various forms of expression that simultaneously interrupt and regenerate the existing coordinates of space and time. Not only is pain invested "with spatio-temporal force," it represents a "public relationship" from which the "desire for language" emerges in ways that differ from context to context.[22] One advantage of this approach is that it maintains pain's character as an irrevocably *Unheimlich* feeling of not-being-at-home—a feeling that can be simultaneously physical and mental, sensorial and psychological. Another advantage is that it highlights how the processes by which pain is delimited and then tolerated—the processes by and through which a society names some experiences as "pain" but not other—is an inherently political operation, one that distributes power and privilege and sets the terms for a sufferer's demand for recognition within a given set of sociopolitical relations.[23] To endure pain, you might say, depends just as much on how a given society recognizes the feeling of pain as it does on the sufferer for whom the feeling of pain constitutes an immediate reality that demands urgent attention and ongoing care.

In the ensuing chapters, I draw on this account to better conceptualize the differences between passive tolerance and active tolerance—that is, between respectively a limiting practice of either repression or self-restraint and an expansive practice driven by the desire to experiment and become otherwise. As I see it, the conceptualization of these two sides is intimately linked to what I have referred to as the theory of active tolerance, which can be characterized as an attempt to switch the focus from an "external" perspective concerned with the limits of tolerance to an "internal" perspective that explores tolerance's sensorially inflected life-world, foregrounding what Jacques Rancière calls the "partitioning of the sensible."[24] Reversing the tendency in contemporary democratic theory to ignore this partitioning, the theory of active tolerance seeks to explain how tolerators make sense of the world—what we can call *mise en sens*—and to show how tolerators stage this sense-making—what we can call *mise en scène*.[25] In relation to both, the theory of active tolerance considers how the endurance of pain generates reasons for, and practices of, becoming tolerant, and how these reasons and practices enable tolerance to work differently according to the context. The question that defines the theory of active tolerance is therefore not how tolerators practice their tolerance *in spite of* the pain they endure; rather, the central question animating the theory of active tolerance is *how* the endurance of pain empowers the desires, powers, and limits of becoming tolerant, and *how* this empowerment stages relationships between tolerator and tolerated. In what way, the theory of active tolerance asks, is the endurance of pain world-making, and how does the endurance of various pains in various contexts contribute to a politics in which the tolerating subject is either passively supportive of the status quo or actively involved in a pluralization of the span of acceptable differences in society?

The very possibility of answering this question hinges on what we saw earlier: that pain signifies an inherently pluralistic experience subject to politicization and reframing. To be sure, there are some regimes of discourse and sensation that frame pain's world-making power as a mode of repression rather than as a mode of empowerment and pluralization. This is especially the case in a liberal, neo-Kantian frame where procedures of justification and reasoning often are so detached from the sensorium of political life that the experience of pain represents a nonthought, too passive and too subjective to be included in the domain of public deliberation.

In this universe, the sufferer is often depicted as an isolated individual for whom the path to recognition is limited to what Wendy Brown, in *States of Injury*, calls "wounded attachments."[26] But this cannot be all there is to the endurance of pain. Consider not just Bacon's Diogenes but also other exemplars important to the argument I am making, including the Stoic conceptualization of *tolerāntia*, Kant's analysis of the sublime, Nietzsche's idea of a gay science, and Merleau-Ponty's embrace of perceptual incompleteness. Highlighting the difficulties associated with a fluid state of affairs in which the arrival of a new identity challenges the existing regime of discourse and sensation—what William Connolly calls "the politics of becoming"[27]—these exemplars encourage us to theorize how the feeling of pain sometimes can designate a transformation whereby one's own identity is opened up to more empowering constellations of self, other, and world, participating in what Spinoza calls the desire to "affect" and "be affected in more ways."[28] The reader skeptical that there is such a thing as an empowering pain vital to contemporary democratic politics will find arguments for this claim in Chapters 2, 3, and 4. For now, the point is simply that it is not implausible to say that when we acknowledge that pain is not just passive and reductive but also expansive and empowering, then tolerance is no longer reduced to a passive practice of *either* restrained respect *or* repressive benevolence. A broader conception of pain highlights the importance of the various sensorially inflected forces that make endurance and resilience seem more or less desirable in their own right; it also encourages us to investigate how these forces can be framed and mobilized to serve a practice of tolerance in which the gain of one does not represent the loss of another.

The theory of active tolerance is one way to identify the conditions needed to empower this vision of acting tolerantly in a world defined by pluralism and interconnectedness. Renewing tolerance's potential as a practice of empowerment and pluralization, questioning the commonplace claim that tolerance is so intimately tied to contemporary liberalism that our commitments to the former depends on our commitments to the latter, the theory of active tolerance strives to show how tolerance once again can become an enabling force vis-à-vis some of the most important sites of contemporary democratic politics. As we shall see, these sites include the politics of becoming (how to encourage greater pluralization), the politics of multiculturalism (how to enable existing configurations of identity and difference to coexist), and the politics of free speech (how to ensure that freedom of expression is used to expand rather than contract the range of acceptable differences in society).

III. A SENSORIAL ORIENTATION TO POLITICS

An important backdrop to the contributions that a theory of active tolerance makes to these three sites of contemporary democratic politics concerns the second main argument developed in this book: an invitation to reorient the ontological assumptions that underpin how we, as political theorists and as members of various democratic regimes, develop our divergent accounts of tolerance as the cardinal virtue of contemporary democracy. Today, most discussions of tolerance are defined by what I earlier referred to as an intellectualist orientation to politics. Although the specific assumptions and implications of this orientation will be elaborated in Chapters 1 and 2, its three central elements can be summarized here: invoking a mind-body dualism in which the mind is defined as superior to the body, an intellectualist orientation to politics holds (1) that the *object* of democratic politics is public reason (defined as procedures for deliberation and justification); (2) that the *purpose* of democratic politics is constitutional law (defined as the shared platform from which issues of justice can be decided in ways that are reasonable, even if not agreeable, to everyone affected); and (3) that the *ideal* of democratic politics is autonomy (defined as the ability to give laws independently of foreign powers and the desires and passions that threaten to interrupt reason's ability to decide on its own, disembodied terms). An intellectualist orientation, thus understood, tracks various historical developments in neo-Kantian philosophy, and it encourages a move, prevalent in contemporary democratic theory, away from the affective intensities and perceptual shifts that underpin the endurance and resilience embedded in the practice of tolerance.

Because of the concerns introduced earlier—in particular the risk of tolerance becoming "impossible" whenever registers of lived experience are either relegated to the unexamined background or considered too particularistic to have any normative import—this book introduces another orientation to politics, one that I call "sensorial." A sensorial orientation to politics may at first seem paradoxical, if not self-contradictory, especially when we consider the orientation's use of reason and reason giving, something that may give the impression that a sensorial orientation to politics merely reproduces the blind spots and double binds it attributes to its intellectualist counterpart. One response to this impression is to recognize that a sensorial orientation to politics indeed is born out of conversations with proponents of intellectualism, and that it therefore is likely to carry various traces of the intellectualist tradition. Another response is to note that rather than refuting reason—and, by extension, language and interpretation—a sensorial orientation to politics seeks to recalibrate its stature in order to better recognize how reasons, too, are ways of sensing the world. A sensorial orientation, in other words, expands the parameters of the discussion to include the more general sensorium of political life, which is taken to be neither completely synergistic nor immediately present, but reliant on representations, images, and memories that situate actual sensory inputs within historically defined regimes of discourse and sensation. How a sensorial orientation to politics develops this perspective on political life—and thus how a sensorial orientation to politics changes the ontological assumptions underpinning discussions of contemporary tolerance—is best understood in terms of various developments in twentieth-century phenomenology and poststructural critical theory.[29]

A sensorial orientation to politics stands on the shoulders of a long tradition in the history of political thought that culminates with various efforts in twentieth-century Continental philosophy, especially those inspired by Husserl's phenomenological investigations and further developed in discussions of embodiment, sexuality, desire, psychology, new media, and techniques of the self. Drawing on these efforts, a sensorial orientation to politics implies first and foremost an interest in sentient beings (in particular human bodies) as generative forces that both are structured by and exceed their place within social institutions and political regimes. Whether described as an ontological lack or as sign of vitality and abundance, sentient beings entail this excess because they are not only the object of sociopolitical pressures but also the source of these pressures. If sociopolitical pressures arise, it is because sentient beings project and live out their own assumptions regarding material needs, psychological well-being, and cultural recognition. Contemporary feminists and critical theorists have long been interested in foregrounding this dynamic chiasm in order both to denaturalize the human body, challenging discourses of physiology and medicine, and highlight the possibility of political resistance granted by embodied differences (whether marked in terms of gender, class, race, or something else). The differences themselves are an important reason sentient beings move and resist the weight of their own past, creating the possibility of a new future. As Elizabeth Grosz notes, "Bodies are not inert; they function interactively and productively. They act and react. They generate what is new, surprising, unpredictable."[30]

As the backdrop to how a sensorial orientation to politics reorients the discussion of tolerance, this account stands in sharp contrast to the mind-body dualism that defines how intellectualism privileges disembodied reason as the proper source of deliberation, law, and autonomy. To emphasize the sensorium as the enabling force behind reason is to undermine the hierarchy that delimits the conceptualization of these terms. And to move beyond this delimitation is to generate a more nuanced conception of how sentient beings participate in the production of regimes of discourse and sensation, as well as how these regimes "frame" the way sentient beings reason with each other.[31] Some of these insights follow from the denaturalization of the body that we have come to associate with contemporary poststructural critical theory. In Michel Foucault's discussion of late-modern governmentality, for example, the denaturalization of the body implies an interest in how political disciplining can be both limiting and enabling, instituting a field of normalcy that not only restricts and constitutes the span of acceptable differences in society but also enables resistance and subversion.[32] Along similar lines, Judith Butler has pointed out how a society's ability to recognize bodies as bodies— what she calls "recognizability"—depends on an ontological framing that contains the seen and sensed without holding "anything together in one place, but itself becomes a kind of perceptual breakage, subject to a temporal logic by which it moves from place to place."[33] To Butler, this breakage assumes the denaturalization of the human body and, by extension, sentient beings: rather than conceptualizing sentient beings as given entities, controlled by the demands of disembodied reason, we must see them as cumulative and accomplished entities that actively participate in the structuring of meaning and recognition, and thus in the various definitions of reason and reason-giving.

A sensorial orientation to politics goes further than this, however. Inspired by Butler's own concern for the unsettling feeling of vulnerability that often follows from the experience of pain and displacement, a sensorial orientation to politics shows how the denaturalization of the body, though valuable in one sense, has had the adverse effect of bypassing how bodily existence is more than just a way of generating a subject recognized by others.[34] That is, a sensorial orientation suggests that bodily existence, in addition to generating individualized subjects of desire, evolves around relations of power and difference that exceed the sentient beings they enable, something that requires a return to Nature as the very source of power and difference.[35] A sensorial orientation to politics thus argues that sentient beings are generative, not only because their bodies are socially constructed but also because their senses communicate with a natural world always-already open to intervention and change. Sentient beings are neither the most interesting nor the most fundamental element of analysis; they stand out as assemblages of bodily material in and through which affective intensities and perceptual shifts wire the body's senses in ways unique to both place and time. According to a sensorial orientation, human bodies "act and react" because their senses presuppose an opening to the world, which situates bodily existence in an environment of feeling and perception, and which makes movement possible, generating context-specific conditions of reason and agency. According to a sensorial orientation, the senses are uniquely situated because they exceed the bodies they serve, and because in that sense they suggest an interiority *and* an exteriority, a nonspace—but a nonspace that generates a more definite world in which sensory inputs help to define a body capable of perceiving itself in a context of smell, taste, touch, sound, and sight. According to a sensorial orientation, representations of this nonspace open the sensorium to political processes that cross-pollinates what the natural sciences describe in neurological and physiological terms with what the humanities describe in either psychological or cultural terms.

These comments highlight an important difference between contemporary poststructural critical theory and the approach suggested by a sensorial orientation to politics. Insofar as the former has left the conceptualization of the senses to the natural sciences, particularly the discourses of physiology and medicine, the wiring of sensorial experience has come to be associated with a turn to nature as a fundamentally organic and precultural category immune to change, incompletion, and difference across its various instantiations. In accepting this view, contemporary poststructural critical theory has more or less tacitly embraced another division of labor between the natural sciences and the humanities, one that erects a new nature-culture dualism on the ruins left by intellectualism's mind-body dualism. This may seem obvious given the interests that situate contemporary poststructural critical theory vis-à-vis the natural sciences, and yet the temptation to replace one dualism with another is what a sensorial orientation to politics seeks to resist. The challenge is to rethink political practices from within the world in which they appear, and therefore to problematize any pregiven separation of both mind and body *and* culture and nature. The sensorial orientation to politics thus shows how reorientation implies major epistemological upheavals, not only for the intellectualism of contemporary democratic theory, which has tended toward a separation of mind and body, ceding the latter to the natural sciences, but equally (and perhaps more importantly) for contemporary critical theorists who have privileged culture over nature and thus seem to have emasculated their own commitment to nondualist theory.

A powerful way of bringing these insights together is to say that a sensorial orientation to politics highlights what Gilles Deleuze and Félix Guattari call the "molecular" level of political life—the level where connections between, across, and within sentient beings are forged through moments of becoming, and where affective intensities and perceptual shifts undergird representations of civilization, meaning, and desire.[36] The move to the molecular level raises the question of how studying the sensorium can change the way we think about politics altogether. On the one hand, the molecular emphasizes how sentient beings, many of which are split against themselves, are the consequence of their concrete determinations, their fluid states, and their interactions with the determinations of other fluid sentient beings (whether human or not). The molecular thus implies a perpetual pluralization, which cuts deeper than the one assumed by most contemporary political theorists, and which demands our renewed attention if we want to understand the changing conditions of conflict and difference, agonism and tolerance. On the other hand, the molecular level also implies a shift away from a belief in the sufficiency of principles and institutions, and instead it turns our attention to the intensities and flows that circulate in and out of these institutions—what Deleuze and Guattari call "micropolitics."[37] As I am studying it, a sensorial orientation to politics combines both aspects: attending to how regimes of discourse and sensation partition the sensible, a sensorially inspired account of politics turns our analytical gaze to the way in which seeing, hearing, smelling, touching, and tasting, as well as lesser-known senses such as balance and acceleration, generate contextually situated beings that seek, and perhaps even desire, to engage proactively with a pluralizing world of difference and conflict. A sensorial orientation to politics, in other words, is both attentive to *and* generative of a world of deep pluralism.

I dwell on these elements of a sensorial orientation to politics because they help us see how a shift to this orientation changes the way contemporary democratic theory engages the politics of tolerance, as well as how it might be possible to buttress a theory of active tolerance responding to changes provoked by globalization, immigration, inequality, and war. A sensorial orientation to politics contributes to both aspects because it challenges all instantiations of dualistic thinking in order to approach modes of thought and action, mind and body, from the perspective of a radical immanence in which the "outside" or "other" is always relative to the infinite possibilities within *this* world. Although this approach is not as orderly as the turn to "reason" in contemporary democratic theory seems to demand, it situates the reasonable within its embodied circumstances, and in this sense it has all the explanatory power of reason and reason-giving. For our purposes, the focus on the sensorium, on the way in which affective intensities and perceptual shifts inscribe themselves on both individual and collective bodies, furthermore has the added bonus of linking tolerance explicitly to the endurance of pain, and thus of engaging the politics of tolerance in a way that seems either forgotten or disavowed. A sensorial orientation to politics reverses our mode of engaging the politics of tolerance because it raises the question of contextual specificity, of who tolerates what, what their differences are, and whether their tolerance contributes to the pluralization of society, so as to more readily historicize, problematize, and transform the function and value of tolerance in democracies where citizens come together in an ongoing democratic struggle against inequality, suffering, and violence. How a consideration of these aspects relates to the ambition of changing the politics of tolerance, reorienting the discursive terrain by bringing pain back in, hinges on three analytical shifts related to how a sensorial orientation to politics defines the object, purpose, and ideal of contemporary democratic politics.

First, because the sensorium implies an open-ended set of potentialities that never appears in completely unmediated or raw terms, a sensorial orientation to politics takes the meaning of tolerance to be always mediated through representations, images, and memories, which can make conflicts seem more or less frightening, more or less affirmative. Even if political life appears to be "nasty, brutish, and short," to use Hobbes's famous phrase about the state of nature, we cannot assume that all reactions to someone or something objectionable (and hence painful) are always or even primarily defined in binary terms, in terms of a drive toward *either* annihilation *or* repression. Correspondingly, we should be careful not to limit the object of contemporary democratic politics to a public reason seeking to regulate the proper course of action according to procedures of deliberation and justification that are untouched by the context in which they operate. Rather, we need to broaden our scope, and look to the regimes of discourse and sensation, which enable citizens to feel, see, and think in the first place, and which thereby prime them to perceive the objectionable as more or less acceptable, more or less tolerable.

Second, because the sensorium is not only constitutive *of* but also contemporaneous *with* the appearance of a political society, a sensorial orientation to politics suggests there is no strict separation, temporal or otherwise, between citizens' "natural" habitat and the normative demands and institutional arrangements that regulate the citizenry whenever it appears in public. Such temporal separation may in fact belie how the structuring of feelings, desires, and perceptions undergirds citizens' commitments to duties and obligation imposed by the societies in which they live. For the study of tolerance, this means that insofar as democratic politics points to a "social contract"—a contract that for the purposes of tolerance delimits the meaning of pain so as to identify who should bear the brunt of suffering—this contract is continuously renegotiated (tested, affirmed, and altered) through practices of contestation and resistance. To be a subject *of* tolerance is to participate in these practices of renegotiation, subjecting one's desires, feelings, and perceptions to a world in which endurance of pain empowers the possibility of agency, legitimacy, and reason.

Third, though the sensorium offers a way of making sense of the world, it does not imply a linear narrative in which citizens move from one state of being to another in order to save their self-interests. Rather than invoking a process of maturation, positing autonomy as the ideal of democratic politics, the sensorium points to a cacophony of impulses, or perhaps better, a heterology of powers and possibilities. As sentient beings, tolerators require a normative model different from the one of autonomy that most contemporary theorists of democracy use to represent and understand them. I am not suggesting that tolerators are without the ability to change the conditions under which they live, or that they do not relate to a desire for some level of self-government; my claim is the simpler one that the ideal of autonomy in contemporary democratic theory persistently misrepresents the relationship between tolerators and their environment as one of either mastery or servitude. Tolerators "act and react." But they also participate in chiasmatic processes of reversibility and folding, pressing back on their own conditions of possibility such that in some instances this leads to a pluralization of differences in society. From the perspective of a sensorial orientation to politics, one of the main challenges that must be confronted if contemporary democratic theory wants to remain relevant in a world of deep pluralism is how to theorize these instances in order to identify new practices of endurance and resilience that can counter the drive toward indifference and intolerance.

IV. TOWARD A THEORY OF ACTIVE TOLERANCE: PLAN OF THE BOOK

The ambition of the next four chapters is to further develop each of these three shifts in order to better appreciate how discussions of tolerance and the sensorium are intimately linked, and how bringing them closer together can point us in the direction of a theory of active tolerance relevant to contemporary democratic politics. Starting from within the intellectualist tradition, offering an immanent critique that gradually moves us toward a sensorial orientation to politics, the chapters show how the theory of active tolerance is one that (1) draws our attention to the sensorial aspects of democratic politics; (2) considers tolerance as an inherently open-ended practice linked to the framing and partitioning of the sensible; and (3) looks for ways, at both the institutional level and the micropolitical level, to make conflict and disagreement a positive resource for empowering as well as pluralizing the span of acceptable differences in society. Another way of saying this is that the theory of active tolerance aims to empower tolerators so that once again they can inhabit what Herbert Marcuse describes as a "partisan goal, a subversive liberating notion and practice."[38] Asking us to consider the endurance of pain as a "want" rather than as a "need," the theory of active tolerance explains, first, how tolerance, despite its nearly universal appeal as a cardinal virtue of contemporary democracy, has come to represent an impossibility that limits rather than augments the desire to experiment and to live otherwise; and, second, how this impossibility can be displaced by reorienting contemporary democratic theory toward a subset of sensorially inflected powers that go beyond self-restraint and repressive benevolence.

Chapter 1 begins with the existing uses of tolerance in public discourse and contemporary democratic theory in order to develop the claim that tolerance has become impossible because of a schism between the justification and the practice of tolerance. The chapter examines three contemporary models of tolerance—"reasonable tolerance," "tolerance as recognition," and "tolerance as superiority"—and shows, through a close reading of the work of Rawls, how the intellectualist orientation to politics expresses itself through a somatophobia that associates sensorially inflected experiences with subjectivity and nihilism, reducing everything sensed or felt to something dangerous, thereby enabling the sense of disempowerment present in both public discourse and contemporary democratic theory. The chapter concludes by outlining the path to the theory of active tolerance, proposing a new critique of pain based on the works of Mill and Nietzsche respectively.

Chapter 2 seeks to make the path to active tolerance more accessible by showing how the genealogy of tolerance exceeds the account that informs most discussions in contemporary democratic theory. The chapter draws on the work of Foucault and Freud to show how contemporary democratic theory has screened off many of tolerance's remainders, making the history of tolerance seem more linear and progressive than it historically has been. To interrupt this impression, pluralizing how we use historical knowledge about the concept and practice of tolerance, the chapter goes on to propose an alternative reading of three of the most important early modern thinkers in the intellectualist tradition: Kant, Locke, and Descartes. My reading of these thinkers develops a countermemory that shows how the intellectualist orientation to politics is shot through with elements of the sensorium, as well as how it is possible to locate elements of the theory of active tolerance within intellectualism itself. Both aspects make it less plausible to say that active tolerance has been lost to a hidden past unavailable for interpretation and mobilization.

Chapter 3 sets out by identifying more self-consciously with a sensorial orientation to politics so as to better develop the main tenets of the theory of active tolerance. Examining the work of Spinoza alongside a line of thought that goes as far back as Seneca (and the Stoics more generally), the chapter situates tolerance within a force field of its own and goes on to examine the experience of pain as an affective mode of being that expresses various degrees of power. The chapter thus substantiates the idea that tolerance is a form of world-making, and that this world-making can be expressed in either a predominantly active or a predominantly passive way, empowering radically different orientations to the endurance of pain. To illustrate the dangers as well as the potential of this ambiguity, the chapter places the theory of active tolerance in relation to three cases of endurance: masochism (Sacher-Masoch), comedy (Dave Chappelle), and torture (the war on terror). Together these cases show how tolerators might desire the endurance of pain in the first place, how it might be possible to displace some of its more disabling effects, what the limits of the endurance of pain might be, and how, as theorists and citizens, we might counter those who use the endurance of pain for undemocratic purposes.

Chapter 4 continues by deploying a sensorial orientation to politics in order to consider the experiences that underpin the theory of active tolerance, and that enables it to make a difference within contemporary conflicts such as the Danish cartoon war. Attending to the plurality represented by the twelve *Jyllands-Posten* cartoons, the chapter suggests that the theory of active tolerance offers a better approach to the challenges that face contemporary democratic politics because it is associated with a framing and sensibility based on what Merleau-Ponty calls "tolerance of the incomplete," a dictum that looks to reorient rather than resolve the background conditions of deliberation and contestation. To see how this might be a better approach, the chapter examines the limitations of existing approaches, in particular those appealing to the morality of personal autonomy and the right to free speech, and goes on to broaden the scope of the discussion, moving from the previous chapter's discussion of tolerance's force field to a discussion of how the plurality of lived experience is framed in conflicts such as the Danish cartoon war. The chapter concludes by considering the implications of this framing for public reason as well as for current conditions of deliberation and contestation.

The Conclusion summarizes the theory of active tolerance, and it highlights the general idea that the endurance of pain is vitally important to a democratic society that actively cares for a radical openness that can bind citizens to see, feel, and think differently.

CHAPTER 1
Impossible Tolerance

Tolerance, the virtue that makes peace possible, contributes to the replacement of a culture of war by a culture of peace.

Declaration of Principles on Tolerance (1995)[1]

Let us suppose it agreed upon, among ourselves, that all of us here are for "tolerance," even if we have not been assigned the mission of promoting it or founding it. We would be here to try to think what "tolerance" could henceforth be.

Jacques Derrida (1998)[2]

I. VISIONS OF TOLERANCE IN CONTEMPORARY DEMOCRATIC THEORY

Among the many attempts to promote tolerance in light of societal changes provoked by globalization and the emergence of new information technologies, the most prominent might be the 1995 Declaration of Principles on Tolerance. Issued by UNESCO to celebrate the United Nation's fiftieth anniversary, the declaration stands out because it places tolerance within a globalized discourse of civilization that splits the international community into two dichotomously opposed characteristics: tolerance and intolerance, peace and war, reason and passion, deliberation and violence, choice and repression, moderation and fundamentalism. At the same time as these dichotomies define tolerance negatively, identifying what tolerators must reject to comply with the international society's principles of citizenship, the dichotomies also help to justify tolerance as a universally attractive concept that people of all stripes can practice without violating their commitment to a certain faith, culture, or creed. The declaration seeks in that sense to acknowledge the ubiquity of disagreement and difference while at the same time supplying the authority needed for tolerance to be normatively binding in a globalized world committed to peace and nonviolence. Not only does the UNESCO declaration legitimize practices of restraint against which past uses of discipline and punishment seem barbaric, it also defines tolerators as leaders of an international movement, one that privileges some as the bearers of dispassionate reason, distinguishing tolerators from competing groups that either haven't "yet" learned how to be tolerant or are unwilling or unable to learn because of an especially dogmatic world-view embedded in their history, religion, or culture.

The effects of the Declaration of Principles on Tolerance are visible on many levels and in many regions of the world. In the United States, the declaration's proclamation of November 16 as an annual International Tolerance Day has become the occasion for NGOs such as Teaching Tolerance to teach school children about tolerance, providing principals and teachers with instruction manuals that promote activities such as "mix it up," where students of one race spend time with students of another race in order to nurture an inclusive school community untainted by racial prejudices and social stereotypes.[3] In Europe, the Declaration of Principles on Tolerance has encouraged establishment of the European Council on Tolerance and Reconciliation, which is another NGO that focuses on monitoring toler-ance in Europe, in particular in relation to the Jewish genocide and the threat of anti-Semitism in many European countries.[4] And finally, in Africa and Asia, the UNESCO declaration's emphasis on tolerance as the way to peace is juxtaposed with the concern that tolerance can be used to justify religiously motivated practices such as female genital mutilation, prompt-ing the United Nations Sub-Commission on the Promotion and Protection of Human Rights to declare February 6 as an International Day of Zero Tolerance for Female Genital Mutilation.[5] Common to these interventions are anxieties about tolerance and its relationship to pain and other sensori-ally inflected experiences of hardship. As tolerance has risen to a superior position within the international community, its practitioners are both implicated in and limited by the struggle to make sense of something as counterintuitive as the link between democratic government and the need to endure some forms of pain though not others.

This chapter looks at the affinities between the Declaration of Principles on Tolerance and the intellectualist orientation to politics that, as I sug-gested in the Introduction, has come to define an increasingly important part of contemporary democratic theory. Inspired by Derrida's interven-tion cited above, my strategy is primarily one of an immanent critique that collects evidence from contemporary texts to disclose blind spots and dou-ble binds that limit how we, as theorists and as members of various politi-cal regimes, have come to think of and practice a given concept. Specifically, my contention is that although the intellectualist orientation to politics embedded in the Declaration of Principles on Tolerance is compelling insofar as it emphasizes the need for a common ground shared by those subject to the demands of tolerance, it nonetheless calls for close scrutiny because its staging of the sensorium—what I call "somatophobia"—runs the risk of turning tolerance into an impossibility.[6] The historical-philosophical context behind intellectualism's somatophobic staging of the sensorium is the topic of Chapter 2. In the present chapter, I limit myself to a discussion of how somatophobia appears in contemporary democratic theory as well as how it turns tolerance into an impossibility, thereby emphasizing the need to reorient the discussion toward a theory of active tolerance based on a critical yet affirmative engagement with pain and its role in contemporary democratic politics. Although the role of pain may have been forgotten, even rejected, it has not disappeared from actual political struggles in which tolerance is seen as either the problem or the solution—as a way of either repressing the span of acceptable differences in society or pluralizing this span so that heretofore marginalized individuals or groups can come into view as constitutive members of the body politic.

Section II of this chapter places the Declaration of Principles on Tolerance alongside three models of tolerance and develops the idea that the intellectualist orientation to politics is marked by a somatophobic staging of the sensorium. Section III focuses on the work of John Rawls to substantiate the stronger claim that intellectualism's somatophobia makes tolerance impossible because it engenders a double bind whereby tolerators must either rise above the sensorium that defines the lives of "ordinary" people or construe the sensorium such that tolerance becomes the cause of what Nietzsche calls *ressentiment*. Section IV begins the work of moving beyond the terms set by intellectualism, placing it alongside a sensorial orientation that conceptualizes the endurance of pain according to its world-making potential, and not as an issue separate from the procedures of reason that, for Rawls and other advocates of intellectualism, are essential to a just and fair society. Section V concludes with a discussion of how to further develop this conceptualization in the context of contemporary democratic theory, as well as how it may pertain to more specific initiatives developed in the wake of the Declaration of Principles on Tolerance.

II. GLOBALIZED TOLERANCE: DIFFERENT MODELS, SAME SYMPTOM?

Written in response to a "rise in acts of intolerance," the Declaration of Principles on Tolerance sets out by invoking a framework of human rights that links tolerance to a Lockean liberalism based on personal choice, religious freedom, and separation of Church and State.[7] The limitations of this version of Locke's liberalism are well known—according to Marx, it requires "every man to see in other men, not the *realization*, but rather the *limitation* of his own liberty"[8]—prompting its followers, including the authors of the Declaration of Principles on Tolerance, to oscillate between recognizing the right to "adhere to one's own convictions" and emphasizing state-sponsored education as "the most effective means of preventing intolerance."[9] The oscillation between these two viewpoints—between individual freedom and collective responsibility—highlights anxieties about the role that tolerance should play in contemporary democratic politics, something that can be further developed by situating the UNESCO declaration alongside three of the most prevalent models of tolerance in contemporary democratic theory. The models, I emphasize, are not necessarily all-encompassing or mutually exclusive; there may well be some characteristics of the UNESCO declaration (and contemporary tolerance more generally) that fit into more than one of the models, and others that do not fit at all. Yet I believe that the models help delimit the discursive terrain of the UNESCO declaration, and that they do so by privileging an intellectualist orientation to politics that associates sensorially inflected experiences with a turn to subjectivism and nihilism. How this comes to be the case requires looking at the Declaration of Principles on Tolerance in relation to each of the three models of tolerance in contemporary democratic theory.

The Model of Reasonable Tolerance

The model that appears most prominently in the Declaration of Principles on Tolerance, and that sets the tone for how tolerance is studied and discussed today, is championed by theorists such as John Rawls, Jürgen Habermas, and Rainer Forst (as well as a host of other political liberals and deliberative democrats).[10] Here, the version of Lockean liberalism introduced above is supplemented by a neo-Kantian notion of reason, which is defined as a universally shared faculty that uses procedures of generality and reciprocity to both contest and displace any criterion for inclusion based on religion, ethnicity, or sexuality. As long as constituents avoid such criteria, theorists of reasonable tolerance argue, they have the same right as everyone else to participate in public discussions about matters of common concern. Tolerance thus is seen as a neutral, colorblind resolution to disagreements about forms of life, religious beliefs, and freedom of expression—what the Declaration of Principles on Tolerance identifies as the single most important condition for "peace and for economic and social advancement of all peoples."[11] The reasonable-tolerance model includes some variance with regard to the role that pain plays in this agenda: whereas one view (the "relaxed view") suggests that the encounter with pain can be domesticated by reaching back to Mill's harm principle, another view (the "strict view") sees pain as external or detrimental to the procedures of generality and reciprocity that define the proper use of reason. Both views, however, embrace the hierarchical separation of mind and body that defines the intellectualist orientation to politics, something that enables both views to associate sensorially inflected experiences with a turn to subjectivism and nihilism. These views see pain as a purely physical phenomenon, and they stage the sensorium as somehow wilder, less agentive, and more directly implicated in conflict, disagreement, instability and violence than any proper use of reason could ever be.

Theorists of reasonable tolerance use this account to argue that tolerators who wish to overcome the normative and political tensions that trouble contemporary democracy must do so by defining themselves independently of the pain they endure as part of their tolerance. According to theorists of reasonable tolerance, experiences of pain are too often grafted onto "religious values and beliefs," which privilege "social homogeneity," putting the "cultural presuppositions" of tolerance into question.[12] Many theorists within the reasonable-tolerance model thus see a tension between, on the one hand, the contextually situated constituent who is driven by feelings and perceptions and, on the other hand, the exemplary citizen who does not justify a principle or policy with reference to feelings and perceptions but instead differentiates between a narrow first-person perspective and a broader third-person perspective, privileging the latter as the proper basis for public reason, thereby downplaying the place of sensorially inflected experiences as motivation for following procedures of generality and reciprocity.[13] Echoing many of the concerns expressed in the Declaration of Principles on Tolerance, theorists of reasonable tolerance point to recent cases such as the French hijab case to highlight the importance of these points. Though most theorists of reasonable tolerance agree with the Muslim minority, and thus argue against those who want to ban the hijab from public schools, theorists of reasonable tolerance also fault the Muslim minority for invoking the pain inflicted by institutional discrimination and social harassment as a reason for resisting the French majority.[14] This invocation, theorists of reasonable tolerance argue, fails to acknowledge that pain is too personal to be shared by others and thus violates the basic principle of public reason: that the reasons citizens give for a principle or policy can be shared, understood, and evaluated by everyone else. Muslims who express their pain, in other words, fall short of being truly tolerant because they allow their ethical beliefs to interfere with the demands of a moral framework in which there is more than one conception of the common good, failing to separate their own conception of the good ("ethics") from common principles and procedures that all reasonable conceptions of the good are said to share ("morality"). As Forst puts it, adding to the view we discussed in the Introduction, true tolerators are those who separate ethics from morality, and who use this distinction to approach "each other as moral-political equals in the sense that their common framework of social life should [...] be guided by norms that all parties can equally accept, and that do not favor one specific 'ethical community.'"[15]

Whether or not this way of defining the norms of deliberation and justification makes tolerance impossible is a question to which I shall return in the next section of this chapter. For now, the important point is to note how the argument invokes an intellectualist orientation to politics, and how this orientation not only substantiates many of the basic claims advanced in the Declaration of Principles on Tolerance but also highlights the influence of a somatophobic staging of the sensorium prevalent in the discussions of contemporary tolerance. On the basis of the presuppositions of the reasonable-tolerance model, we might say that somatophobia is a staging of the sensorium that entails (1) a notion of reason as universally accessible, and as constituted in ways that are fundamentally different from the body and its sensorially inflected experiences (whether painful or not); (2) a notion of democratic politics that emphasizes order and stability rather than change and contestation (it is significant, though, that citizens who follow the procedures of reason have the right, perhaps even a duty, to contest each other as well as those constituents who are unreasonable—what doesn't change is the nature and meaning of reason itself); (3) a desire to enhance pluralism though an overlapping consensus based on reciprocity and generality; (4) a commitment to religious, political, and social tolerance within the limits of reason; and (5) a notion that all forms of intolerance are motivated by citizens who have been overtaken by their passions, and who therefore are prone to hatred and bigotry, obstructing reason's quest for justice, human dignity, and a peace that, as Kant claims, will put "an end to all hostilities."[16]

The second model that resonates with the Declaration of Principles on Tolerance is the tolerance-as-recognition model. Key thinkers here are Charles Taylor, Anna Elisabetta Galeotti, and other theorists who respond to the reasonable-tolerance model by looking at how late-modern, secular democracies can expand the limits of pluralism and publicly recognize the value of especially cultural differences. According to the recognition model, the intellectualist orientation to politics prevalent in the works of Rawls, Habermas, and Forst is in need of a contextualization that emphasizes the historical (and therefore also finite) nature of reasonableness.[17] To enforce this contextualization, turning it into a political virtue that resonates with the changed conditions of government, contemporary democratic theory should avoid assuming the universality of reason, and instead encourage multicultural societies to publicly recognize cultural differences as essential to their bearers. This is not as self-referential as it may sound, theorists of recognition insist. Insofar as citizens come from different cultural backgrounds, and insofar as they do not share the same notion of reason, their ability to make differences visible may have a positive effect on their deliberations. Making differences visible may also enable some citizens to see their own identity in another, more critical light, and in this sense it can empower the flexibility needed for citizens of various stripes to negotiate the challenges provoked by globalization, immigration, inequality, and war. As one recognition theorist notes, "symbolic recognition indirectly redraws the map of the standards of action and belief a society accepts."[18]

The importance of the symbolic dimension of democratic politics may help to explain why the authors of the Declaration of Principles on Tolerance focus on expanding the limits of public deliberation so as to ensure that cultural differences are not only seen but also voiced. The expansion appears especially valuable as an antidote to a politics of misrecognition, which the declaration takes to be intolerable because "it can lead to frustration, hostility and fanaticism."[19] The UNESCO declaration mirrors here the basic claim of the tolerance-as-recognition model, which also holds that misrecognition must be avoided because it can inflict pain to such a degree that it undermines the possibility of authenticity and personal autonomy. "Nonrecognition or misrecognition can inflict harm, can be a form of oppression, imprisoning someone in a false, distorted, and reduced mode of being," says Taylor at the outset of his discussion of why recognition is so important to social and political well-being.[20] And, Taylor goes on to argue, anticipating what the Declaration of Principles on Tolerance refers to as "harmony in difference,"[21] the way to prevent such harmful distortions is to ensure that diverse languages, traditions, and narratives can flourish in places where no cultural consensus can be found. As Taylor puts it in relation to the value of a bilingual community in Quebec, Canada: "Policies aimed at [cultural] survival actively seek to *create* members of the community, for instance, in their assuring that future generations continue to identify as French speakers. There is no way that these policies could be seen as just providing a facility to already existing people."[22]

Much of what I argue later in this chapter (and indeed throughout the book) is indebted to Taylor's insights regarding the insufficiencies of a purely procedural conception of reason. At the same time, however, I am not convinced that the investment in visibility and voice actually uproots intellectualism's somatophobic staging of the sensorium as subjectivist and potentially nihilistic. This is partly a matter of doubting the nature-culture dualism that some recognition theorists have raised as an alternative to the classical mind-body dualism.[23] But there is also another concern: like the Declaration of the Principles of Tolerance, the recognition model has a limited understanding of pain, one that seems to follow from linking harm to misrecognition. Assuming that pain is primarily incapacitating and nonagentive in nature, Taylor and other recognition theorists have tended to focus on how citizens can overcome their suffering through a more wholesome, communitarian, and authentic mode of being. Pain, we might say, following the model's revision of Locke's liberalism (and contemporary democratic theory more generally), is contrary to the view of the modern citizen as someone who seeks to "master" her own future in ways similar to how Hegel resolves the master-slave dialectic through the slave's sublimation of the master's desire for domination and sovereignty. Part of this sublimation is a transition from "pure" nature to what is postulated as a self-governing mode of being for which the sensorium is something to be mastered through cultural practices and institutional arrangements. Insofar as both forms of mastery entail seeing the sensorium as an obstacle to—and not a part of—reason and agency, deliberation and autonomy, we may say that the turn away from pain as a sensorially inflected experience remains operative in the model of recognition as well as in the international discourse invoked by UNESCO's Declaration of Principles on Tolerance.

Another way of saying this is that the actual difference between the models of reasonableness and recognition is less about intellectualism and somatophobia and more about how to define their implications for tolerance as the enabling condition for peace and nonviolence. Although the two models of tolerance disagree about how citizens might invoke pain as a reason for political action, they agree with the Declaration of Principles on Tolerance that pain itself does not constitute anything affirmative—that contemporary tolerance is about the avoidance of pain. For theorists of recognition, this difference expands the politics of tolerance in ways that the reasonable-tolerance model does not. On the one hand, the tolerance-as-recognition model seeks to historicize as well as contextualize the causes of misrecognition and intolerance—in particular how the causes of these phenomena are embedded in social and political institutions, and how these institutions exercise power in ways that create economic as well as symbolic inequalities among different constituencies (whether defined in religious, social, or cultural terms). On the other hand, the model also seeks to rework the ideals that contemporary democratic theory has come to associate with Lockean tolerance (justice, deliberation, liberty, and so on) and that still inform conflict resolution in multicultural societies in both Europe and elsewhere. Together, these tenets, which are part historical-contextual and part normative-reconstructive, generate a number of political alternatives embedded in the Declaration of Principles on Tolerance, including a revised "overlapping consensus model" (Taylor) and the concept of "toleration as recognition" (Galeotti).

Superior Tolerance

If the first two models of tolerance are relatively easy to identify within the Declaration of Principles on Tolerance, the third model—what I call the superior-tolerance model—appears more surreptitiously as the element that both sustains and undercuts the appeal to tolerance in a globalized world committed to peace and nonviolence. The superior-tolerance model, we might say, is simultaneously more conservative and more radical than the other two models of tolerance: at the same time as the model privileges a narrower group of people who know what tolerance "really" means, it reworks the other two models' somatophobia, turning their limited conception of pain into an often militant opposition to constituents who reject the "true" definition of what it means to be tolerant of others. Notwithstanding tolerance's inclusive appeal, the superior-tolerance model thus captures the concept's darker side and shows how it might be that tolerators, thanks to their tolerance, can claim a privileged position vis-à-vis the tolerated.

One way to appreciate the work done by this combination of inclusion and exclusion is to examine how official documents such as the Declaration of Principles on Tolerance divide the international community into two dichotomously opposed characteristics: tolerance and intolerance, peace and war, reason and passion, deliberation and violence, choice and repression, moderation and fundamentalism. Adding to what we already have seen, these dichotomies enable the UNESCO declaration to privilege tolerance as the solution to the problem of intolerance, while at the same time it avoids the difficulty of explaining how the struggle for tolerance itself might be tainted by the violence attributed to acts of intolerance. Whereas the Declaration of Principles on Tolerance explicitly places the category of intolerance, and more generally the many imperfections of our current age, inside a historical time subject to contestation and critique, the declaration says little if anything about tolerance's own history, depicting it as a "moral duty" enforced by "the standards set out in international human rights instruments."[24] This rather ahistorical conception of tolerance places the community of tolerators in a superior position vis-à-vis constituencies who (on this view) still haven't learned how to be tolerant of others. On the one hand, the conception severs the community of tolerators from the context out of which the urge to act intolerantly is said to arise. On the other hand, the conception also ensures that when tolerators set out to replace "the culture of war by a culture of peace,"[25] they can do so knowing that the justification for their actions won't be threatened or undermined by the violence associated with such change. The superior-tolerance model develops, in other words, a sense of immunity that protects tolerators from anxieties about their own finitude and imperfections. Not only does the superior-tolerance model depict tolerators as always-already reasonable (and hence moderate and deliberative), it gives them the confidence needed not to question how their own claim to reasonableness mirrors the so-called intolerant ones' insofar as both groups invoke a limited set of sensorially inflected experiences in order to cultivate and sustain their various perceptions of what it means to believe and to know.

For our purposes, the superior-tolerance model is particularly interesting because it highlights what most contemporary democratic theorists seek to downplay: that tolerance is more than a secular concept, and that its sense of superiority is secured by way of tolerance's historical ties to Christianity and Western civilization.[26] From Paul's "Second Letter to the Corinthians," which sees tolerance as a way to endure the pain of original sin,[27] to Locke's *Letter Concerning Toleration*, which combines a justification for tolerance based on reason with one based on Christian dogmas,[28] we find a genealogy that is Eurocentric, and that grows out of a Westernized conception of reason combined with a Christian orientation to the world. Although this genealogy is not mentioned in the Declaration of Principles on Tolerance, it buttresses the declaration's claim to superiority, pinpointing the extent to which tolerance is a uniquely Western concept, shaped by two thousand years of Christian history, and limited to constituencies that either belong to this history by birth or are willing to assimilate to it and make it their own. This privileging of Christianity operates even in today's globalized world because so many of the attempts to promote the values of tolerance, both domestically and internationally, assume a Christianized conception of belief and knowledge.[29] According to Jacques Derrida, who distances himself from tolerance's claim to superiority by proposing "another tolerance," this means that we should be careful not to assume that tolerance is unequivocally universal, and that we instead must approach tolerance as a limited virtue, one that historically has been the secret of the Christian community, which has used tolerance to set an example for other believers who also need to endure various pains caused by internal disagreements, political conflicts, and anxieties about life after death. In Derrida's words, "the concept of tolerance, *stricto sensu*, belongs first of all to a sort of Christian domesticity. It is *literally*, I mean behind this name, a secret of the Christian community."[30]

Another reason for attending to the superior-tolerance model focuses more directly on the place of pain within a staging of the sensorium that associates sensorially inflected experiences with a turn to subjectivism and nihilism. Insofar as this association is tied to the history of Christianity and Western civilization, and insofar as both Christianity and Western civilization sustain the somatophobia that underlines the other two models of tolerance, we might say if pain is brought back in under the auspices of an intellectualist regime of discourse and sensation, it is done in a way that both acknowledges and reworks pain's limited potential, replacing the secular-physiological account of pain with a political-theological account in which pain stands out as the sign of a necessary, if not meaningful, punishment for the sins and misdeeds that individuals and communities have committed in *this* life. Pain—and the endurance thereof—becomes here the virtue of a citizen who turns intellectualism against itself, and who does not distinguish between political views and religious beliefs. Another way of saying this is that a reintroduction of pain legitimized by the superior-tolerance model represents the flip side of somatophobia because it expresses itself either through resentment and demand for revenge for one's suffering (the "aggressive view") or through meditation on the fragility of the human condition (the "introspective view"). Although the responses differ in their orientation to society, they both embody a predominantly *re*-active endurance in which tolerance entails a zero-sum game between the tolerator and the tolerated: whereas the aggressive view puts the burdens on the tolerated, redoubling the infliction of pain in an attempt to diminish the tolerated's presence, the introspective view steps back in order to protect itself from further suffering. Both views represent in this sense a limited conception of pain, one that can be used to justify a militant opposition to constituents who reject the "true" definition of what it means to be tolerant of others.

The discussion of how UNESCO's Declaration of Principles on Tolerance embodies three models of tolerance in contemporary democratic theory has now come full circle. To be sure, the mapping proposed here does not necessarily capture everything there is to say about how tolerance is understood and practiced today; indeed, my argument in the coming chapters is that elements of another, more empowering tolerance subsist within current discussions of democratic pluralism, pointing us in the direction of a theory of active tolerance attuned to the changed conditions of citizenship and government. My point, however, is that turning to this theory is not truly possible unless we first appreciate how the intellectualist orientation prevalent in contemporary democratic theory has created the discursive conditions for a somatophobia that relegates pain (and the sensorium more generally) to the unexamined background. Of particular interest here is how the preceding discussion suggests that somatophobia not only privileges a detachment from sensorially inflected experiences such as pain but also opens up the possibility of an immanent opposition—a turning operation, to use Hannah Arendt's expression[31]—one that stages the sensorium in such a way that when it is overturned, it aggressively unleashes the passions and violence that the various appeals to reason and recognition hoped to repress, if not displace or overcome. The challenges associated with this turning operation are evident in a number of contemporary conflicts, including the French hijab case, which may involve a moral question about who has the right to decide what citizens should wear in public, but also, and perhaps more importantly, evolves around "collective anxiety" and "resentment over visible cultural difference,"[32] generating what Joan Scott describes as "growing hysteria."[33] Hysteria is indeed a good candidate for describing how intellectualism's staging of the sensorium expresses itself. As pain is relegated to the unexamined background, and as this relegation restricts the return of pain to a *re*-active mode of endurance, hysteria occurs because the demands of intellectualism limit the expression of the pains that tolerators are expected to endure, creating the need to either mute pain itself or express it indirectly—through secondary symptoms that are meant to relieve the tolerator from the distress caused by the initial pain. The result is not unlike the one we find in conflicts such as the French hijab case: a zero-sum game where each side expects the other side to bear the burden of moderation, and where a feeling of intractability takes center stage because neither the tolerator nor the tolerated wants to shrink his or her presence to make room for the other side of the relationship.

III. RAWLS AND THE IMPOSSIBILITY OF BEING TOLERANT

The prevalence of the intellectualist orientation to politics in both official documents such as the Declaration of Principles on Tolerance and the various strands of contemporary democratic theory raises the question whether there is something about an intellectualist orientation to politics that cuts deeper than simply troubling tolerance from within its own presuppositions. One way to ask this question is to consider the extent to which the turning operation mentioned above is incidental or intrinsic to an intellectualist orientation to politics: Are the limits of an intellectualist orientation to politics restricted to the possibility of immanent opposition in which tolerance, more or less fortuitously, morphs into something other than the intended goal of reason and recognition—what the Declaration of Principles on Tolerance calls "harmony in difference"[34]—or are they more fundamental because intellectualism's somatophobic staging of the sensorium undercuts the very empowerment of tolerance, making it *impossible*, and not simply more difficult or self-contradictory, to become tolerant on the terms set by intellectualism itself? My claim is that it is the latter, and to see why I suggest that we look closer at the underlying presuppositions of the intellectualist orientation to politics, using the work of John Rawls as our focal point. As the previous section suggested, Rawls occupies a privileged position in contemporary discussions about how to conceptualize tolerance because his work is seen as (1) essential to the definition of tolerance, (2) representative of the challenges facing contemporary secularism, and (3) pivotal for a turning point that simultaneously removes tolerators from their Christian roots and encourages them to return to these roots. Moreover, for our purposes, Rawls's work is particularly interesting because it prefigures the intellectualist terms by which tolerance becomes detached from the endurance of pain. Rawls's point is that citizens are right to treat the endurance of pain as opposed to the ideals and norms of tolerance, and that they must do so, even if it troubles their ability to practice tolerance in a world defined by greater pluralism and a higher degree of interconnectedness.

Rawls's justification of this argument begins with a critique of the utilitarian doctrine, which right before the publication of *A Theory of Justice* was the dominant approach in political philosophy.[35] As is well known, Rawls criticizes the utilitarian doctrine because its emphasis on pleasure and pain gives "no reason *in principle* why the greater gains of some should not compensate for the lesser losses of others; or ... why the violation of the liberty of the few might not be made right by the greater good shared by many."[36] To avoid this violation, Rawls develops a four-step procedure that he wants citizens to follow. The procedure embodies a neo-Kantian conception of reason, and it establishes Rawls as one of the principal architects of the intellectualist orientation to politics in contemporary democratic theory. Put schematically, the procedure runs like this: first, citizens should identify tolerance as part of the democratic tradition to which they belong; second, they should subject this intuition to what Rawls calls "the original position" to ensure that tolerance is more than just a modus vivendi; third, they should elevate tolerance to a principle that is congruent with what it means to be reasonable; and fourth, they should insert this principle back into public discourse, presenting the principle as a demand of reason that all members of society ought to recognize as part of the democratic tradition. As Rawls argues, reasonable persons should be careful not to justify or evaluate the value of "diversity" and "plurality" according to either the utilitarian doctrine or any other doctrine claiming to know what is universally good:

> The essential point is this: as a practical political matter no general moral conception can provide a publicly recognized basis for a conception of justice in a modern democratic state. The social and historical conditions of such a state have their origins in the Wars of Religion following the Reformation and the subsequent development of the principle of toleration, and in the growth of constitutional government and the institutions of large industrial market economies. These conditions profoundly affect the requirements of a workable conception of political justice: such a conception must allow for a diversity of doctrines and the plurality of conflicting, and indeed incommensurable, conceptions of the good.[37]

Before we turn to the blind spots and double binds that might follow from this argument, it is important to note that Rawls does not always adhere to a strict version of the intellectualist orientation to politics, especially not when it comes to the so-called democratic tradition, the appeal to which Rawls thinks is crucial if conceptualizations of justice and tolerance are going to have any real impact on practices of citizenship and public deliberation more generally.[38] Rawls develops this argument by suggesting that the democratic tradition names a set of public opinions and precepts that, in ways not always anticipated by the Declaration of Principles on Tolerance, have evolved over a longer period of time. Emphasizing the importance of events such as the Reformation and the ensuing Wars of Religion, the democratic tradition brings the political context back in, and, according to Rawls at least, it reminds everyone of why tolerance is so important to the possibility of a just and stable society. The democratic tradition does so because it places moral principles in a context of plurality and disagreement, and because it sees this context as a necessary feature of late-modern political life. The democratic tradition, you might say, is the bridge that links contemporary democratic theory to the history of what Rawls calls the "fact of pluralism"—that is, to how political institutions, social norms, and moral ideals have evolved, not only through appeals to reason and recognition but also through the messy politics of passionate advocacy, violent resistance, revolutionary practice, and careful maintenance.

Rawls's references to the democratic tradition are worth emphasizing because they show how thin the line can be between an intellectualist orientation to politics and a sensorial orientation to politics, and how each orientation, when mobilized in relation to the other, can enhance elements in both. Pushing this mobilization further seems promising because it could bring discussions in contemporary democratic theory closer to an understanding of how alternative practices of tolerance can pluralize the span of acceptable differences in a world defined by contestation and interconnectedness. Not only would the mobilization of both orientations help to expand the notion of pluralism as a "fact," emphasizing the many trajectories that circulate in and out of the democratic tradition, it would also enable us to develop a set of new terms that would acknowledge more fully reason's finitude as part of a historical process in which regimes of discourse and sensation help to define what counts as reasonable, alerting us to the link between the principles that regulate public deliberation and the sensorial forces that make citizens see reason as the proper way to resolve conflict and disagreement at any given moment.[39] As I see it, the importance of considering these aspects follows from Rawls's own references to the democratic tradition: rather than disavowing the importance of context, they encourage us to see the democratic tradition as the impetus for theorizing about democracy, sending us down a path where it no longer seems right to define reason independently of context and where we must instead examine how changes in the historical context produce changes in the meaning of reason.

Although such considerations resonate with Rawls's aim of generating a vibrant and expansive sphere of deliberation and public reason, they do not figure prominently in his own work, in part because he remains wedded to the idea that reason itself can and should remain untouched by gestures toward context and the sensorium.[40] This makes good sense if the goal is to establish an overlapping consensus, appealing to a higher moral ground that aims to justify the right balance between equality and inequality, freedom and unfreedom. But it may also create an impasse that shows how tolerance becomes impossible when inflected by an intellectualist orientation to politics: not simply more difficult or self-contradictory, but blind to, even detached from, its own conditions of thought and action. Consider especially the difficulties of both recognizing the importance of context because it invigorates public deliberation *and* insisting on the need to overcome this affirmation in the interest of ensuring that the principles of reason are universal or at least general in the sense of being shared across cultural, religious, or social divides. Embedded in Rawls's conceptual language, the tension between these two demands invokes a double bind intrinsic to how intellectualism envisions the way tolerators might respond to contestation and disagreement: *either* tolerators rise above the sensorium that defines the lives of those who are not yet tolerant, invoking a superiority that limits the inclusiveness of tolerance itself, *or* they embrace the sensorium along the lines discussed in the previous paragraph, in which case they can be charged with undermining the procedures of generality and reciprocity that is said to define reason itself. Neither outcome seems to be a foregone conclusion, and yet, even though the space between the two sides of the double bind is significant, it is left untheorized by Rawls and the majority of contemporary democratic theorists who follow his intellectualist orientation to politics.

A good way to develop an appreciation of how the double bind works— and to better understand its implications—is to focus on two areas, the first of which concerns one of the five conceptual components that most contemporary democratic theorists see as critical to the circumstances of tolerance: the objection component.[41] As noted in the Introduction, the objection component is typically conceptualized with reference to expressions of disgust or repulsion, and the component thus appears to be the closest the extant literature comes to something like endurance and the sensorially inflected experience of pain. On the Rawlsian account, however, expressions of disgust and aversion are regulated by neo-Kantian principles of reason, which ensure that only objections that are "normatively substantive" are included as legitimate objections, ruling out context-specific objections based on personal preferences and idiosyncratic traditions.[42] An objection to same-sex marriage based on arguments from the New Testament, for example, is "unreasonable" because it excludes non-Christians, and because it posits a right to marriage without making it available to all members of society.[43] Conversely, an objection to torture is not only legitimate but also incontestable because no "reasonable" person would want to endure and reciprocate the pain suffered by the tortured.

Despite the attractiveness of such moral proceduralism, there is an inherent problem here, especially if we consider Rawls's own oscillation between context and reason. To contextualize an objection, we might say, is to uncover its internal complexity, and to show how the reasons that sustain the objection are mixed up with emotion and agony, feeling and perception, all sensorially inflected experiences structured by regimes of discourse and sensation. This is often the case even when it comes to so-called absolute objections, which, as Preston King has pointed out, obtain their "absoluteness" from comparative judgments that frequently change from context to context.[44] To acknowledge the importance of context is to acknowledge the potential contingency of all objections, and to analyze each of them, not according to their moral standing, as Rawls initially envisions it, but according to their various and changing intensities, durations, and consequences. Promising in its own right, this approach contradicts the neo-Kantian concept of reason as untouched by the sensorial dimensions of human experience, and thus it highlights the tension between acknowledging the work done by these dimensions and maintaining that the procedures of reason are the same across place and time. Indeed, if someone tried to invoke both claims at the same time, the outcome would most likely be deemed unsuccessful when judged by Rawls's own standards: whereas the side of reason would see the turn to context as undermining the need for moral certainty, the contextual side would see the emphasis on reason as undermining the powers needed to tolerate (or not tolerate) the continued presence of whatever is perceived as being objectionable in any given situation. The uncertainty created by these opposing judgments suggests that a tolerator who follows Rawls's line of thinking is likely to face a difficult situation in which she, contrary to what Rawls anticipates, is fundamentally unsure about whether she is right to perceive something or someone as objectionable, and thus whether or not her actions will be recognized as "tolerant."[45] Might this not undermine the desire to become tolerant in the first place?

The other area where Rawls's oscillation between context and reason seems to trouble the empowerment of tolerance relates to the depiction of intellectualism as a mode of theorization that justifies norms and principles by way of reason alone. In Rawlsian theory, the challenge to this depiction follows from the emphasis on a "sense of justice," which moves citizens "by ends and ideals of excellence," invoking a set of "moral feelings" organized around "a liability to humiliation and shame."[46] Rawls may mean to put the emphasis not on "sense" but on "justice," but if we take the former seriously, we can identify a number of ways in which the outcome undermines the reasonableness he posits. Most obvious is how the reference to "sense," as well as to "humiliation and shame," is in tension with his commitment to a justification of tolerance based on procedures of reason untouched by the sensorium that sustain the citizenry's attitudes and sentiments vis-à-vis issues regarding justice and pluralism. This tension, we should note, is not limited to Rawls's earlier works but appears also in the later works, including *Political Liberalism*, where he emphasizes the need to endure what he calls "the burdens of judgment."[47] In both cases, the idea is to introduce a set of feelings and perceptions that on the one hand entail a certain disposition or ethos, acknowledging the finitude of reason, and on the other hand run counter to the intellectualist orientation on which Rawls and others base their criticism of competing approaches to democratic theory.[48] One way to read this tension is to place it alongside our earlier discussion of context, and to emphasize how both the turn to context and the interest in feelings such as humiliation and shame redouble the ambiguities of Rawls's intellectualism, augmenting the sense of impossibility that arises when citizens have to both acknowledge and disavow their entanglements with sensorially inflected experiences. Another way to read the tension is to say that even when the intellectualist orientation to politics appears at its most stringent (as it does in Rawls's work), it relies on feelings and perceptions that exceed citizens' ability to reason independently of who they are as embodied beings situated within a sensorially inflected context. If this is the case, then perhaps we should say that there is no such thing as a purely intellectualist orientation to politics. Indeed, if there is no sense of justice without a liability to humiliation and shame,[49] and if the ability to judge is characterized by an uncertainty that seems burdensome, then the conclusion might well be that intellectualism itself is a way of engaging what it seeks to disengage: the sensorium and its role in defining the conditions of thought and action in a world of deep pluralism.

Whichever way we read it, the important point here is that the reference to feelings such as humiliation and shame troubles the basic drift behind Rawls's argument: that tolerance, as an inclusive and deliberative practice of reasonable citizens, can mitigate the tension between two opposing viewpoints, especially in a world like ours challenged by globalization, immigration, and so on. The reason the various references to humiliation and shame trouble this argument does not necessarily lie with humiliation and shame themselves, which, as Christina Tarnopolsky has pointed out, can unsettle "one's 'blind' or unthinking identification with an image or ideal, which can actually be a good thing if who we are cannot be fully captured by an overly unitary or fantastical standard."[50] In Rawls, however, this recognition of finitude and difference is limited because the pain that undergirds the liability to humiliation and shame heightens the importance of context, which, as we saw earlier, is defined either in opposition to reason or as an appendix undoing the intellectualism from which Rawls's criticism of other approaches to justice and democracy springs. In both cases, the ability to endure pain, either through discursive communities or through virulent lines of flight and world-making, is left untheorized, enabling the turning operation we discussed in the previous section of this chapter. Pain, we might say, does appear at the heart of Rawlsian theory, but because it is limited to something as self-negating as a liability to shame and humiliation, it fails to take on any affirmative role in the pursuit of pluralism and democracy. That is, rather than pluralizing pain, allowing some of its forms to appear as an opening to the world of deep pluralism, whether defined in religious, cultural, social, or sexual terms, Rawls's intellectualism turns it inward, to the inner life of the human self, invoking a mode of politics based on disavowal and self-denigration rather than empowerment and engagement.[51]

Limiting pain to a person's inner life is a historical practice that, as I indicated at the outset, is the topic of the next chapter (Chapter 2). What I want to stress here is how Rawls's intellectualist orientation to politics tends to make tolerance impossible because it splits, in ways similar to what I suggested earlier, the practice of tolerance into two equally flawed choices. Why be tolerant, citizens might ask, if tolerance does not address the complex range of motives, feelings, and reasons that sustain our objections to a practice, tradition, belief, or idea? Conversely, citizens might ask, how to be tolerant if tolerance is too context-dependent to actually fulfill the demands of reason? Each question harkens back to the turning operation discussed in the previous section, and this helps to explain how tolerance can sanction its own paradoxes and transgressions as it encompasses everything from reasonableness to benevolent superiority. Apart from the apathy that may arise from not knowing what tolerance actually means, let alone how to engage its internal conflicts, the affinities between these outcomes may well foster an antagonistic relationship between tolerator and tolerated, one that threatens to undermine the aim of becoming tolerant. Rather than being a source of affirmation, the tolerated may be why tolerance fails. "My" tolerance, a reasonable person might say, is impossible because "your" demand to be tolerated is too difficult to comprehend or engage in any meaningful way. Here, tolerance turns into intolerance, setting up the kind of *ressentiment* that externalizes pain and turns endurance into a matter of holding someone else responsible for one's suffering. As Nietzsche puts it, *ressentiment* implies a situation in which "every sufferer instinctively looks for a cause of his distress; more exactly, for a culprit, even more precisely for a *guilty* culprit who is receptive to distress."[52]

I have dwelt on these aspects of Rawls's work to show how intellectualism itself is a way of way of engaging what it seeks to disengage—the heteronomous world of sensorially inflected experiences—and to suggest how nurturing an interest in the sensorium more generally is important, not only because it can bring the discussion of tolerance closer to the circumstances in which tolerators live and act, but also because it might displace the risk of a double bind that threatens to turn tolerance into an impossibility. I use the term *impossible* in a stronger sense than the one discussed by most contemporary democratic theorists, including the philosopher Bernard Williams. According to him, tolerance seems impossible because it implies the acceptance of beliefs that the tolerator finds "deeply unacceptable."[53] For Williams, however, this impossibility is surmountable if we distinguish between the belief in question and the person holding this belief, and then use the latter's right to hold certain beliefs as a reason for granting tolerance of what we otherwise find unacceptable. Tolerance is *possible*, Williams says, as long as the good "is found not in that belief's continuing but in the other believer's autonomy."[54] This solution has merit but may not be sufficient for grasping how tolerance is felt and how it often appears as a practical impossibility. As our discussion has shown, tolerance becomes impossible when we expect tolerators to identify with two opposing demands—a sensitivity to political context *and* a commitment to abstract reason—and when our conceptual apparatus doesn't offer a vocabulary that enables tolerators to see, let alone challenge or rework, the connection between these two. Tolerance becomes impossible, we might say, the moment we stage the sensorium through a somatophobic language that associates sensorially inflected experiences with subjectivism and nihilism. Not only does such a staging of the sensorium undercut the enabling conditions of reason and agency, it makes it impracticable to be tolerant in the way currently envisioned in both public discourse and contemporary democratic theory.

Another way of saying this is that reorienting the discussion of tolerance toward an interest in pain and the sensorium of political life more generally may be a particularly promising way of responding to the intractability that has come to define contemporary tolerance conflicts such as the French hijab case. The challenge is to supplement, if not redefine, current efforts to promote tolerance so that our conceptual apparatus becomes more attuned to the role pain plays in democratic politics. What is needed is not just a declaration of principles on tolerance, let alone a proclamation of a specific day as the annual day of tolerance celebrated by the United Nations and other international institutions; rather, in addition to scrutinizing the inequalities prompted by globalization and the success of new information technologies we need a better conceptualization of what pain does, and how it might be an intrinsic feature of democratic subjectivity, whether we understand the latter in terms of demands for social recognition and individual rights or in terms of contestation and experimentation. Such conceptualization may not automatically resolve the intractability of the existing terms of political conflict, but it may help us see how tolerance once again can become a progressive practice that aims to empower and pluralize the span of acceptable differences in society as well as to generate the modes of subjectivity needed to support such orientation to contemporary democratic politics.

IV. THINKING CRITICALLY ABOUT PAIN

In the remaining part of this chapter, I want to begin considering how one might bring such an alternative conceptualization into conversation with the terms privileged by the intellectualist orientation to politics. The first thing that stands out is how the link between somatophobia and the impossibility of tolerance draws our attention to the path along which tolerance could become more than a practice of passive restraint defined by various appeals to reason, recognition, and superiority. Unlike most critiques of tolerance, which interpret the limitations of an intellectualist orientation to politics as a reason to replace tolerance with a different set of practices, our discussion suggests that the issue is less whether contemporary democratic theory should be "for" or "against" tolerance, and more whether there are alternative ways of imaging the links among the sensorium, regimes of discourse and sensation, and the conception of tolerance as the endurance of pain.[55] Imagining these links differently does not in and of itself guarantee a more active tolerance, but it does encourage us to develop a critique, which avoids collapsing pain into one feeling, one experience, and instead pluralizes pain's many meanings in order to engage the diverse worlds, experiential registers, and agentive capabilities that the encounter with something painful might invoke. As discussed in the Introduction, my hunch is that such a critique will be essential to the theory of active tolerance and democratic subjectivity more generally. If contemporary democratic theorists relax the demands of an intellectualist orientation to politics, if they engage endurance and resilience from a critical perspective that neither moralizes nor simply celebrates pain, then it might be that new orientations toward pain's world-making potential open up: its meanings may become more sharable, its differences may become more visible, its agentive capacities may become more resilient, and as a result its political futures may become more affirmable. It is, of course, important that each of these elements of the critique (meaning, difference, agency, and potentiality) be mobilized in relation to all the others. Without this mobilization, one could end up with an account of democratic politics unable to explain how the same pain can work differently across time and place, or with a naïve masochism that assumes what John Durham Peters, in *Courting the Abyss*, calls a sensibility of "homeopathic machismo," that is, a sensibility in which the very presence of pain is celebrated as a sign of social progress and civic virtue.[56]

But I am getting ahead of myself. Before trying to sort out how modes of endurance might figure affirmatively within an alternative account of the challenges facing contemporary democracy, we must first examine the assumptions that can sustain an understanding like the one just outlined. Particularly important in this regard is a consideration of how a sensorial orientation to politics might broaden our conception of pain, and how such a broadening might mitigate the risk of tolerance becoming an "impossible" practice. To this end, consider here two seemingly very different formulations, by Friedrich Nietzsche and John Stuart Mill respectively:

> Pain is something different from pleasure—I mean it is *not* its opposite... Pain is an *intellectual* occurrence.... There is no pain as such.... The really specific thing in pain is always the protracted shock, the lingering vibrations of a terrifying *choc* in the cerebral center of the nervous system:—one does not really suffer from the cause of pain..., but from the protracted disturbance of equilibrium that occurs as a result of the *choc*. Pain is a sickness of the cerebral nerve centers.... [One] does *not* react to the pain. Pain is subsequently projected to the wounded place.... It is a mere place-sign.[57]

> What means are there of determining which is the acutest of two pains, or the intensest of two pleasurable sensations, except the general suffrage of those who are familiar with both? Neither pains nor pleasures are homogenous, and pain is always heterogeneous with pleasure. What is there to decide whether a particular pleasure is worth purchasing at the cost of a particular pain, expect the feelings and judgments of the experienced?[58]

Even though Nietzsche and Mill often are portrayed as standing on opposite sides in the discussion of tolerance—a difference to which I shall return below—the two formulations just cited suggest a set of commonalities that are worth stressing in relation to the limitations of intellectualism and a move toward a sensorially oriented understanding of the work done by pain. Most obvious is how both Nietzsche and Mill emphasize the bodily processes that sustain the sensorium, and that I have argued should figure prominently in the conceptualization of democratic politics. Both, as I read them, suggest an account of pain as a world-making experience that develops the feeling of displacement by generating context-specific ways of feeling, seeing, and speaking.[59] Nietzsche and Mill elaborate on this account by placing themselves outside the dominant ways of defining pain: neither, for example, believes in the existence of an essence, which, as one historian of political thought recently has suggested, would make it possible to expect "all living creatures" to have the "same capacity of feeling pain."[60] Nietzsche and Mill contest this view, each in his own way, drawing our attention to how the capacity of feeling pain is contextually defined by a set of distinct linkages among symbolic practices, physiological structures, and contingently situated conditions of affect and perception.[61] Nietzsche and Mill also depart from other dominant approaches, prominent especially in psychoanalysis and literary criticism, which use the critique of essentialism to denaturalize the body, turning the critique of pain into a cultural analysis that downplays or ignores issues of physiology, affect, perception, and movement. Rather than reducing pain to *either* a physical event *or* a cultural phenomenon, Nietzsche and Mill seem to share an interest in the intersection of the two. That is, they focus on the ambiguous sites where neither side of the nature-culture dualism has been fully settled, and where, as Nietzsche puts it, the "protracted disturbance of equilibrium" prevents us from speaking of pain "as such."

A good way to lend more specificity to this understanding of the work done by pain is to look more closely at Nietzsche's somewhat aphoristic comments cited above. The first thing that stands out is how the comments appear to scorn the Cartesian theory of pain—the so-called specificity theory, which posits that special pain receptors in the skin relay sensory input to a special pain center in the brain, which then tells the body how to eliminate or prevent more damage to the skin tissue.[62] Nietzsche scorns this theory by pointing out how speed overflows conscious agency, and how, in moments of harm and danger, individuals would put their lives in further jeopardy if they waited for the "bell of consciousness" to ring.[63] In moving away from the specificity theory, however, Nietzsche does not revert to earlier conceptions such as either Aristotle's notion of pain as pure emotion or a Christian model of pain as divine punishment. Like the Cartesian theory they precede, these accounts do not probe the linkages among pain, the sensorium, and the work done by regimes of discourse and sensation. Nietzsche underscores these linkages by suggesting that pain is a "place-sign," which is "subsequently projected to the wounded place."

What Nietzsche has in mind when he makes this suggestion is not always clear. We might think that the reference to a place-sign projected to the wounded place means that Nietzsche agrees with the view advocated by an intellectualist orientation to politics, and that he sees pain as a purely subjective experience, one that individuals invoke whenever they find it convenient or necessary to make sense of their personal lives. This convergence is ultimately misleading, however, especially since Nietzsche associates subjectivism with the doctrine of free will, which he abhors and aims to displace in all of his writings. Given this, it seems more appropriate to interpret his remarks regarding pain as a place-sign as emphasizing how pain does not have an ahistorical essence, and how, as a sensorially inflected experience, it is framed by regimes of discourse and sensation. The regimes help to define what a given society should count as painful as well as how members of that society should react to the encounter with this feeling. Regimes of discourse and sensation do so because they work at the intermediate level of embodied existence—what Deleuze and Guattari, in a Nietzschean vein, call the "molecular level": as regimes of discourse and sensation regulate the meaning of pain as a place-sign, they decide who get access to this sign, and who can use it as a justification for attention and care.[64]

Further support for this reading can be found in Nietzsche's discussion of what we might call the temporality of pain. Though pain has no essence, Nietzsche argues, it does have a temporal dimension, one that he, not unlike Mill, describes in terms of a "protracted shock," a "disturbance of equilibrium," and "lingering vibrations"—all of which inhabit a certain relationship in time that defines the sufferer's mode of being. The temporality of pain, we might say, points to an act of creation, which gives the feeling its distinctively political character. Even at its most "passive," the endurance of pain can turn its alleged passivity into something active, something generative. To emphasize this point, both Nietzsche and Mill suggest, perhaps rather paradoxically, that pain is different from—and not simply opposed to—the feeling of pleasure.[65] From a democratic theory perspective, this suggestion is significant because it frees pain from notions of dissatisfaction and invisibility, often tied to ontologies of either lack or perfection, and instead foregrounds other possibilities, including that of pain as a world-making experience, defined on par with the one of pleasure, and yet characterized by textures, capabilities, relationships, and meanings.[66] On this account, pain is always in the process of becoming "painful." One might even say that pain inaugurates the most important process of becoming because it deals with moments of disequilibrium, protraction, and vibration, which circumscribe the very possibility of becoming (understood as the transition from one state of existence to another). Is pain the affect that defines the "becoming of becoming"? The question is not only rhetorical. As Nietzsche says, even in situations where suffering and wretchedness dominate, we find that a "powerful will might exist, a Yes to life, a need for this predominance." And, he goes on to say, if "the pleasure is to be very great, the pains must be very protracted and the tension of the bow tremendous."[67]

Nietzsche points here to a sensorially inflected conceptualization of the work done by pain, one that not only avoids the intellectualism and somatophobia that risk making tolerance impossible but also anticipates the broader conception of pain as a feeling of displacement discussed by Heidegger in *Being and Time*. Nietzsche, together with Mill, helps us see how this feeling of displacement can be conceptually as well as politically productive, pointing us in the direction of what best can be described as a continuum along which regimes of discourse and sensation structure the meaning and status of pain as a sensorially inflected experience.[68] At one end of the continuum, we find a subset of pains, which Wendy Brown has developed in terms of what she calls "wounded attachments"[69] and that we, inspired by Nietzsche's discussion of *ressentiment*, could call "painful pains." At this end of the continuum, the basic situation is one where the sufferer sees endurance as a zero-sum game and therefore separates himself or herself from the world of differences so as to externalize and individualize the blame for the pain endured.[70] At the other end of the continuum, this response is challenged by a different subset of pains, which we, in vein similar to Nietzsche's more affirmative depictions of pain, could call "pleasurable pains." Pleasurable pains disrupt existing precepts so as to empower or inhabit a new modes of being, and they suggest in that sense a situation more akin to the one of an artist who struggles with unconventional modes of expression, or a political activist who practices nonviolence to challenge an unequal distribution of power and privilege. In both of these cases, the need for blame is displaced because the endurance of pain is perceived as a plus-sum game where the right mix of conditions and encouragements makes the very presence of pain ethically affirmative as well as politically valuable. Pain is perceived in this light because it augments the sufferer's ability to think and act, and because it thereby enables him or her to do things he or she could not otherwise do. Rather than representing something undesirable, pain signifies here a condition of empowerment and pluralization.

As indicated in the Introduction, pleasurable pains are not as unusual as they might seem, and in fact they can be detected in interventions ranging from the Stoic concept of *tolerāntia* over Kant's concept of the sublime to Merleau-Ponty's embrace of perceptual incompleteness. Much of the discussion in the chapters to come revolves around an attempt to develop and substantiate this experience of pain in relation to the many challenges facing contemporary democracy, including globalization, immigration, inequality, and war. In order to prepare this discussion, however, we first need to note how the continuum mentioned above differs from the terms that currently define contemporary democratic theory, and thus how it can mitigate some of the blind spots that turn tolerance into an impossible practice. The continuum intervenes into these blind spots by exploring the in-between space left untheorized by Rawls—the space between reason and the sensorium—and by avoiding associating sensorially inflected experiences with subjectivism and nihilism. The result, I argue, suggests a number of insights that both conceptually and politically reorient the discussion of tolerance.

At the conceptual level, the continuum mitigates the risk of tolerance becoming impossible because it neither moralizes nor celebrates pain but instead seeks to mobilize the various elements necessary to differentiate the very experience of pain. As we just saw, the continuum emphasizes the value of context-specific meanings, embraces the differences that lie within all modes of perception and affect, pluralizes the range of agentive capacities, and foregrounds pain's potential as a world-making experience. Attention to these elements can alert us not only to practices of endurance and resilience that go beyond the idea of a zero-sum game but also to another way of tackling the difficulties the objection component poses if one follows an intellectualist orientation to politics. Shifting the focus away from a double bind in which tolerators must justify their conception of the objectionable with reference to *either* reason *or* the sensorium, the continuum suggests that the important question tolerators should ask themselves is not so much whether their objection is morally justifiable in the neo-Kantian sense of being "normatively substantive" but whether the pain embedded in the objection exposes them to a vulnerability around which new connections can be mobilized: Is the endured pain empowering in the sense of drawing attention to alternative ways of living? If so, how can this pain become part of a desire to belong to a world of deep pluralism? This approach builds on the constitutive role played by the sensorium, and it allows us to see why the "reason" citizens should become tolerant might be a wish—or, perhaps better, a "want"—rather than a "need." If the objectionable is embodied by a pain that, on the one hand, displaces one's sense of security and, on the other hand, enables a transition that augments one's ability to think and act, then tolerance no longer has to be a second-best option that one accepts against one's better wishes. Rather than being associated with a demand to restrain oneself, tolerance can now become an expansive practice of affirmation and engagement.

At the political level, the continuum outlined above changes our orientation to tolerance in ways that can be best developed by returning to one of the issues that do separate Nietzsche and Mill, the significance of becoming tolerant. As is well known, Mill and Nietzsche seem to differ widely on this issue: whereas Mill links his account of pain to a theory of tolerance based on contestation and free speech, a theory that subsequently has been either debunked or reduced to accommodate Rawlsian intellectualism, Nietzsche appears to draw the opposite conclusion, suggesting that tolerance implies a disdain for the politics of difference and becoming.[71] This disagreement, however, narrows if we consider how Nietzsche cultivates an appreciation of what the endurance of pain can do outside the intellectualist orientation that neither he nor Mill adopts. The two converge here around the idea that a certain endurance is indispensable to the politics of empowerment and pluralization, while they diverge on how to situate this endurance within a framework of political institutions and social knowledge. Unlike Mill, who simultaneously defers knowledge of pain to "the feelings and judgments of the experienced" *and* insists on building a society based on a calculation that weighs pain against pleasure, Nietzsche seems more radical in his approach, expanding on a view that, as we shall see in Chapter 2, reaches back to Kant and others. On Nietzsche's account, there is no neutral way of weighing pain against pleasure, especially if we accept Mill's claim that pain "is always heterogeneous" with pleasure. Nietzsche, moreover, contests the idea that the sufferer has special access to pain's meaning. To say the sufferer knows best, Nietzsche argues, may actually bring back an essentialism that ignores the regimes of discourse and sensation underpinning the encounter with something painful. To avoid this complicity, Nietzsche wants sufferers to resignify pain in such a way that detachment from its immediate urgency becomes possible, and a comprehensive critique of various regimes of discourse and sensation can take its place. As Nietzsche suggests in the section of the *Will to Power* cited earlier, since one "does not . . . suffer from the cause of pain," it may be possible to change the conditions under which suffering seems necessary.

In the debate between Mill and Nietzsche, the most important thing is to keep the disagreement alive, and not try to either privilege one thinker over the other, or collapse the difference between them. Nietzsche, I believe, is right to point out that regimes of discourse and sensation are responsible for how pain is felt and perceived in this or that situation, and this fits well with our previous discussion of how changes in context and tradition often affect our judgments about what is right and what is wrong. But the role played by regimes of discourse and sensation does not necessarily mean that the politics of tolerance should be indifferent to how sufferers are positioned in relation to the work done by these regimes. In some cases, the pain may be so intense and traumatic that Nietzsche's demand for detachment from one's experience can seem impossible, even cruel. Similarly, in cases such as the French hijab case where a minority's experience of pain is silenced or unacknowledged, a first step toward reconfiguring power and privilege is often to publicize testimonies from constituents who feel violated or harmed. Not only do these testimonies have an emotional appeal, which can charge the desire to act and speak up against discrimination and inequality, they may also remind the majority of its finitude and context-specific ways of perceiving pain. There is, we might say, no need to choose between presumptively acknowledging a sufferer's account of pain *and* critically engaging the regimes of discourse and sensation that structure this account. Maintaining both aspects at the same time may in fact be one way of cultivating the vocabulary needed for the tolerator and tolerated to not only express but also contest and reconfigure the pain endured on each side of the relationship.

V. TEACHING TOLERANCE

The objective of this chapter has been to examine the limitations of an intellectualist orientation to politics, and to show why an interest in tolerance as a sensorially inflected experience does not necessarily lead to subjectivism and nihilism. Even though circumventing this assumption does not in and of itself guarantee a more robust theory of active tolerance, it does point in that direction when it broadens our conception of pain so as to pluralize the endurance of pain and the various kinds of sociopolitical relations empowered by this endurance. The reorientation of the discussion of tolerance appears here as an inherently political operation where context-specific regimes of discourse and sensation stage the sensorium and thus define how constituents with differing beliefs and outlooks perceive and engage each other. To better appreciate the openings created by this perspective, our terms for thinking about tolerance must follow four specific conditions, all of which track the general shifts suggested by a sensorial orientation to politics, seeking to invigorate the discussion of what tolerance could and should mean in a world of deep pluralism.[72] First, the terms for thinking about tolerance must avoid dichotomous accounts of the body politic, which divide citizens into mutually exclusive categories of reason and passion, peace and war, deliberation and violence, moderation and fundamentalism, tolerance and intolerance. Second, the terms for thinking about tolerance must no longer associate the sensorium with a drive to intolerance (or violence), which puts tolerance on the side of a reasonableness that is defined as universally the same and independent of context-specific modes of perception and affect. Third, the terms for thinking about tolerance must theorize pain from a critical perspective, which does not assume the presence of a single essence but instead focuses on how the encounter with something painful relies on—as well as engenders—context-specific modes of perception and affect, each defined by various and changing intensities, consequences, and durations. Fourth, the terms for thinking about tolerance must contest whatever somatophobic tendencies they embody in order to focus on the affirmative role that pain can play in the constitution of social bonds and political obligations.

Together, these four conditions define the baseline for a theory of active tolerance. Even though the implications of this theory cannot be unfolded until later, we can, by way of conclusion, speculate on how the four conditions listed above suggest an approach unlike one of the initiatives sparked by UNESCO's Declaration of Principles on Tolerance: the idea of teaching tolerance to grade schoolers across the United States. If the current way of teaching tolerance is based on the idea that tolerance is different from violence and that tolerators are defined by their ability to abstract from their own experience of pain, then the alternative suggested by a sensorial orientation to politics pulls in the other direction, bringing pain back in so as to better cultivate the requisite practices of endurance and resilience that enable citizens to deal with pain and extend beyond it. The idea is not to celebrate pain uncritically, but to develop a richer, more nuanced vocabulary around which the contestation and reconfiguration of pain can occur in a world of deep pluralism. Inculcating this vocabulary to citizens of all ages means pursuing a pedagogical approach different from the one dominant today. Rather than using activities such as "mix it up" to encourage students from diverse racial background to identify what they have in common, the same activities might be used to create an alternative conversation in which students recount their encounters with social discrimination, economic inequality, and existential suffering. The idea would be to bring pain back into the conversation and to develop an acknowledgement of the struggles and hardship that shape our perceptions of power and privilege. The means for such a conversation should not be limited to a staged meeting during lunch break, but would include art projects, physical education, community work, dance classes, creative writing, and band practice.[73] With these sensorial experiences as their backdrop, some students might be more receptive to learn about the fear of bullying that keeps some of their peers from speaking up and participating in extracurricular activities; other students might find that their divergent backgrounds do not preclude a shared sense of hardship, one with which they struggle on an everyday basis and one that can be empowered by sharing it with others; and still other students might begin to think about how to organize across class and race barriers prevalent in their local neighborhoods. Teachers and principals will then seek to augment the stakes of these conversations by situating the interpersonal experiences of pain within a historical perspective. Rather than privileging the Jewish genocide as the ultimate sign of intolerance, something that tends to limit the practice of tolerance to those who experienced the Holocaust and that tends to define intolerance in rather crude terms analogous to genocide, teachers and principales might instead use a broader array of examples so as to better historicize the existence of intolerance, bringing more people into the conversation about what tolerance can and should mean. Finally, rather than proclaiming one day a year to be "tolerance day" and another to be "zero-tolerance day," school officials could merge these proclamations in an attempt to remind their students how tolerance and intolerance are intimately linked and how both revolve around issues about the need to endure pain within societies in which there are no shared standards for thought and action. The conversations promoted by these changes do not guarantee that students will redefine the limits of tolerance, but the conversations may nonetheless be effective because they become part of an attempt to reorient the very terms by which such limits are conceived, contested, and revised.

How might contemporary democratic theory contribute to this more pluralistic approach to teaching tolerance? One way is to pluralize and defamiliarize the examples we use to discuss tolerance so as better to discern the conditions under which the practice of tolerance is either active or passive. Another way, which is the one to which I shall turn presently, is to reexamine to the history of tolerance in order to clarify why contemporary democratic theory has come to think about pain as it does—as private and purely physiological—and how the history of political thought itself remains rich with examples that contradict this view. My wager is that excavating some of these examples may generate a sort of countermemory important to a new orientation to tolerance.

CHAPTER 2
Remembering Tolerance

The historical sense gives rise ... to a use of history that severs its connection to memory, its metaphysical and anthropological model, and constructs a countermemory—a transformation of history into a totally different form of time.

Michel Foucault (1971)[1]

I. TOLERANCE IN THE HISTORY OF POLITICAL THOUGHT

If the history of political thought is the study of how knowledge about politics develops over long periods of time, then there may be no better way to approach this study than through an engagement with the many discussions of tolerance that have taken place ever since the concept made its first appearance in the Graeco-Roman world. Shaped by innumerable painful encounters, the history of tolerance demonstrates, perhaps more powerfully than suggested in the previous chapter, how social struggles, cultural transformations, technological innovations, institutional revolutions, religious conversions, and even geological earthquakes influence people as they receive, evaluate, and use knowledge about political structures and their consequences for social relations and human existence more generally. From the perspective of the present, this accumulation of knowledge may seem to generate a fairly coherent image, much in the way Descartes thought clear and distinct sense perception would help align past experiences with sensory input from the present.[2] But if we look back, tracing the discussion of tolerance from the present to the past, we can see how diverse and contingent the history of tolerance actually is. Knowledge about tolerance is defined differently in different places and at different times, and it rarely points to a linear development in which changes from one meaning to another emerge seamlessly. The absence of linearity indicates a general principle of temporality in the history of political thought, which in turn resembles the experience of pain insofar as it evokes a sense of displacement, exposure, and vulnerability. As Foucault puts it, "to follow the complex course of descent is to maintain passing events in their proper dispersion; it is to identify the accidents, the minute deviations—or conversely, the complete reversals—the errors, the false appraisals, and the faulty calculations that gave birth to those things that continue to exist and have value for us."[3]

Inspired by Foucault's genealogy of descent, this chapter turns to interpretations of early modern thinkers such as Kant, Locke, and Descartes in order to examine how uses of historical knowledge are mobilized, and how they can be reoriented to better engage the challenges facing contemporary tolerance. The turn to the early modern period is motivated by an appreciation of the period as a particularly fecund resource for reorienting the discussion of tolerance, *as well as* by a tendency, shared by advocates and critics of contemporary democratic theory, to simultaneously privilege the period and either homogenize the period's diverse insights or dismiss them as largely irrelevant to knowledge about tolerance as it is practiced today.[4] My contention is that both approaches reflect a deep-seated disavowal of what tolerance has meant, does mean, and can mean, and that they therefore represent a significant obstacle to the ambition announced earlier: to further Mill's and Nietzsche's insights about the world-making potential of pain so as to pluralize the way tolerance is imagined and taught in societies where there are no universally shared standards for thought and action.[5] As I argue below, rather than opening up to the possibility that tolerance could be more than a passive practice of either restraint or repression, the disavowal risks screening off an engagement with the plurality of historical knowledge, empowering the kind of dichotomous thinking that more often than not turns tolerance into an impossible practice in which tolerators must both affirm and negate the role played by sensorially inflected experiences. The double bind associated with this impossibility emphasizes the need to change how historical knowledge is enlisted and engaged in contemporary discussions of tolerance.

Before getting too deep into this argument, one might ask whether an engagement with the history of tolerance really is the proper way to relax the kind of dichotomous thinking that limits our ability to grasp how citizens become tolerant of each other. The suspicion that it might not is raised because tolerance appears to assume a disavowal of its own history, something that is evident not only in contemporary democratic theory, which, as Wendy Brown has pointed out, tends to eschew "comprehension

of its *historical* emergence,"[6] but also in many contemporary tolerance conflicts, including the French hijab case, where divergent interpretations of
history encourage a "clash of civilizations" because constituents either do
not share the same historical backgrounds or, via French colonialism, share
more than they avow. Both outcomes have become so commonplace that it
is tempting to ask whether there is any use in returning to history, and if
there is, whether one can do so without creating a parallel universe with no
effects on how contemporary democratic theory and public discourse more
generally have come to understand tolerance. Is it possible, one might ask,
to reorient the discussion of tolerance if the very terms of this reorientation are defined by a discourse that either disavows the plurality intrinsic
to the history of this practice or limits the plurality to a linear progression
toward something like reasonableness and recognition as the primary, if
not sole, goal of democratic politics?

In what follows, I acknowledge the difficulties posed by this question but
hope nonetheless to move forward in order to show how attention to other
ways of becoming tolerant is suggested, even encouraged, by the history of
tolerance in general and the early modern period in particular. Extending
the immanent critique developed in the previous chapter, my aim is not to
invoke a perspective external to contemporary interpretations of the early
modern period but rather to examine these interpretations paraliptically,
by which I mean a double perspective that devotes one eye to uses of historical knowledge and another to various insights obscured by these uses.
This double perspective is close to what Foucault, in this chapter's epigraph,
calls "countermemory," and it sets the terms for a mode of remembering
that resists the terms set by the intellectualist orientation to politics.[7]
Parallel to the temporality of descent, and much like an affirmative endurance of pain, the idea is to expose the intellectualist orientation to politics
to the plurality embedded in its own history, invoking a witnessing that
sees displacement and vulnerability as potentially world-making because
they draw our attention to the new and the unforeseen. The witnessing
performs, you might say, the active tolerance it seeks to remember. On the
one hand, the witnessing maintains the history of tolerance in its "proper
dispersion," which also means identifying the "accidents," "deviations," and
"errors" that subsist within those early modern thinkers whom contemporary discussions of tolerance have canonized. On the other hand, the
witnessing embraces discontinuities in the history of political thought, and
it does not identify any one ideal as the bedrock of tolerance (e.g., Rawls's
overlapping consensus or Habermas's communicative rationality). As we
shall see, the upshot is a historical sensibility that mobilizes sensorially
inflected registers of affect and perception to explore the extent to which

the most common way of remembering tolerance in contemporary democratic theory is but one way of articulating the concept's history.[8] To tell the history of tolerance in the finest possible way, I argue, is to activate the concept's historical plurality so as to both empower and pluralize our divergent images of what tolerance has meant, does mean, and can mean. This way of telling the history of tolerance does not add up to an independent theory of active tolerance, but it may provide the resources with which to expand the account privileged in contemporary democratic theory and public discourse more generally.

Section II elaborates on how contemporary democratic theory has mobilized the early modern period in ways that have contributed to a disavowal of the plurality of insights embedded in the history of tolerance. Sections III, IV, and V set out to counter this disavowal by returning to the same early modern thinkers who have been privileged by contemporary democratic theory, but this time with the ambition of interpreting their works paraliptically, looking to excavate some of the insights obscured by contemporary uses of historical knowledge. Focusing on some of the lesser known aspects of the works by Kant, Locke, and Descartes, sections III, IV, and V show not only how the early modern period supports the general drift of contemporary democratic theory but also how various early modern "encounters" with the sensorium of political life points us in the direction of a more active tolerance than the one present in contemporary discourses on tolerance. Section VI concludes with a discussion of how excavating these encounters is part of a sensorial orientation to politics, and how the history of tolerance, approached as a lived experience in time, once again can contribute to a democratic theory that sees politics as a way to care for a radical openness that binds us to feel, see, and think differently.[9]

II. DISAVOWAL IN CONTEMPORARY DEMOCRATIC THEORY

To see how contemporary discussions of tolerance have come to disavow some of the many insights developed by early modern canonical thinkers, let's look first at the memories of tolerance that circulate in and out of interpretations of the work of Kant. Whereas most contemporary democratic theorists take Kant's work to be of highest importance, it wasn't until Rawls's *A Theory of Justice* (1971) that Kant's status as a "democratic" thinker was established, prompting Michel Freeden to suggest that if political liberalism (and contemporary democratic theory more generally) is as successful as it claims to be, "the Western liberal tradition . . . would have to be retold from a new horizon of experience."[10] Emphasizing the importance of narrative and retelling, Freeden poses the question of how to engage gaps and discontinuities in the history of political thought: Are gaps and discontinuities signs of multiple memories, do they encourage us to think differently about how to recount the history of tolerance, or do they represent a fundamental challenge to our ability to make tolerance, or anything else, for that matter, universally binding?

The question is directly linked to Kant's own critique of tolerance, which anticipates how Goethe and other German Enlightenment thinkers limited the value of tolerance to nothing but a "passing attitude."[11] In his 1784 essay "An Answer to the Question: What Is Enlightenment?" Kant develops an earlier version of this claim by distinguishing between an "enlightened age" and "enlightenment," and by arguing that the former is reached through a maturation process in which the use of "public reason" gradually becomes the governing source of morality and deliberation. Intrinsic to the process is a shift from "tolerance" to "freedom of religion," which Kant favors because it represents the best way "out of barbarism," allowing men "to use their own reason in all matters of conscience."[12] To illustrate his point, Kant enlists Frederick the Great (1712–1786), whom he praises for having refused the "presumptuous title of tolerant (*den hochmütigen Namen der Toleranz*)" despite his tolerance of Jews and other non-Christians.[13] The way Kant frames his argument makes it doubtful he would want us to define tolerance as a cardinal virtue of contemporary democracy. Not only does Kant think that tolerance is unable to generate the kind of respect for the moral law that could make it universally binding, he also seems to argue that a society of tolerators is doomed to fail because it remains tethered to the interests of the sovereign who may or may not see religious freedom as the best way to develop and secure his power. Both arguments make tolerance a less-than-secure guide to Kant's "kingdom of ends," challenging tolerance's status as a means or endpoint of contemporary democracy.

How contemporary democratic theorists in particular treat Kant's critique of tolerance tells us a different story, however. Although no one claims that Kant wrote extensively about tolerance as a concept in its own right, a majority of contemporary democratic theorists interpret his work as if he could have analyzed it in this way, choosing either to interpret tolerance as the hidden key to Kant's emphasis on public reason (the "hermeneutical" strategy) or to develop a conception of tolerance that Kant himself would have challenged, but that in fact fulfills the spirit of his philosophical project (the "revisionist" strategy).[14] The latter strategy is particularly important to theorists associated with the reasonable-tolerance model discussed in Chapter 1. Rainer Forst, for example, limits Kant's critique to what he calls a "permission conception," leaving room for a Kantian alternative closer to the true meaning of tolerance.[15] Rawls, in his discussion of Kant, bypasses the critique to focus instead on offering a historical argument according to which the expanded pluralism that followed in the wake of the "Wars of Religion" and the appearance of "large industrial market economies" makes it necessary to develop a neo-Kantian approach freed of Kant's now controversial metaphysics.[16] And Habermas, drawing on the work of Forst, goes one step further and suggests that we read the history of tolerance as the gradual evolution of a "mutual perspective-taking," which may have originated in the work of Pierre Bayle, but which we now associate with Kant's philosophy. According to Habermas, "ever since the days of Spinoza and Locke the philosophical justification given for religious tolerance points the absolutist state in a direction away from *unilaterally* declared religious toleration...and towards a conception of tolerance based on the *mutual* recognition of everybody's religious freedom."[17]

Even if these accounts make sense from the standpoint of the present, it could still be the case, as I would indeed argue, that how contemporary democratic theorists define them is structured such that they disavow many of the insights developed by Kant and other early modern thinkers, foreclosing a more pluralistic and open-ended engagement with tolerance as a sensorially inflected experience of becoming. Disavowal is a term Freud introduces to analyze an experience that first acknowledges and then displaces an unwelcome fact of reality. Freud elaborates on this tension by suggesting that moments of disavowal come into being through a "screen memory," which he describes as a practice of remembering in which a limited set of recollections hides a more ambiguous field of experiences, events, and epiphanies.[18] Interpretations such as the ones cited above are like Freud's screen memories. When contemporary democratic theorists such as Forst, Habermas, and Rawls claim that the philosophy of Kant helped move the history of tolerance from one position to another (from "unilaterally declared religious toleration" to "mutual recognition of everybody's religious freedom")—or when they either minimize the relevance of Kant's critique of tolerance or limit the emergence of tolerance to a specific epoch (the "Wars of Religion following the Reformation" and the emergence of "large industrial market economies")—what they often displace in the name of a generalized history of tolerance are the many ambiguities and struggles that accompanied these arguments and developments in time. Did the Reformation really make it imperative to act more tolerantly compared to when there was only one Christian Church? Did institutional innovations in the early modern period embody a progression toward mutual perspective-taking, or did they primarily redistribute power in a way that pleased some constituents more than others? Did Kant merely mean to debunk one conception of tolerance, or did he see tolerance as being tied to a different history than the one we tell today? Questions such as these may not be answered unequivocally, but when we discuss them in relation to a metanarrative of some sort, we risk deflecting attention away from how events and ideas relevant to the history of tolerance harbor multiple meanings, some of which can be mobilized for different purposes according to the context. The issue, we might say, is not simply *what* the history of tolerance should look like, but *how* we as political theorists and as citizens of democratic regimes engage or enlist historical knowledge more broadly understood. For purposes of excavating tolerance's plural meanings, reorienting the terms of the discussion in contemporary democratic theory, the latter is important because it may signify a willingness to expose one's account of tolerance's history to internal pressures and external challenges, and because it thereby can come to represent a first step toward expanding the concept's appeal beyond its current impasses and double binds.[19]

The reluctance to embrace this step more fully so as to expand the history of tolerance beyond its contemporary neo-Kantian providence is felt in a number of areas important to the argument developed here. Most importantly, in redirecting the early modern discussions of tolerance along the lines proposed by Forst, Habermas, and Rawls, contemporary democratic theorists have tended to focus on how the practice of tolerance has ushered in individual rights and greater respect for difference, and they have in that sense tended to read the history of tolerance progressively, as moving from "less" to "more," alighting on those parts of Kant's philosophy where history is assumed to work toward a certain endpoint, generating what Freeden calls "a non-history... elevated to the rank of history."[20] Though this tendency appears most explicitly in Habermas's insistence on a progressive movement toward "mutual perspective-taking," we find it both in Rawls's notion of a historical break that made it necessary to become more tolerant than before, and in the emphasis on what Forst calls the "mutual respect" conception as the proper endpoint for the theory of tolerance.[21] These readings are not blind to other conceptions of tolerance, but because they interpret the alternatives in relation to Kant's, which sets the standard for a successful account, the readings have engendered a relatively closed system of assumptions that one must embrace in order to decide which conception of tolerance is the most reasonable or liberal one. The most troublesome aspect of this system is not that it privileges a certain outcome (all readings do this in some way or another) but that it does so without engaging the resources embedded in the system's underlying appropriations, exclusions, and remainders. At the moment when conceptions of tolerance can be classified as "reasonable" or "unreasonable," what we face is a turning point in the history of tolerance, which limits rather than broadens the concept's ability to pluralize the range of acceptable differences in society. Once principles of reason have been naturalized—once the principles have been detached from their belonging to changing perceptions of time, history, and memory—the reference to anything sensorial, including pain, will be enough to cast suspicion on those who insist on its relevance to democratic theory. Once contemporary democratic theory has displaced sensorially inflected experiences, questions about who should bear the brunt of suffering no longer bring up an interest in what the endurance of pain has meant or could mean.

The other area where it is possible to detect a reluctance to pluralize tolerance's historical meanings relates to how contemporary democratic theory invokes a set of linkages across the early modern period, which then is positioned at the center of the future of democratic politics. Consider here how the contemporary neo-Kantian framework is placed alongside not only Locke's conception of tolerance, which is said to have "launched"[22] the liberal tradition, but also thinkers such as Descartes, who is said to have inaugurated liberalism's "disengaged perspective"[23] in response to the "crisis of the European mind."[24] How these linkages are developed in contemporary democratic theory once again comes close to what Freeden calls "non-history...elevated to the rank of history."[25] In relation to tolerance, this way of construing history appears to invoke three distinct norms: (1) to insist on placing texts concerning the concept and practice of tolerance in their historical context, ordering their relationship chronologically, while (2) pressing for the universalization of liberalism at the same time, ensuring (3) that especially early modern texts are interpreted and weighed according to how well they anticipate the demands of a neo-Kantian framework yet to come. Together, these norms create the appearance of a progressive history that legitimates the disavowal of other insights important to the early modern period.[26] Indeed, if Kant's prominence in contemporary democratic theory points to a narrative that forecloses an engagement with alternative readings of the early modern period, might we not say that the interpretations of Descartes and Locke as neo-Kantians yet to come returns this limitation back into history, creating a consistency that restricts our interpretative freedom, limiting how we remember what tolerance has meant, does mean, and can mean?

The concern raised here is neither that contemporary democratic theory links discussions of tolerance across time (all histories do that to varying degrees), nor that contemporary democratic theory tends to privilege the works of Descartes, Locke, and Kant (all three thinkers, each in his own way, stand out in the history of tolerance). Rather, the peculiar challenge posed by the norms just outlined hinges on what Foucault calls "the chimeras of the origin"[27]: the moment when historical interpretation becomes too concerned with drawing a straight line through past, present, and future—the moment when engagements with the past are governed by a desire to master a certain trajectory in time—what we encounter is an idealization of the origin, which solidifies the reluctance to expand the history of tolerance because it either institutes a nostalgia for the past or, as is perhaps more likely in the case of contemporary democratic theory, justifies a benchmark against which historical evolutions can be evaluated as a process of either decay or progress. Although this desire for cohesiveness may seem inevitable, especially if we consider its ability to generate a sense of meaning and orientation, the upshot is a tendency to block rather than engage history's own potential for empowerment and pluralization. Governed by the desire for consistency and cohesiveness across various historical epochs, our ability to engage and interpret texts according to the context and purpose becomes less available, and it thus becomes harder to excavate the overlooked or unexplored potential embedded in concepts such as tolerance.

What, one might ask, are the general lessons that follow from this new approach to the link between contemporary discussions of tolerance and various interpretations of thinkers in the early modern period sustaining these discussions? The most obvious lesson might be that tracking how contemporary democratic theorists have screened off an engagement with the broader history of tolerance allows us to see how uses of historical knowledge add to the impossibility that, as we discussed in Chapter 1, has come to define the practice of tolerance. The uses of historical knowledge do so because they screen off insights that do not fit into a narrative of progress and reason, and because in that sense they add weight to the somatophobic language so characteristic of an intellectualist orientation to politics. Less obvious, but equally important, is that by identifying how various moments of disavowal limit our appreciation of the history of tolerance, we may actually be in a better position to see how one might engender a reorientation of the contemporary discussion of tolerance. That is, even if contemporary democratic theorists such as Forst, Habermas, and Rawls encourage us to interpret the early modern period through a certain screen memory that disavows many of the insights articulated by the period's canonical thinkers, and even if disavowal itself works by erasing its own conditions of possibility, it would be wrong to assume that there is no other way of mobilizing the history of tolerance, especially since disavowal too has a history, which, despite attempts to appear otherwise, may belong to the discourses and experiences that have shaped contemporary discussions of tolerance in contingent and often contradictory ways.[28] Another way of saying this is that since acts of disavowal put aside but never completely obliterate the object of their concern, it follows that we at least presumptively should acknowledge the possibility of excavating some of what has been disavowed, and thus of witnessing and remembering the history of tolerance through other "screen memories" than those that filter accounts by contemporary neo-Kantians such as Forst, Habermas, and Rawls.[29] Apart from enriching our understanding of what tolerance has meant, does mean, and can mean, an interest in responding differently to history's own plurality might also bring us closer to tolerance's potential for empowerment and pluralization. Not only can resistance to existing screen memories unsettle our established conceptions of certain events and texts, it might (I stress *might*) mobilize a greater appreciation of the unseen or new, creating the conditions for more pluralistic conceptions of feeling, seeing, and knowing.

III. KANT: ACTIVE TOLERANCE AND THE VITALITY OF PAIN

To put this intuition to work, consider here a different way of witnessing intellectualism's canon, one that, in the paraliptical mode discussed at the outset of this chapter, begins with the analysis of pain that Kant develops in Part I, Book II of *Anthropology from a Pragmatic Point of View* (1798).[30] The analysis, which stands out because it features the doubling of activity and passivity that defines most of Kant's critical philosophy, appears to modify at least parts of Kant's overall orientation toward personal autonomy and transcendental reason, and it may in that sense represent a counterpoint embedded in the same intellectualist orientation that seeks to disavow a more sensorially attuned strand subsisting within especially the early modern history of tolerance.[31] As noted in Chapter 1, elements of this history appear to have survived in the form of what Rawls calls "the burdens of judgment" and our "liability to humiliation and shame"—terms that may not fully embrace the sensorium but nonetheless recognize its role in relation to thought and action. Attending to this role in more detail is important because it troubles our tendency to separate the two and thus can put pressure on intellectualism's own presuppositions, opening it up for a discussion of the many ways in which a person or society can endure—perhaps even affirm—experiences of pain.

Contrary to what we learn from most contemporary democratic theorists, Kant contributes to this project by noting a tension intrinsic to the experience of pain. On the one hand, Kant defines pain as displeasure through sense, insisting that even though pain is enjoyment's counterpart, it still carries a vitality that sees danger, risk taking, and vulnerability as part of world-making.[32] On the other hand, Kant also seeks to limit this vitalism so that it doesn't affect the principles and procedures of reason. As "affect," pain is distinctively nonreflective, which means that it works by suspending the mind's composure, generating an element of surprise that "shuts out the sovereignty of reason."[33] The tension between these elements of Kant's analysis is well expressed in the following passage:

> Small inhibitions of the vital force mixed in with advancements of it consti-
> tute the state of health that we erroneously consider to be continuously felt
> well-being; when it fact it consists only of intermittent pleasant feelings that
> follow one another (with pain always intervening between them). Pain is the
> incentive (*der Stachel*) of activity, and in this, above all, we feel our life; without
> pain *lifelessness* would set in.[34]

Kant appears to envision two scenarios that follow from the claim that without pain "lifelessness would set in." Both scenarios challenge intellectualism from within its own presuppositions, but they differ in how they conceptualize the power of pain itself. In the best-case scenario, pain is only temporary and can therefore be endured without any real concern for the well-being of reason. In the worst-case scenario, pain grows into a passion, which lingers on as a "sickness that comes from swallowing poison."[35] The second scenario appears to be why, if not Kant himself, then at least neo-Kantian contemporary democratic theorists have disqualified pain from the domain of reason and morality, and thus from the discussion of how to secure the right to tolerance. Neo-Kantian contemporary democratic theory, you might say, privileges an understanding of pain in which the sufferer's experience is either morally irrelevant or detrimentally opposed to the realm of the normative, to the operations of reason, and thus to the selection of principles and rights that define how individuals and groups can coexist even though they do not belong to the same culture, ethnicity, religion, social class, or sexual orientation.

Now, what would happen if we mobilized Kant's initial understanding of pain as vital and therefore as potentially world-making? Would such mobilization reveal elements of an active tolerance challenging our present-day image of tolerance as either restraint or repression? Maybe so, but it is important to note that although Kant's understanding of pain as world-making is surprisingly close to the Nietzschean one I discussed in Chapter 1, there are some important differences that must be noted. Whereas Kant, in a footnote to the *Anthropology*, approves of the Milanese philosopher and economist Pietro Verri (1729–1799), who, in a short treatise *On the Nature of Pleasure and Pain*, argued that "the only moving principle of man is pain," Nietzsche uses the exact same quote to draw a distinction between the notion that pain moves by virtue of being the opposite of pleasure and his own intervention, which, as we discussed in Chapter 1, tries to displace the traditional opposition between feelings of pleasure and pain.[36] This difference suggests two divergent understandings of the vocation accompanying the engagement with pain and pleasure: Nietzsche collapses the distinction between pleasure and pain in order to challenge the demands of morality, and Kant sees the distinction as part of the passage through which morality comes into being in a world characterized by finitude, vulnerability, and uncertainty. For Kant, that is, pain reveals in a more limited way than for Nietzsche how sensorially inflected experiences empower as they point us toward new ways of perceiving, judging, and knowing.

That said, Kant's emphasis on pain as the "incentive of activity" does challenge the notion that pain is uniquely passive—with no agentive capacity of its own—and by shifting the attention away from Kant's intellectualism, one could therefore read some of his works as harboring elements of an active tolerance, which in turn would be different from the established alternatives—be it the one Kant criticizes in the 1784 Enlightenment essay, or the one that most contemporary democratic theorists associate with Kant's own work.[37] Additional clues to this argument appear in the analysis of the sublime, which Kant includes in the *Anthropology* but develops more fully in the *Critique of Judgment* (1790), drawing on themes introduced in *Observations on the Feeling of the Beautiful and the Sublime* (1764). What emerges from these discussions is the idea that sublimity is similar to "a feeling of displeasure"[38] that can become empowering in and of itself: pushing the faculties of experience beyond transcendentally established categories of reason and knowledge, revealing a power essential to all modes of judging (what Kant calls *Urteilskraft*), the sublime invokes a dissenting feeling of pain that finite beings must endure in order to both affirm and reconfigure their own finitude. The endurance anticipates Nietzsche's idea that a subset of pains can be a way to remember the past without assuming a hidden origin or positing a future *telos*, and in that specific sense it points to a more empowering practice of tolerance, one in which the ability to tolerate what seems painful participates in the quest for new connections across differences embedded in various images of self, other, and world.

Another way of saying this is that Kant's many encounters with pain's world-making potential trouble the disavowal that has pushed contemporary democratic theory away from the idea that tolerance, as a sensorially inflected experience of becoming, can be more than a passive stance expressed through either restraint or repression. Kant's encounters with pain's world-making potential reverses this reluctance by enabling us to see how tolerance need not be limited to the domains of religion and social diversity but also can apply more broadly to situations where the encounter with pain disrupts preconceived notions of self, other, and world. In these situations, tolerance is irreducible to the framework of individual rights that currently is seen as a guarantor of a tolerant society but from a genealogical perspective is better viewed as on the side of the lifelessness that Kant says we fall into without endurance of pain. In these situations, tolerance is a way of "feeling" life, one that seeks to affirm the subsets of pains that pluralize and empower new connections across established categories of feeling, judging, and seeing. In these situations, tolerance challenges the perception of the world as given more or less definitively; it seeks instead to replace this perception with an openness that evaluates new constellations of identity and difference less on the basis of their claim to a higher truth and more on the basis of their capacity for affecting and empowering others. In these situations, tolerance is a vital and life-giving force, one that is at its noblest when it actively seeks out new ways of encountering the world. What a world-making power tolerance can be!

Intrinsic to this practice of tolerance is a sense of history different from the one assumed by Forst, Habermas, and Rawls. That is, as Kant's encounters with pain and the sublime engender a world that resists existing categories of reason and knowledge, and as the resulting endurance and resilience expose the faculties of judgment and sensation to new modes of thought and action, tolerance itself becomes a way to experience time differently, replacing the notion of time as linear progression with what Deleuze, in his discussion of Kant's sublime and its similarity to Shakespeare's *Hamlet*, calls time "out of joint."[39] An experience of disjointedness is neither ahistorical nor apolitical, but instead highlights the very contingency of what a concept such as tolerance has meant, does mean, and can mean. Tolerance of sublime pain, for example, may follow from the encounter with natural phenomena (Kant's preferred examples are "mountains," "storms," and "earthquakes"), but it can also be linked to images of existential suffering (Francis Bacon's "Study after Velázquez's Portrait of Pope Innocent X" is a good example), transnational terror (think of the images of the World Trade Center's twin towers collapsing on September 11, 2001), and divine violence (as in the Book of Job). All these examples illustrate the kind of "monstrous" horror Kant describes as "an indeterminate concept of reason."[40] And yet their implications point in multiple directions, encouraging us to approach them as the starting point for thinking politically in time, and not, as in the case of Forst, Habermas, and Rawls, as an obstacle to sociability and community.[41] To engage historical events and texts through Kant's encounters with pain's world-making potential is to pluralize our sense of time, even if in so doing we step into a heterogeneous domain of thought and action characterized by the sensorium's indeterminacy and unruliness.[42]

IV. LOCKE: ACTIVE TOLERANCE AND THE DOCTRINE OF *ADIAPHOR*

The question we now need to consider is whether Kant's interest in a more active tolerance is a singular event in the canon of early modern thinkers, as it is conceived by the intellectualist orientation to politics, or part of a broader countermemory, one that acknowledges the inherent plurality Foucault associates with the history of political thought. Parts of the answer to this question were foreshadowed by the discussion in Chapter 1 where I suggested that Mill's work, together with Nietzsche's, entails a critique of pain that affirms a sensorial orientation to politics and that in this sense represents a strand of thinking different from the intellectualist one prevalent in contemporary democratic theory. I now want to consider this answer in a bit more detail, and in the somewhat different context of early modern political thought—in particular as we find it in the works of two early modern thinkers who also are depicted as important proponents of intellectualism: John Locke and René Descartes.

To see how Locke's work goes beyond the idea of tolerance as passive, we first need to challenge his place within a purely intellectualist orientation to politics, and instead explore the parallels between Locke's interest in the sensorium and Kant's analysis of pain in the *Anthropology*. Like his friend Thomas Sydenham (1624–1689), known as the English Hippocrates, Locke was associated with the Oxford School of Physiology, which reworked the Cartesian theory of the body, putting greater emphasis on medical experiments as well as on developing a more corpuscular concept of matter.[43] Sydenham devoted his studies to epidemic constitutions and pain medicine; Locke focused more exclusively on the empiricist epistemology sustaining these studies. Traces of this interest that *qua* its empiricism seems closer to a sensorial orientation to politics than Kant's transcendental idealism appear in *An Essay Concerning Human Understanding* (1690), where Locke locates pain alongside pleasure as "simple *Ideas*, which we receive from both *Sensation* and *Reflection*," and which linger on as individuated "Constitutions of the Mind."[44] Locke uses this framework to suggest that pain arises in relation to an uneasiness of the mind, which in turn leads him to an insight similar to the one Kant proposes one hundred years later: that pain implies a vitality that incites action by transposing sufferers from one state of affairs to another. Unlike Kant, Locke links this world-making capacity to the vocabulary of Good and Evil, underscoring, as Nietzsche does too, how sensorially inflected experiences always intersect with questions of morality and politics: "Things then are Good or Evil, only in reference to Pleasure or Pain.... We name that *Evil*, which *is apt to produce or increase any Pain, or diminish any Pleasure in us; or else to procure us any Evil, or deprive us of any Good.*"[45]

To the extent that this interest in pain persists throughout Locke's work, we might say something is amiss if we follow the trend in contemporary democratic theory, and define Locke's conception of tolerance as the anticipation of a neo-Kantian framework yet to come.[46] What is amiss becomes clearer if we consider the doctrine of "things indifferent" (*adiaphor*), which is a doctrine that Locke first examines in *Two Tracts on Government* (1660),[47] and a doctrine to which he returns in the second half of the first *Letter Concerning Toleration* (1689)—a text whose Latin title (*Epistola de Tolerantia*) itself suggests an interest in how and why to endure pain.[48] In the *Two Tracts*, Locke argues that (1) there are things indifferent to salvation and blessedness, (2) things indifferent concern aspects of religious worship not mentioned explicitly in the Scripture, and (3) civil government has a right to legislate things indifferent in order to maintain the peace and security of the commonwealth. Of these claims the latter is by far the most controversial as it legitimizes certain limits on religious freedom. Locke appears to realize this in the *Letter Concerning Toleration*—perhaps because his exile in Holland gave him a more visceral sense of the pain and suffering that such limits can cause—and eventually turns his interpretation of things indifferent into an argument in favor of not only individual freedom but also a certain forgetfulness and detachment in disputes over religion. In the *Letter*, Locke argues this with an eloquence that exceeds even his own standards of writing:

> [If] I be marching on with my utmost vigour, in that way which, according to the sacred geography, leads straight to *Jerusalem*; why I am beaten and ill used by others, because, perhaps, I wear not buskins; because my hair is not of the right cut; because, perhaps, I have not been dipt in the right fashion; because I eat flesh upon the road, or some other food which agrees with my stomach; because I avoid certain by-ways, which seem unto me to lead into briars or precipices; because, amongst the several paths that are in the same road, I choose that to walk in which seems to be the straightest and cleanest; because I avoid to keep

company with some travellers that are less grave, and others that are more sour than they ought to be; or in fine, because I follow a guide that either is, or is not, clothed in white, and crowned with a mitre? Certainly, if we consider right, we shall find that for the most part they are such frivolous things as these, that, without any prejudice to religion or the salvation of souls, if not accompanied with superstition or hypocrisy, might either be observed or omitted; I say, they are such like things as these, which breed implacable enmities among Christian brethren, who are all agreed in the substantial and truly fundamental part of religion.[49]

If I suggest that we focus on the sensorial elements of this passage, highlighting Locke's interest in pain rather than the mind-body dualism that according to other interpretations forms the dominant horizon within which the doctrine of indifference operates in the early modern period, it is for at least two reasons.[50] First, although the doctrine of indifference seems to conjure up a mind-body dualism similar to the one that underpins the neo-Kantian framework of Forst, Habermas, and Rawls, Locke's tropes and imagery point in a less dualistic direction, bringing the sensorium back into view, demonstrating how influential sensorially inflected experiences can be when it comes to ways in which potential tolerators might perceive and judge each other. The focus on walking, speed, geography, eating, hygiene, clothing, sociability, and mood—all of these sensorially inflected experiences may seem "indifferent," even "frivolous," and yet they suggest a strong sense of finitude embedded within Locke's account of early modern political subjectivity. As the Lockean subject enters into the world of differences, marching on with "utmost vigour," he or she is not a person detached from his or her environment, but rather someone who stands forth, who encounters the possibility of living otherwise and thus becomes susceptible to feelings of insecurity and vulnerability. Displacing the mind-body dualism assumed by intellectualistic interpretations of Locke's work, the doctrine of indifference depicts the political subject as a person who risks being "beaten and ill used by others," and who struggles with this risk as he or she navigates various domains of conflict and disagreement.[51] Locke's early modern political subject, we might say, is indifferent in a worldly manner, from within the world of bodily affects, and not from disengaged perspective in which lived experience is separate from one's mental conceptions of what is right or just.

Second, approached sensorially, Locke's doctrine of indifference supplements the susceptibility to insecurity and vulnerability with a resilience, which augments rather than conceals an individual's desire to expose himself or herself to others. The affirmation of this resilience, which remains one of the most promising aspects of Locke's work, is doubly interesting because it does not eliminate pain as such, but instead, in a vein similar to Kant's sublime, seeks to reorient pain's debilitating effects, acknowledging the ubiquity of pain while inaugurating the distance necessary for a person of indifference to empower new modes of thought and action in a world of deep pluralism. Now, initially, this resilience was not incompatible with an interest in individual rights and popular sovereignty, especially since Locke's doctrine of indifference originally was conceived as a minority doctrine subject to criticism and scorn. Only later, after the relegation of the sensorium to the unexamined background and the reification of an intellectualist orientation to politics, is the link between indifference and resilience displaced by a more hegemonic theory of rights, which sees the desire to expose one's insecurity and vulnerability as a threat to the very possibility of an autonomous rights bearer. As already indicated, Locke's doctrine of indifference resists this interpretation from within the early modern period itself. Turning, or, perhaps better, *re*-turning our attention to the sensorium of the lived experience of politics, we find Locke's doctrine of indifference highlighting the different ways in which resilience is (or can be made) relevant to the politics of deep pluralism, resisting the tendency to see indifference as a practice of disembodied skepticism, countering the domestication of Locke's work as a neo-Kantian paradigm yet to come.

Granted these considerations, we might say that the passage cited above stands out because it depicts the tolerator as a struggling person who is simultaneously assertive *and* cautious, troubled *and* indifferent, embodying the various cross-pressures that a tolerator must endure in order to become tolerant of others.[52] There is a temporal dimension to these cross-pressures worth emphasizing as it resonates with the one evoked by Kant's encounter with sublime pain. Most obvious is how the person depicted in the passage cited above is someone who walks through the world, *in time*, experiencing a historical meaning that connects the past with the future, empowering the confidence needed to make the leap from the first person singular (*I*) to the first person plural (*we*). At the same time, however, the person depicted is not someone who is completely consumed by or irrevocably attached to the history of his or her own experiences. Indeed, as Locke's depiction leaps from the particular *I* to the general *we*, appealing to a shared time that is yet to come, the person is freed from the past so that he or she can enter into a new relationship with the world writ large. There is, we might therefore say, an agonistic attitude embedded in Locke's account of what it means to be simultaneously vulnerable and resilient, indifferent and proactive: even if some experiences are essential to *my* history, the same experiences may also seem contingent, and in this sense "indifferent," especially if placed alongside other considerations concerning the future, about how to live well in a different time and context (what Locke refers to as "the salvation of souls").

Together, these two elements—the desire to expose oneself through indifference and resilience on the one hand, and on the other the ability to free oneself from the demands of chronological time—suggest a historical sensibility, which is close to the one we find in the theory of active tolerance, and which calibrates the endurance of pain so that potential tolerators come to acknowledge their attachments to the past while affirming the contingency of the attachments' future. "Recognize that your history as a social being is how you have become who you are today, but don't think it exhausts who or what you might become in the future"—this may be the slogan for a historical sensibility that doesn't expect tolerators to disavow historically situated disagreements in order to overcome the inclination for intolerance, repression, and violence. Nietzsche, in *On the Genealogy of Morality* (1887), suggests something similar when he points out that active forgetting "is not just a *vis inertiae*... but rather an active ability to suppress, positive in the strongest sense of the word."[53] Locke adds to this argument an account of why active forgetting can be so difficult to accomplish, especially when it comes to articles of faith broadly understood— what Locke, in the passage cited above, calls the "truly fundamental part of religion."[54] The reason articles of faith pose such a challenge is not their religious nature per se, but rather because they encourage tolerators to disavow certain unwelcome facts of reality *as well as* help to instill a set of normative demands that justify this disavowal retroactively. A person seeking to affirm tolerance's potential for empowerment and pluralization struggles with this dimension of political life as he or she steps onto the embodied terrain that wires the sensual and the cognitive, the prospective and the retroactive, the past and the future.

The empowering and pluralizing potential embedded in these elements of Locke's doctrine of indifference is perhaps felt most strongly by those who are new to Locke, and who have not yet learned about how his work is said to anticipate a neo-Kantian framework yet to come. My aim here has been to sustain this impression in order to shed light on a countermemory subsisting within the intellectualist tradition, one that allows us to see a set of connections between Kant and Locke that otherwise might not emerge. The norm for these connections is best expressed by Merleau-Ponty's account of the chiasm as both "overlapping and fission, identity and difference"[55]: whereas Kant's sublime attends to the sensorial world in rather extraordinary circumstances that uproot an existing perception of time, Locke's indifference attends to the same world in circumstances of everyday life where practices of resilience and forgoing can empower new modes of communication and sociability among individuals who disagree about the best or most just way to secure joy and happiness in this life or the one hereafter.

V. DESCARTES: ACTIVE TOLERANCE AND THE HUMAN MACHINE

The possibility that early modern thinkers important to today's intellectualist tradition can be linked in a more chiasmatic manner highlights one of the most important assumptions underpinning the project undertaken here: that temporality exceeds chronological time, and thus that we may see historical memory as radically open, resisting the idea that there is an origin from which experiences and texts can be linked into *one* history of tolerance. Although such a conclusion may seem debilitating because it interrupts our bodies' deep-seated desire for a sense of orientation, which often presupposes a linear conception of time, the opposite may also be the case: the idea that there is no origin invites, perhaps even encourages, us to inhabit historical memory differently.[56] As I suggested earlier, this is especially true for the theory of active tolerance, which probes alternative "habitations" of historical memory because they help to pluralize our conception of temporality, and because in that sense they serve to both disclose and augment the potential embedded in the concepts such as tolerance.[57] Taking issue with the idealization of origins, in other words, is not to disavow history (such as it is), but rather to show that insofar as perceptions of history begin *in* time, beginnings themselves are constructed such that they fold past, present, and future into one text, one world. The challenge is to destabilize, if not uproot, the presumed uniformity of this construction in order to enable history's many advances to shine forth in their own right, and not as "accidents," "deviations," and "errors" that contradict the presumed logic of historical progress. The latter need not be the only way to proceed. As Foucault puts it, the more historical the genealogy of descent becomes, the more it proceeds "in the manner of the pious philosopher who needs a doctor to exorcise the shadow of his soul."[58]

To further develop a pluralized approach to historical knowledge, consider here the third—and for our purposes final—thinker important for the connection between early modern political thought and contemporary discussions of tolerance: Descartes. Hardly a theorist of tolerance himself, Descartes is a central thinker who helped shape contemporary views of the sensorium, in particular when it comes to conceptualizing the human body and its encounter with pain.[59] Considering Descartes's contribution can thus give us a better sense of why we have come to approach the experience of pain the way we do, and how this approach is shot through with incompleteness and potential for reorientation.

A good place to start is the *Treatise of Man*, in which Descartes famously asserts that he supposes the body "to be nothing but a statue or machine made of earth, which God forms with the explicit intention of making it as much as possible like us."[60] Although this image seems to suggest that the body is divinely ordained, Descartes goes on to argue, in a more naturalistic vein, that what really moves the body are the finer "animal spirits" that subsist within the body's blood and that penetrate into the pineal gland "situated near the middle of the substance of the brain," passing from "there into the pores of its substance, and from these pores into the nerves."[61] As a prototype of our contemporary conception of sensorially inflected experiences, this depiction of the nervous system enables Descartes to show how external stimuli provoke the need for bodily movement, but also to argue that the body moves only if the brain tells it to do so. The brain holds this power, we learn over the course of Descartes's examination, because it appears on both sides of the causal chain, and because in that sense it is able to work back on the sensorium, which is what causes the body to react in the first place. Emphasizing the dynamic character of the brain, Descartes illustrates this scheme of reaction and action by way of a fountain keeper who, stationed at the fountain's tanks, seeks to control the flow of water running through the pipes: "when there shall be a rational soul in this machine, it will have its chief seat in the brain and will there reside like the turncock who must be in the main to which all the tubes of these machines repair when he wishes to excite, prevent, or in some manner alter their movements."[62]

In positing a rational soul at the helm of embodied experience, Descartes comes close to an early version of the neo-Kantian mind-body dualism, but Descartes affirms, more actively than contemporary neo-Kantians, the need for philosophical thought to situate both sides of the dualism within historical time, emphasizing how each side of the dualism is shot through with elements of the other.[63] This consideration is especially important for Descartes's "specificity theory of pain," which, as I noted in Chapter 1, is a theory that has left a lasting mark on discussions of pain in both contemporary philosophy and medicine.[64] According to the specificity theory, pain occurs in four steps, each of which mirrors Descartes's general depiction of the interplay between external stimuli and internal movement. Ordered schematically, the four steps are (1) tearing of the skin activating designated nerve lanes in the body, (2) these nerve lanes communicating the sensation of injury to a pain center in the brain, (3) the pain center evaluating the input to determine whether or not pain is actually occurring, and

(4) if the evaluation is positive, the pain center communicating back to the affected areas of the skin, causing a reaction similar to when "pulling on one end of a cord, one simultaneously rings a bell which hangs at the opposite end."[65]

The metaphor of the brain ringing a bell in response to pain is both suggestive and odd, raising the question of whether Descartes sees pain as a mechanically defined experience that follows a linear mode of causality, or as an extended feeing that inscribes itself on the body and in some sense has a history of its own. Is the path from sensory input on the skin to the pain center in the brain (and back again) a linear one, or does it fold past, present, and future together in plural and complex ways? The answer to this question is not immediately clear, since Descartes sometimes speaks as if the body and the mind operate independently of each other. At other times, however, Descartes seems to challenge his own views, bringing forth a sensorial orientation that interestingly underpins certain aspects of early modern political thought. The sensorial orientation is especially evident in some of Descartes's other works in which he, much like Nietzsche, and not unlike Kant and Locke, resists the temptation to assume a strict separation between cause and effect, pleasure and pain, and instead examines pain as a passion, which "produces in the soul first the passion of sadness, then hatred of what causes pain, and finally the desire to get rid of it."[66] The key here is to note how pain evokes a sense of duration, and how in that sense it turns into a transient yet extended feeling of history, exceeding an action schema based on a mechanical conception of linear causation. The sense of nonlinear duration is especially felt during the middle stage—what Descartes calls "hatred of what causes pain"—a stage during which pain is not simply a cause of action but also that which embodies the person of hatred as an agent in *this* world. For a person of hatred, pain is simultaneously the reason for action and the outcome of action, and it can therefore turn into a world of its own, one in which time is seen as circular rather than linear. Evoking what Talal Asad, in a different context and for other purposes, calls a "practical relationship inhabiting time,"[67] the middle stage of pain collapses the difference between cause and effect, enabling pain to morph into other states of being, among them "sadness," "hatred," and "anger."[68]

If we think of pain in the terms just proposed, then we might say that to endure pain is to participate in a process that, because it evolves outside a linear conception of time, is inherently open-ended, subjecting it to contestation and resignification, making it more likely that a practice of active forgetting such as the one subsisting in Locke's doctrine of indifference is both possible and desirable.[69] The first of two domains in which

Descartes expands his view on this possibility is in relation to phantom limb pain. First reported by the French army surgeon Ambroise Paré (c. 1510–1590), phantom limb pain was originally seen as a challenge to a new philosophical reasoning based on observable evidence rather than belief and superstition. Why trust the method of observation if pain could be caused by an absence indicating the nonmaterial quality of all human experience?[70] Highlighting the interplay among sensory input, nerve lanes, and the brain, Descartes turns this problem into an advantage by arguing that the absence of a physical referent is a sign that pain has less to do with an injury or wound of some kind, and more to do with the flows and intensities that circulate across and within the parts of the body and mind. Phantom limb pain, in other words, is a mediated experience, one that is subject to intervention and manipulation, and not an experience given once and for all. Here's how Descartes explains it, using the example of a girl who continues to feel pain in her injured fingers after her arm has been amputated at the elbow:

> The only possible reason for this is that the nerves which used to go from the brain down to the hand now terminated in the arm near the elbow, and were being agitated by the same sorts of motion as must previously have been set up in the hand, so as to produce in the soul, residing in the brain, the sensation of pain in this or that finger.[71]

As a model for thinking politically about the endurance of pain outside chronological time, this example of phantom limb pain is interesting in a number of ways. Most obvious is how the example illustrates why pain has no "origin" and why it therefore can be both everywhere and nowhere. As indicated by Descartes's example, the reason for this elusiveness is that although one would expect the feeling of pain to originate in the amputated limb, it is the brain's mapping of the body (and not the limb itself) that determines whether or not the experience is perceived as painful. Moreover, since this mapping does not occur without the body's participation, the outcome must be a circular, even cyclical experience, one that leaves ample opportunities for manipulative interventions, some of which either augment or silence certain nerve lanes. The upshot is what the neuroscientist V. S. Ramachandran recently has characterized as an "echolike 'wha wha' reverberation and amplification of pain": "When we experience pain, special pathways are activated simultaneously both to carry the sensation and to amplify it or dampen it down as needed. Such 'volume control'...is what allows us to modulate our responses to pain effectively in response to changing demands."[72]

The other domain in which Descartes develops pain's capacity for world-making outside chronological time relates to what André Gombay calls Descartes's "inner masochism." Focusing on Descartes's concept of "inner emotions," emotions that are aroused by the soul itself but not separate from the body, and on which "our good and ill depend chiefly,"[73] Gombay lists the various places in Descartes's oeuvre where Descartes acknowledges how the same experience can engender a conflict between the passion of pain and an inner emotion of joy. From the ambiguous mourning of a wife whom the husband "would be sorry to be brought back to life" (Descartes's words) to the performance of a Greek tragedy that moves both actors and the audience, what we find is a world of experiences that split our being into opposing feelings without foreclosing an increased sense of empowerment. Gombay takes this to mean that inner emotions are modes of self-affirmation, which in turn leads him to suggest that a wider array of pains can empower an awareness of one's existence as a thinking soul, bringing past, present, and future together in ways that exceed chronological time. As Gombay puts it, "Perhaps among the mental conditions that he [Descartes] wants us to recognize by speaking of inner emotions, lies not just what he calls 'intellectual joy,' but something else, more complicated—we might call in 'inner masochism,' might we not?"[74]

Whether or not masochism is the appropriate term to use in relation to the theory of active tolerance is a question to which I shall return in Chapter 3. For now it suffices to note that the possible presence of an inner masochism in Descartes's work points to a more general drive in the early modern period, one that approaches the endurance of pain affirmatively—both as a necessary feature of political life and as a desirable practice in and of itself. The existence of this drive is not as surprising as it may seem at first. From Hobbes's social contract, which replaces unfettered freedom with fear of punishment, over Locke's doctrine of indifference as a form of active forgetting, to analyses of the sublime (Kant), self-regarding harm (Mill), and even the burdens of judgment (Rawls)—in all of these discourses we find insights concerning the importance of endurance and resilience with regard to principles of government and sovereignty. The ubiquity of endurance and resilience is well captured by Elizabeth Wingrove, who, in her discussion of the social contract tradition more generally, points out that the most central question all forms of government must answer before they can claim to be legitimate is "how, what, and when to suffer?"[75] Descartes's contribution to this question is the claim that the endurance of pain can work not just negatively, as a mode of acquiescence and repression, but also affirmatively, as a transformative mode of resistance and subversion. Relaxing the demands of chronological time, Descartes's work points to a future past in which the endurance of pain is seen as world-making, not only because it empowers one's ability to act and to think, whether as an individual or as a community, but also because it augments one's connections and engagements with the world writ large.

VI. REMEMBERING TOLERANCE DIFFERENTLY

As noted at the outset, the objective of this chapter is twofold: to examine how uses of historical knowledge empower as well as restrict the discursive terrain sustaining the discussion of tolerance in contemporary democratic theory; and to mobilize a countermemory that reorients the terms of this discussion by interpreting the linkages between contemporary democratic theory and the early modern period paraliptically, invoking a screen memory different from the neo-Kantian one associated with the works of Forst, Habermas, and Rawls. On the basis of what we have seen in the previous three sections, we might say that the countermemory stands out because it approaches the sensorium of political life, not as a remainder that must be displaced because it represents an unwelcome fact of reality but rather as the starting point for bringing forth some of the heretofore unexplored potential embedded in the history of political thought. The countermemory sees historical time as radically open-ended; it highlights the possibility that the endurance of pain in some contexts can be world-making rather than world-shattering; and it cultivates an active forgetting that acknowledges the significance of past experiences for one's current existence while also challenging their tendency to limit one's desire to experiment and live otherwise. Although these elements do not in and of themselves constitute an independent theory of active tolerance, they amount to a countermemory that cuts across the historical narrative underpinning how contemporary democratic theory envisions the best way to conceptualize the politics of tolerance. Contesting this aspect of contemporary democratic theory through an engagement with some of the lesser known aspects of the works of Kant, Locke, and Descartes, the countermemory broadens our sense of tolerance's history, and it thus enables us to better grasp how the theory of active tolerance can be brought back into view in ways that resonate more directly with ongoing concerns about the changed conditions of citizenship and pluralism.

One way to make these resonances more tangible is to compare the efforts undertaken in this chapter with the work undertaken by the nineteenth-century archeologist Giuseppe Fiorelli (1832–1896), who is best known for his work at the Ancient city of Pompeii, buried in ashes when Mount Vesuvius erupted in 79 AD.[76] Provoked by the discovery of several cavities left in the hardened lava, Fiorelli's work is particularly interesting for our purposes because it represents an attempt to unearth a feeling of pain that was caused almost two millennia earlier. Fiorelli's work exhumes the memory of this feeling, not by claiming to access the past directly, pretending to rescue the Graeco-Roman world from the passage of time, but by creating a new technique for historical excavation, filling the cavities left by the bodies with plaster of Paris, enabling his archeological team to bring back full-sized replicas of the men, women, and children no one had been able to see or touch since the day of the eruption. The upshot of these excavations is a ghostly presence that appears to be "real" because it connects elements of the past with concerns in the present, which in turn enables a new future—be it in the current city of Pompeii, in museum halls across the world, on various websites posted on the internet, or any-where else where Fiorelli's replicas can be seen and perhaps even touched. In all of these sites we encounter a mode of witnessing that empowers the future by giving new meaning to a traumatic encounter with pain in the past. Exhibitions of Fiorelli's replicas jumble the chronology of past, present, and future. And they form what Foucault calls a countermemory, one that transforms our historical sensibilities "into a totally different form of time."[77]

Insofar as this chapter has attempted something similar, we may say that the outcome is a set of untimely yet empowering resonances that reorient our way of remembering what tolerance has meant, does mean, and could mean. An important consequence of this reorientation is that we need not draw the same conclusion that a majority of contemporary critical theorists have drawn more recently, namely, that the best way to overcome the difficulties associated with contemporary tolerance is to inaugurate a radical break with the past so as to open up to a set of new practices that, so goes the argument, are better equipped to address the challenges posed by the world of deep pluralism.[78] If one should be reluctant to affirm this approach unreservedly, it is not because the approach underestimates the impasses that can turn tolerance into a passive practice of benevolent superiority, but rather because it allows intellectualism and the neo-Kantian framework to define how we construe and interpret the history of tolerance. My concern is that a concession of this kind takes us back to the sense of impossibility that, as we saw in Chapter 1, troubles contemporary tolerance. Not only does ceding the history of tolerance to the neo-Kantians limit our access to alternative meanings of tolerance, restricting rather than expanding the history of tolerance itself, it screens off an engagement with how other practices of democracy, too, demand a certain endurance of pain, replacing renewed interest in this endurance with a dichotomous view that associates tolerance with only one of the two sides in contemporary democratic theory. This view, together with a limited appreciation of tolerance's many contributions to the history of political thought, maintains tolerance in its current double bind, even as the disempowering effects hereof seem clearer than ever.

As we shall see next (Chapter 3), these remarks do not mean that we shouldn't learn from discussions of tolerance in contemporary critical theory. My point here is simply to suggest that tolerance has meant much more than what it means today, and that there are ways of excavating these meanings so as to mobilize tolerance's heretofore unexplored potential for empowerment and pluralization. One of these ways is to witness the linkages between contemporary democratic theory and early modern political thought paraliptically, with an eye to what some of the early modern thinkers privileged by contemporary democratic theory obscure and yet presuppose. As we have seen in the present chapter, this approach is particularly powerful because it acknowledges tolerance's many remainders—its "accidents," "deviations," and "errors"—as a constitutive part of what it means to think and act tolerantly. Might this acknowledgment not be a better starting point for a theory of active tolerance that cares for democracy's radical openness, binding citizens to feel, see, and think differently?

CHAPTER 3

Affirming Tolerance

The conclusion . . . is that the realization of the objective of tolerance would call for intolerance toward prevailing policies, attitudes, opinions, and the extension of tolerance to policies, attitudes, and opinions which are outlawed or suppressed. In other words, today tolerance appears again as what it was in its origins, at the beginning of the modern period—a partisan goal, a subversive liberating notion and practice. Conversely, what is proclaimed and practiced as tolerance today, is in many of its most effective manifestations serving the cause of oppression.

Herbert Marcuse (1965)[1]

However, nobody as yet has determined the limits of the body's capabilities.

Baruch Spinoza (1677)[2]

I. SPINOZA AND THE THEORY OF ACTIVE TOLERANCE

Like other attempts at reorientation, the discussion in this book has now come to a point where the shift from one orientation to another requires that we focus less on what the shift negates—the tendency to limit tolerance to a practice of restraint and repression—and more on what the shift affirms: a theory of active tolerance attuned to the changed conditions of citizenship and democratic pluralism. Although the previous two chapters sought to recover elements of this theory, our discussion has up to now been defined by the terms set by the intellectualist orientation to politics. The objective of the next two chapters is to take a step beyond this orientation in order to theorize what Herbert Marcuse, in the epigraph cited above, identifies as a mode of partian politics in which tolerance uproots the power of the majority, resisting the repression of political differences, embodying "a subversive liberating notion and practice." Apart from explicating the sensorial character of tolerance, expanding the sensorium's role across various domains of contemporary politics, my contention is that a theorization of democratic politics that does not foreground the positive element of Marcuse's critique risks overlooking the plurality and affirmative potential embedded in the practice of tolerance. If Marcuse's distinction between active tolerance and passive tolerance rings true, and if tolerance has moved from an active practice of empowerment and pluralization to a passive practice of restraint and repression, then the very idea of a turning point should be the center of our attention.[3] What are the powers that turn tolerance from one state or another? Can't—or better, don't—these powers evoke alternative, more affirmative ways of acting tolerantly?

The present chapter pursues this question by turning to another early modern oeuvre that both inspires and troubles contemporary critical theory: Spinoza's philosophy of immanence.[4] Resisting the branch of critical theory that Marcuse's critique inspired, championing a sensorial orientation to politics that more self-consciously breaks with the intellectualist tradition, Spinoza's philosophy of immanence seems especially apt at grasping the various sides of tolerance because it conceptualizes pain as an expressive power open to contestation *and* affirmation, critique *and* reconfiguration. As we shall see, the oscillation between these aspects appears most powerfully in what I call the "tragic moments" of Spinoza's philosophy of immanence, by which I mean those moments of the *Ethics*, in particular as they appear in books III and IV, where the ideal of ethics—beatitude, or joy—is simultaneously posited and contradicted, and where the outcome suggests a degree of pain that, depending on how it is endured, affects our capacity for thought and action.[5] The ambiguity of this affection suggests that the tragic moments are where the powers that move tolerance from one state to another (and back again) are most directly felt. Whereas some might see Spinoza's tragic moments as a failure of philosophizing, I see them as the starting point for theorizing how tolerance can become a practice of empowerment and pluralization. Spinoza's sense of the tragic is an affirmative one; it entails engaging the endurance of pain as part of a desire to augment and pluralize the distribution of power and privilege.[6]

Another way of saying this is that the argument of this chapter follows Marcuse's analysis of tolerance as having two sides, while it at the same time resists Marcuse's corollary claim: that active tolerance was present only "at the beginning of the modern period," and that it now, as a consequence of the concept's co-adaptation by the modern State, has been lost to a past unavailable for interpretation and renewal. My concern is that such a claim overemphasizes the work done by the modern State, and that it therefore undercuts the sensitivity to pain and power that many contemporary critical theorists seek to revitalize in their analyses of the conceits that they argue limit the pursuit of political emancipation, social justice, agonistic respect, and true democracy.[7] Here, Spinoza's contribution to the discussion of tolerance has the added benefit of encouraging both advocates and critics of contemporary democracy to explore the many forces that subsist above and below the modern State, highlighting the potential for resistance and subversion in various subject formations, including those that we normally call "repressive." Although attention to this potential does not preclude the possibility that tolerance becomes passive, it may help us theorize an active tolerance defined by a set of attachments and commitments other than the ones that have come to define tolerance as a "nonpractice" featuring tolerators who seek to protect the State against contestation and resistance.[8] The idea is not to deny or protect power; it is to find ways of enduring pain so that power can be shared maximally, enabling diverse constituents to create new and more expansive connections in a world of deep pluralism. Or, at least, that is my wager.

Section II introduces the idea of a force field unique to the practice of tolerance, mobilizing Spinoza's distinction between *potentia* and *potestas* to show that how tolerance shifts between its active and passive sides depends just as much on the desires and affective intensities embedded in this force field as it does on the various strategies mobilized by the modern State to soothe or repress resistance to its use of disciplinary power. Section III looks more closely at the power that makes tolerance desirable in the first place and suggests that a subset of pains—what I in Chapter 1 referred to as "pleasurable pains"—are especially empowering because they evoke the subversive and liberating practice Marcuse associates with tolerance's active side. Section IV looks at three examples of social life (masochism, comedy, and torture) to examine and make more tangible the conditions under which tolerance's active side might enable both the tolerator and the tolerated to expand their presence in the world. Section V concludes with a general characterization of the theory of active tolerance.

II. THE POWER OF BEING TOLERANT

Among the many challenges that a sensorial orientation to politics must address with regard to tolerance, the most daunting is how to conceptualize tolerance as a practice separate from other ways of relating to difference and disagreement. As noted in the Introduction, the extant literature on tolerance has until now addressed this challenge by emphasizing the interplay between five components, among which the most prominent are the "objection" component and the "acceptance" component.[9] Although a sensorial orientation to politics shares the intention behind this approach—to show conceptually how tolerance differs from other practices—it also suggests that the price for focusing exclusively on each of the five components has been inattention to tolerance as an open-ended practice that evolves, not simply because it is possible to connect the five components in diverse ways, but also because each component is subject to affects and other sensorially inflected powers, all of which help to define and mobilize the component's meaning in this or that context. Another way of saying this is that attention to the sensorial dimension of tolerance is important because it brings forth the plurality and politicality embedded in the practice of tolerance. Not only does attention to the sensorium allow us to conceptualize how various constituents can identify with the need for tolerance and yet disagree profoundly about what tolerance should mean in this or that context, it also gives us the perspective needed to conceptualize how tolerance can be passive *and* active, repressive *and* enabling.

A sensorial orientation to politics develops this conceptualization by encouraging us to focus on what I, inspired by Spinoza's philosophy of immanence, will refer to as "the force field of tolerance."[10] Foregrounding the importance of the sensorium of political life, tolerance's force field suggests another way of delimiting the circumstances of tolerance, one that unlike the extant literature on tolerance sees power as a broader category of bodily potentiality present at all levels of lived experience, including conceptually defined perceptions of what should count as "objectionable" or "acceptable" (or both). In Spinoza's terms, tolerance's force field implies a dynamic process of becoming wherein affects and other sensorially inflected powers sustain the endurance of some experiences of pain but not others, and where tolerance's plurality and politicality is directly linked to the possibility that tolerators might differ from one another insofar as their bodies move "at varying speeds" (EIIp13ax2). How these speeds present themselves—how the speeds are encountered and sustained as either "active tolerance" or "passive tolerance"—hinges fundamentally on the range of gravity points embedded within tolerance's force field; how each of these gravity points either intensifies or relaxes the connections, intensities, and thresholds that sustain the endurance of some but not other experiences of pain; and how these connections, intensities, and thresholds facilitate a sense of agency and orientation necessary to move tolerators in this or that direction. Adding to what we already have seen, taking up the thread suggested by Mill's and Nietzsche's critique of pain, the approach suggested here thus encourages us to see tolerators as political agents who are defined less by preestablished understandings of the "objectionable" and the "acceptable," and more by the various degrees of bodily power associated with the practice of tolerance. Highlighting the latter, tolerance's force field moves our focus from an external perspective concerned with the limits and alleged passivity of tolerance to an immanent one that explores the sensorially inflected life-world in which tolerators think and act.

As I use the term, there are two ways of studying the plurality and politicality embedded in tolerance's force field: one that looks at the range of opportunities and relationships presenting themselves as a consequence of acting tolerantly, or what we can call the power derived from being tolerant; and another that explores the range of affects making tolerance seem desirable in the first place, or what we can call tolerance's own power. The remaining part of this section addresses the former of these two aspects, focusing on the agency and desire associated with the power derived from being tolerant. In the next section (Section III), I then take up tolerance's own power in order to identify the pull of becoming tolerant in an active manner that expands rather than contracts opportunities for empowerment and pluralization.

Agency and the Power of Being Tolerant

Since the power derived from being tolerant speaks directly to concerns raised by contemporary critical theory, it may be helpful to begin by examining the range of possibilities embedded in this power. Wherein, we might ask, consists the power derived from being tolerant, and how does it delimit a tolerator's relationship with the belief, practice, person, or tradition of which or whom she disapproves? Motivated by the idea cited as this chapter's second epigraph—that the body's capabilities are yet to be determined (EIIIp2s)—Spinoza's philosophy of immanence addresses this question by emphasizing a set of intuitions regarding tolerance and power that depart from the ones we might associate with contemporary critical theory. Rather than assuming that the power derived from being tolerant serves the interests of the State, contesting the idea that tolerance offers what Wendy Brown, in *Regulating Aversion*, calls "a robe of modest superiority in exchange for yielding,"[11] Spinoza encourages us to pluralize this aspect of tolerance's force field, introducing a distinction between the way modern state power subordinates the tolerating body—what Spinoza would call tolerance's *potestas*—and the subversive power whereby the tolerating body exceeds this subordination—what Spinoza would call tolerance's *potentia*.[12] The distinction between these two powers is important, first because it suggests there is no single gravity point that rules tolerance's force field at all times and in all contexts, and second because it avoids underestimating the ability of tolerators to mobilize tolerance against the interests of the State. Although the distinction between *potestas* and *potentia* does not imply that tolerators are masters of their own fate, or even the most powerful of the actors involved in the politics of tolerance, it is meant to suggest that where power is involved (and this includes both tolerance's *potestas* and tolerance's *potentia*) we should be careful not to assume that the power derived from being tolerant always reduces or eliminates the plurality and potentiality embedded in tolerance's force field.

To illustrate what this means more correctly, consider Seneca's epistle "On Ill-Health and Endurance of Suffering" (64 AD).[13] An important part of the archive that informed Spinoza's own training as a philosopher in seventeenth-century Amsterdam, one could read this epistle as advancing a male-dominated virtue ethic, and indeed Seneca does seem to reserve the power of endurance and resilience for only one of the sexes.[14] But perhaps more interesting is how Seneca interrupts his own argument—first by scrutinizing the desirability of tolerance, encouraging us to consider the elements that make tolerance virtuous, and second by examining torture as the most extreme case in which tolerance, understood as the endurance of pain, can be practiced. Refusing to condone torture, using it, like his father (Seneca the Elder), as a "hard case" for teaching students how to address difficult legal and moral issues, Seneca asks whether the person who tolerates torture is as powerless as we often are led to believe.[15] His answer is revealing: although the tortured is forced into a situation that he or she did not seek, and although the situation is fundamentally and undeniably unequal, the tortured can exploit tolerance to invoke a nobler stance, which serves to exhaust the torturer's repressive use of power. By tolerating torture, taking its meaning and significance beyond the intentions of the person or institution authorizing it, the tortured can reclaim the power that the torturer uses to inflict physical harm and mental suffering, thereby reversing the terms of their relationship. Whether or not this reversal is available to everyone is not immediately clear from Seneca's discussion. What is clear, however, is that although torture never can be desirable, it might be that the tolerance by which it is endured has a virtuous quality that "is to be desired." As Seneca puts it, in the case of torture, endurance may "be the only virtue that is on view and most manifest; but bravery [*fortitudo*] is there too, and endurance [*patientia*] and resignation [*perpessio*] and long-suffering [*tolerāntia*] are its branches."[16]

More than anyone else, it is Spinoza who enables us to appreciate the potential embedded in this conceptualization of the power derived from being tolerant. Building on Seneca's discussion, agreeing that we approach tolerance as an ennobling practice of endurance and resilience, Spinoza leads us to see that what Seneca develops as a possibility for resistance embedded in tolerance's force field in fact is an intrinsic feature of all relationships constituted in and through the power derived from being tolerant. Spinoza leads us to this insight by linking his own conception of power as both *potestas* and *potentia* to a discussion of how all force fields, including the one of tolerance, tend to exceed their own limits owing to the sensorium's heteronomous character.[17] If a force field defined by an assemblage of connections, intensities, and thresholds represents more than the sum of its parts, it is not because the force field belongs to a preconstituted universe of desires and interests that determine how finite beings should act—Spinoza rejects this view by reiterating the distinction between *potestas* and *potentia*[18]—but rather because it is empowered by the sensorium, which constitutes all finite beings and yet exceeds any desire for mastery and control that a State, a person, or some other concrete form of power might express.[19] The sensorium goes beyond this desire because it is bound by no other law than its own, and because in that sense it expresses the highest degree of potentiality, one that does not appear as such but rather expresses itself through a multiplicity of finite beings, or perhaps better, bodies, each defined by divergent degrees of affectively imbued contractions and expansions (see EIP16&34). The variation implied by this expression is the main reason tolerance's force field—and with it the power derived from being tolerant—always-already entails the possibility for subversive resistance that Seneca identifies in his discussion of tolerance and torture. Not only is there no higher power than the sensorium, the powers derived from it must be seen as dynamic potentialities that develop over time without a final plan or a predetermined objective. In the case of tolerance, this means we must conceptualize the power derived from being tolerant as inherently open-ended: imbued with the potential to be active *and* passive, enabling *and* repressive, it embodies a plurality that can be mobilized for different purposes in different contexts.

An important consequence of the conceptualization suggested here is that it helps to interrupt the assumption organizing the current discussion between advocates and critics of contemporary tolerance, namely, that power and tolerance represent a zero-sum game in which citizens are self-constituted subjects endowed with the power to choose their own conception of good.[20] Though Brown and other contemporary critical theorists insist on the impossibility of such a subject, detailing how practices of citizenship are shaped through regimes of discourse and sensation that both enlarge and reproduce "modern political power," they still tend to limit tolerance to a "choice or ability," which "is cancelled by mandate on one side and passivity on the other."[21] Spinoza's pluralistic conception of power suggests there is something counterintuitive, perhaps even self-defeating, about this account. If the basic intuition in contemporary critical theory is right, and if we accept that citizens are shaped by powers they don't control, then it does not seem to follow that tolerance is impossible, or repressive, or irrelevant to new practices of democratic politics. Such a conclusion may indeed defeat its own purpose because it mirrors rather than displaces the terms that govern the contemporary discussion of tolerance, and because it thereby contributes to the image of tolerance as a passive nonpractice, obscuring new lines of thought for which restraint and repression do not exhaust what tolerance's force field has meant, does mean, and could mean.[22] Although tolerance may have become synonymous with the modern liberal State, although tolerance has been liberalized and can change only to extent that it acknowledges its dependency on the principles of contemporary liberal democracy, there is nothing intrinsic to this process suggesting we can or should rule out the possibility of tolerance becoming an active source of empowerment and pluralization that once again counters the desires of the modern State or some other finite power.

To be sure, one could object that Seneca's and Spinoza's conceptualizations of the power derived from being tolerant are outdated, and that citizens now live in a new set of circumstances in which tolerance's empowering and pluralizing potential has been "lost" (as Marcuse claims it has). In response to this objection, consider another case closer to the time of Marcuse's essay: the 1961 Freedom Riders of the U.S. civil rights movement.[23] Although none of the Freedom Riders referred directly to either Seneca or Spinoza (at least not to my knowledge), one could interpret their actions as invoking a set of powers and practices that are similar to the ones both philosophers privilege in their discussions of how and why to endure pain. Like Seneca and Spinoza before them, the Freedom Riders did not desire pain actively, and yet their responses were hugely empowering—both in their way of meeting violence with nonviolence (as the Freedom Riders did on their bus ride through the segregated South) and in their way of using endurance and resilience to challenge discrimination and inequality (as the Freedom Riders did by tying their nonviolence to principles of justice and inclusion). Given the risk of entering the segregated South, and their getting on Greyhound buses that transported them into places and situations they did not control, we might say the Freedom Riders practiced an active tolerance, which is different from the contemporary account of tolerance as a passive nonpractice linked to a politics of restraint and repression. Exceeding both possibilities, the Freedom Riders show, not simply in theory but also in practice, how the power derived from being tolerant sometimes amounts to a practice of pluralization, which can turn pain's world-making capacities against the ones inflicting harm and suffering, undermining the claim that to become tolerant is *either* a choice achieved by an act of free will *or* a process of subordination and repression.[24]

Whether or not additional conditions must be fulfilled before the power derived from being tolerant can contribute to a politics of empowerment and pluralization is still an open question to which I shall return later in this chapter. At this point, however, my main concern is to examine how the power derived from being tolerant works and how it swings from one side to another. In this regard, the preceding discussion suggests five requirements that must be established concomitantly in order to ensure that the power derived from being tolerant contributes to a politics of empowerment and pluralization. In no particular order, the five requirements are that (1) endurance of pain is acknowledged as a precondition for acting politically in a world of inequality and exploitation; (2) endurance of pain is seen as exemplifying a condition of finitude and vulnerability shared by constituents divided by ideology, race, and religion; (3) endurance of pain is used to communicate conviction and inclusion, not apathy and exclusion; (4) endurance of pain is mobilized not to dominate or repress but to affirm a presumptive generosity toward others; and (5) endurance of pain is desired as way of challenging and reconfiguring an often unequal distribution of power and privilege. Together, these five requirements illustrate how the power derived from being tolerant can exceed the interests and desires of the modern State, and thus show how one might counter the claim that tolerance has become a repressive nonpractice with a pluralizing (and, in this sense, empowering) account of the subversive power derived from being tolerant. Although the five requirements do not exhaust everything there is to say about the power derived from being tolerant, they represent an important contribution to how tolerators might identify with this power, shifting tolerance from a passive nonpractice that serves the interest of the State to an active resistance that empowers and pluralizes the range of acceptable differences in society.

Desire and the Power of Being Tolerant

Another important aspect of the power derived from being toleant concerns the relationships that emerge as a consequence of acting tolerantly. What, we might ask, drives tolerators to affirm the various powers derived from being tolerant, and how does this drive shape the way tolerators engage each other as members of a pluralistic society in which all of us "are either in motion or at rest" as our bodies move "at varying speeds" (EIIp13ax2)? Plunging even deeper into the sensorium of democratic politics, Spinoza begins to answer this question by challenging a tendency, widespread in his own time, to separate the "faculty of sensing" (EII49s) from the "laws of Nature" (EIIIpref).[25] To avoid this separation, Spinoza, like Seneca before him, defines tolerance's force field as a response to what he initially calls the "evils that arise from dissipation, envy, avarice, [and] drunkenness,"[26] emphasizing the problem of how and why we sometimes "patiently bear whatever happens to us that is contrary to what is required by consideration of our own advantage" (EIVap32).[27] This way of delimiting tolerance is significant because it simultaneously acknowledges the power of certitude—understood as "self-interest" or "advantage"—*and* emphasizes the power of restraint, expressed as the ability to "patiently bear" the encounter with something or someone of which or whom one disapproves.[28] According to Spinoza, the combination of these two powers is not always or even primarily a product of liberalism's regime of discourse and sensation—as Brown and other contemporary critical theorists suggest it is—but arises from the "external causes" that undercut the ability to act and think freely. Not only do external causes evoke sad affects and complex passions (what Spinoza calls "passive emotions"), they empower something similar to what we might call a tragic condition of Being, one in which thoughts and actions push finite beings in directions they either didn't anticipate or would prefer not to pursue. Like Antigone or Oedipus before them, Spinoza's finite beings are prone not only to encounter a fundamental disagreement across claims to self, other, and world but also to find ways of living with this disagreement. As Spinoza puts it, reminiscent of the chorus in Sophocles' *Antigone*: "In so far as men are subject to passive emotions, to that extent they cannot be said to agree in nature" (EIVp32).[29]

The key point, at least with regard to noting the relationships derived from the power of being tolerant, is that not only are finite beings "right" to endure the world of external causes, they can practice this endurance so as neither to contradict their own power nor to depend on someone else losing his or her power. Building on Seneca's conception of tolerance, Spinoza does not envision the capacity to "patiently bear" as a second-best option, but instead suggests that it is an inherent part of the ability to open oneself to the world in order to engage with other finite beings (human or nonhuman). According to Spinoza, the point is not just that finite beings are "infinitely surpassed by the power of external causes" (EIVp3). Rather, the point is that though the world of external causes may empower finite beings in a manner that can seem frustrating, even painful, their ability to act and think is constituted in and through this world. This ontological condition suggests that all finite beings are subject to forces they don't control, which in turn highlights their vulnerability and dependency on other finite beings. From a Spinozan perspective, the vulnerability and dependency is crucial to any conception of what it means to live affirmatively, that is, to any conception of how to augment one's power within a network of other finite beings. As Spinoza argues, conjoining the Stoic conceptions of *convenientia* and *tolerāntia*, insofar as finite beings affirm and value the power of external causes, "the endeavor of the better part of us is in harmony with the order of the whole of Nature" (EIVap32).[30]

From a Spinozan perspective, then, the power derived from being tolerant has the potential to constitute an affirmative desire that finite beings can share even though their perceptions of the desire differ radically, and even though the difference itself can be a cause of conflict and disagreement. In addition to what we already have seen, Spinoza encourages us to think about the power derived from being tolerant in these terms by suggesting that the desire to "persist in [one's] own being" (EIIIp7) is directly linked with the desire to both "be affected in more ways" and to affect "other bodies in more ways" (EIVp38). What this means, I think, is that if one wants to maintain or augment one's power in the interest of persistency, then one must first expose oneself to the worldly forces that define life as such, acknowledging vulnerability and dependency on others as an essential component of what it means to live an affirmative life that maintains or augments one's power within a network of other finite beings. The tolerance that this exposure requires encourages tolerators to privilege one of the gravity points embedded in tolerance's force field, one in which the object of tolerance—the tolerated—is both a cause of disapproval and a source of power. In this gravity point, tolerators subvert existing constellations of movement and rest in order to share and augment their differential powers. In it, tolerators grow the number of connections in the world and hope to expand their power both as an individual and as a community. In it, tolerators embody the certitude needed to put themselves in places or situations that enrich their rapport with the world while presumptively affirming the vulnerability and dependency of every finite being.

Although there is still more to say about the politics sustaining a gravity point like this one, we can now say something more general about how a sensorial orientation to politics conceptualizes the power derived from being tolerant, and how it contributes to the main reason for turning to Spinoza's philosophy of immanence: to develop and affirm a theory of active tolerance attuned to the changed conditions of citizenship and democratic government. As we have seen, Spinoza's pluralistic conception of power is particularly helpful in this regard because it shows how tolerance and power do not constitute a zero-sum game, at least not necessarily, and because in that sense it brings us closer to the active side that Marcuse's 1965 critique highlights but never develops in greater detail. The idea, we might say, is to cultivate a resilient orientation to the endurance of pain, which enables tolerator and tolerated to expand their presence in the world and allows both sides to affirm the desire to affect and be affected in different ways.[31] The upshot is neither contemporary liberalism nor critical theory (as we know it), but rather an admixture that draws our attention to the affirmative role tolerance can and does play across various domains of contemporary democratic life. Unlike most contemporary models of tolerance, which conceptualize tolerance as a way of either respecting the other by restraining oneself (Forst) or shoring up one's identity at the expense of someone else (Brown), Spinoza's pluralistic conception of power points to a situation in which the power derived from being tolerant is mobilized so as to enable both the tolerator and the tolerated to expand their divergent presences in a world of deep pluralism. As suggested above, the theory of active tolerance sees this expansion as the primary aim of the power derived from being tolerant.

III. THE PULL OF BECOMING TOLERANT

If the affirmative consequence of acting tolerantly is an expansive sense of power—and if this expansion is linked to a shared world of finitude and vulnerability—then the next question is how tolerators become interested in this constellation of power and tolerance in the first place. Unlike most advocates of contemporary tolerance, a sensorial orientation to politics addresses this question by focusing less on the punitive side of tolerance—on the legally and morally codified limits that tolerators cannot transgress—and more on the enabling side of tolerance, on what I earlier named the second aspect of the force field of tolerance: the power of tolerance. As I use the term, the power of tolerance stands out because it highlights the assemblages of connections, intensities, and thresholds that make the endurance of some but not other experiences of pain attractive, and because in that sense it delimits a tolerator's life-world from other possible life-worlds. Another way of saying this is that the power of tolerance represents the "pull" of becoming tolerant: that is, the power of tolerance endows tolerators with a sense of orientation and agency as it pulls them toward either restraint and repression (passive tolerance) or empowerment and pluralization (active tolerance). Attending to the power of tolerance is thus crucial if we want to conceptualize how tolerators can disagree profoundly about what it means to be tolerant, and, perhaps just as importantly, if we want to appreciate how tolerators can mobilize the power derived from being tolerant so as to be more or less expansive, more or less enabling.

Spinoza's philosophy of immanence contributes to an examination of these aspects by showing how affects, whether joyful or sad, help to empower our ability to think and act. "By affect," Spinoza says at the outset of Part III of the *Ethics*, "I understand the affections of the body by which the body's power of activity is increased or diminished, assisted or checked, together with the ideas of these affections" (EIIIdef3).[32] The easiest part of this definition might be the claim that affects move bodies with a degree of power specific to each and every affect. Although this claim seems intuitively correct—try to recall the power you experience when feeling sad or joyous—it says nothing about how affects can make bodies move, let alone how this movement can become part of the mind. Spinoza answers both concerns by emphasizing that affects are "*of* the body" and that "*by which* the body" moves. On the one hand, affects empower because they share a materiality with the bodies they move. On the other hand, this empowerment—this affection—is irreducible to both body and mind, being that "by which" both move. What this "by which" means, Spinoza suggests, is that affects empower a person from the outside in, making themselves felt through their own degree of power. Affects are thus neither private nor incontestable; they appear from within the sensorium as causes no one can control, often meaning different things to different people. As affects empower various modes of action and thought, they simultaneously tend toward difference *and* identity.

As I suggested earlier, we should be careful not to characterize this conception of empowerment such that we replace contemporary democratic theory's view of the citizen as a self-constituted individual with a parallel view that moves the claim to autonomy from one ontological category (e.g., the individual) to another (e.g., affect). To be sure, at the most general level—what Deleuze and Guattari refer to as the "plane of immanence"[33]—affects do seem to constitute a self-empowering joyfulness that has the power to define expressions of thought and action without external influence. This empowerment amounts to what Spinoza calls "active emotions," which in turn represent the goal of Spinoza's ethics.[34] At the level of finite beings, however, affects are often both mobilized *and* experienced as external causes that subvert the autonomous movement of action and thought from the outside in. Invoking what I earlier referred to as the tragic condition of Being, Spinoza's philosophy of immanence develops this difference by distinguishing between the general category of affects and the subcategory of affects that Spinoza calls passions (*passiones*).[35] The latter represents an immanent challenge to the joyfulness that Spinoza's interpreters typically associate with his vision of ethics and politics. Not only do passions cause men to be "not so much active as passive,"[36] their ubiquity undermines the pursuit of pure joy insofar as they prevent finite beings from governing their own thoughts and actions. Passions "overtake" the directions of finite beings and evoke what Davide Panagia calls the "heterology of impulses" from which the new and unforeseen can emerge.[37] Passions express a "difference," an impure potentiality, which is why they tend to empower lines of flight that no office, person, or philosophy can ever master without relying on something or someone other than itself.

For our purposes, the power embedded in all passions is particularly important because Spinoza associates passion more directly with pain than with pleasure (EIIIp11s).[38] Rich in meaning, Spinoza uses the Latin *tristitia* to suggest that pain is not just a physiological phenomenon associated with injury or harm; it also includes a wider range of pains that the Ancient Greeks describe as *penthos* or *kèdos*, and that we today would translate as adversity, sadness, sorrow, violence, mourning, suffering, or melancholy.[39] Exceeding the modern definition of pain as private and noncommunicative, these experiences express a loss that limits finite beings in terms of their affective powers—what Spinoza characterizes as a transition from a "state of greater perfection" to a "state of less perfection" (EIIIdef.aff3). The "perfection" absent in pain is not pregiven, as this would contradict Spinoza's definition of perfection in terms of degrees of power, and the loss must therefore be defined in relative terms, in terms of more or less.[40] What is pain relative to? Pain, Spinoza says, is relative to the level of activity present at the moment of transition: "the greater the pain, the greater the extent to which it must be opposed to a man's power of activity" (EIIIp37proof). The corollary of this relation is that finite beings tend to shun pain because it undoes their ability to persevere and become self-generating sources of acting and thinking. Pain embodies in this sense the opposite of what Spinoza calls the *conatus* (EPIIIp7&9) that drives all finite beings to overcome the influence of external causes and persist infinitely in their own being: "we endeavor to remove or destroy whatever we imagine to be opposed to pleasure and conducive to pain" (EIIIp28).

Notice here how Spinoza distinguishes between the pain's empowering potential and the person or community embodying this potential. Although a person or community may see pain as an obstruction to self-preservation, pain itself is defined by its "passionate" character, which in turn means it evokes a power of its own. This claim sets Spinoza's account of pain apart from the account that underpins most discussions in contemporary democratic theory,[41] instead situating it closer to the countermemory that subsists within the early modern period in general and Kant, Locke, and Descartes in particular.[42] What Spinoza shares with these thinkers is the idea that pain, despite its disagreeable qualities, mobilizes a counterpower that both repels and attracts potential tolerators into a world of endurance and resilience. At the same time pain brings forth the tragic condition of Being, undermining the ability of finite beings to persevere in their own being, it also empowers thoughts and actions that can inspire and even sustain social movements, political agendas, and other modes of community building. Whether these movements, agendas, and communities pull tolerators toward tolerance's active or passive side depends, as we saw earlier, on the gravity point empowering the actual encounter with this or that pain. Given this, we might say pain's affective power is one of affirmation *and* negation, activity *and* passivity—a strange and bizarre experience indeed!

To get some traction on the possibilities embedded in this experience, we now need to consider how pain of various sorts can be endured differently across contexts and situations. How is it, we might ask, that pain's affective power can be expressed differently, and what might this difference tell us about the turning point that shifts the power of tolerance between an active side and a passive side? In a scholium on the degrees of power that separate one category of passion from another, Spinoza begins to address this question by encouraging us to see how pains can empower various modes of actions. Here's how he formulates the issue:

> We see then that the mind can undergo considerable change, and can pass now to a state of greater perfection, now to one of less perfection, and it is these passive transitions [*passiones*] that explicate for us the affects of Pleasure [*laetitia*] and Pain [*tristitia*]. So in what follows I shall understand by pleasure "the passive transition of the mind to a state of greater perfection," and by pain "the passive transition of the mind to a state of less perfection" (EIIIp11s).

It is hard to overestimate the significance of this scholium for the purposes of conceptualizing the power of tolerance. The first thing to note is that pleasure and pain are not the same, at least not on the surface. Whereas the former leads to a state of greater power, the latter leads to a state of lesser power, confirming what Spinoza already has defined as the essence of pain. Still, beneath this difference we find a striking similarity, which indicates that even though pleasure and pain pull in opposite directions, they both express elements of a subtler, more general experience of pain. One way to describe this pain is to say it cuts through the fabric of Being as it traces the decay and rebirth of embodied life, empowering new constellations of thought and action while also subverting the autonomous self-government that persons and collectives desire in the interest of self-preservation.[43] Against his stated goal, Spinoza highlights the existence of this pain when he shows how even the most desirable pleasures are less joyous than they appear at first sight, and thus how the tragic condition of Being is an enduring feature of affective life.[44] Titillation, for example, is painful because it affects only one part of the person, creating a feeling of disequilibrium (EIIIp11s). Love, another important pleasure, is not as joyous as we think because it hinges on an "external cause" that may or may not be permanent (EIIIdef.aff6). Finally, Spinoza suggests that hope never loses sight of a painful fear, arising from what he calls an "inconstant pleasure" (EIIp18s2). In all of these experiences, we find a subsisting pain that finite beings must tolerate if they want to live and engage with each other. Their coexistence, you might say, makes them vulnerable in love, hope, and titillation.

Now, since the pain subsisting in all passions is not always expressed identically, it is important to foreground the plurality embedded in the power of tolerance. One method of doing so is to introduce two subsets of experiences, both of which expand on insights associated with the thinkers we already have discussed, in particular as they pertain to the critique of pain suggested by Mill and Nietzsche.[45] Each subset empowers a unique conception of orientation and agency that pulls tolerators toward one of tolerance's two sides; together they outline a continuum along which the vulnerability of passionate life is experienced as enabling or repressive, pluralizing or limiting, active or passive.

At one end of the continuum, we find what I call "painful pain," which entails a conception of orientation and agency in which pain is experienced as doubly painful because it captures the feeling of vulnerability discussed above as well as the conventional definition of pain as a world-shattering event. For our present purposes, painful pain is particularly interesting because it embodies an experience that separates the tolerator from the world of external causes, who in turn interprets the feeling of vulnerability as a sign of failure and weakness. The tolerator does so not only because any specific pain is perceived as a world-shattering event that diminishes the forces needed to expand one's presence in the world, but also because pain in general is juxtaposed to the very practice of power, thereby creating the appearance of a zero-sum game in which only the relative absence of pain entails a sense of fulfillment.[46] Painful pain is thus the closest we come to the discussion of tolerance in contemporary critical theory. Embodying an experience that Wendy Brown calls "wounded attachment," painful pain represents the passive side of tolerance's power.[47]

Across from the subset of painful pains is another subset, which may be experienced as painful in the general sense but nonetheless provokes a feeling of pleasure because vulnerability here is experienced as a means of augmenting one's power, drawing the sufferer/tolerator into, not out of, the surrounding world of external causes. For our purposes, we might characterize this conception of orientation and agency as an experience of "pleasurable pain," which resembles what Spinoza calls the affect of *hilaritas* (EIIIp11s), unique because it uplifts and energizes without achieving complete bliss.[48] If painful pain turns the feeling of vulnerability into a reason for victimization, pleasurable pain does the opposite: as it affirms the world of external causes, the experience of pleasurable pain empowers a resilient endurance that allows tolerators to develop a set of relationships based on mutual contestation, agonistic respect, and existential uncertainty. These practices may be painful because they subject tolerators to forces they don't control, but they can also be pleasurable insofar as they draw the very same tolerators into a network of new possibilities, empowering connections that strengthen one's belonging to the world. Pleasurable pain, you might say, empowers the active side of tolerance's power. Indeed, if Spinoza privileges a gravity point in which the desire to persist in one's being connects with the desire to be affected in more ways, it might well be that pleasurable pain is both the cause and the effect.

Another statement of this is that pleasurable pains constitute an active power that, from within tolerance's force field, draws tolerators into a gravity point in which the gain of one does not constitute the loss of another: as pleasurable pains work to delimit the range of possible encounters within tolerance's force field, so a relationship that expands the worldly presence of tolerator and tolerated becomes more and more likely; and as tolerator and tolerated orient themselves to a relationship like this one, so the drive and power to affirm pleasurable pains becomes both more probable and more desirable. The virtuous circle suggested by this gravity point complements our previous discussion of the five requirements needed to mobilize the power derived from being tolerant in an expansive manner. In both cases, the key is not to assume that pain automatically or necessarily contradicts a politics of empowerment and pluralization. At the same time pain marks a worldly decay, it may also belong to an enduring resilience subsisting within various practices needed to empower and pluralize the span of acceptable differences in society. The pleasure derived from this expansion does not erase the experience of pain saturating the tragic condition of Being but instead may make it "tolerable" in an empowering and pluralizing manner.

IV. TOWARD A POLITICS OF ACTIVE TOLERANCE

In the remaining part of this chapter, I want to explore the politics behind such an active tolerance by considering three examples that because they depart from the usual cases discussed in the literature on tolerane illustrate some of the lesser-known possibilities for empowerment and pluralization embedded in tolerance's force field. The three examples are Sacher-Masoch's masochistic contract, Dave Chappelle's reversal of racial epithets, and the justification of torture used during George W. Bush presidency. Like some of the other examples encountered so far, in particular the 1961 Freedom Riders, Seneca's enobling stoicism, and Ancient Greek tragedy, the three new examples focus explicitly on the endurance of pain and the powers associated therewith. However, they go one step further in clarifying the circumstances that orient tolerators toward the several gravity points within tolerance's force field, and as such they contribute to a better understanding of the forces that either obscure or mobilize the endurance and resilience needed to subvert what Marcuse calls the "manifestations serving the cause of oppression."[49] As we shall see, the three examples contribute to our understanding of these forces—and thus to the theory of active tolerance—by defamiliarizing tolerance's assumed character as a passive nonpractice, turning our attention toward the world-making character of pain as well as the kind of disciplinary work that posits practices of endurance and resilience as enabling or repressive, pleasurable or painful. Since these aspects are most explicitly thematized in the case of Sacher-Masoch's masochism, it is here I begin the discussion.

Sacher-Masoch's Subversive Contract

Although the link between masochism and an affirmative conception of tolerance may not seem readily apparent—especially if we consider the commercialization of the masochist in contemporary popular culture—I want to suggest that there are elements of the former that are important to the latter.[50] To see why, we must understand masochism in relation to the more familiar terrain of the social contract, which, as noted in Chapter 2, includes practices for "learning how, what, and when to suffer."[51] Like the social contract, masochism develops its account of these practices by underscoring how submission and domination are "concomitants of human *perfectibilité*."[52] Unlike the social contract, however, masochism does not see the endurance of pain as limited to a politics of social repression, but rather as a key to another, more affirmative world of difference and disagreement. Permitting, even demanding, practices of resistance and subversion, masochism does not become "real" until the two parties involved break and then reconstitute their contractually established relationship. Masochism offers in this sense a prism for thinking about a practice of tolerance that turns modern self-government inside out: not only does masochism illustrate a radical affirmation of pain, it also shows how this affirmation can be mobilized so as to both acknowledge and resist structures of inequality and oppression.

To make this more tangible, consider Sacher-Masoch's 1870 novel *Venus in Furs*.[53] A key text in the history of masochism, *Venus in Furs* starts out as a fairly conventional love story between the main character, Mr. Severin, and a young woman, Wanda, whom Mr. Severin envisions as the Ancient Venus who acts like a "wild animal, faithful or faithless, kindly or cruel, depending on the impulse that rules her."[54] Repulsed at first, Wanda is gradually seduced by this "classical" representation of love, and she eventually agrees to a contract in which she promises to "appear as often as possible in furs" on the condition that Mr. Severin in turn give up his name to satisfy "all the wishes of his mistress, [and] to obey all her orders" (220). The equilibrium achieved by the contract is short-lived, however, and the affections that Mr. Severin and Wanda have for each other are soon replaced by a basic disagreement about who has the right and the duty to do what when. After one of their quarrels, Mr. Severin goes so far as to flee Wanda in order to begin a new life untouched by his desire for her domination. The escape is unsuccessful, and to punish Mr. Severin for thinking that he could free himself—and to show that she is the real "sovereign" unbound by the contract's law—Wanda takes Mr. Severin to a nearby vineyard where her black female helpers whip his body as they use his limbs to plough the soil. Although the punishment is humiliating, Mr. Severin does not object; quite the contrary, in fact. Rather than seeing Wanda's punishment as a failure of self-government, Mr. Severin sees it a sign of his love and commitment to her. Thanking Wanda for bringing him "back to life" (262), Mr. Severin insists that his punishment represents the most pleasurable of all things, what he calls "a wild and supersensual pleasure" (268).

Saturated with a sense of how contradictory the endurance of pain can be, it is scenes like this one that illustrate how masochism might contribute to the discussion of the possibilities for empowerment and pluralization embedded in tolerance's force field. Most obvious is *Venus in Furs'* treatment of power as the starting point for the appreciation of any social relationship (as opposed to a feature of social life that one should disavow or displace). *Venus in Furs* is doubly interesting in this regard because it links differences in power to a productive tension between two kinds of inequality: an oppressive kind of inequality and an enabling kind of inequality.[55] To wit: although Mr. Severin encounters Wanda as a human being and as such approaches her as someone who demands his submission, he also sees her as Venus—that is, as a cosmic power embodying everything life can be, including "wild," "voluptuous," "cruel," and "beautiful." The ability to see her in this light is crucial for his empowerment, because he desires the inequality represented by Wanda/Venus not because it is a form of repression but because it marks the existence of another, more empowering world. Like an active tolerator who desires the tolerated, Mr. Severin is drawn into the world of Wanda/Venus because it represents the most powerful of all worlds, and because it exposes him to life at its fullest, allowing him to resist established conventions of affect, perception, and sociability.[56]

Mr. Severin's claim that the noblest of all worlds is simultaneously "wild," "voluptuous," "cruel," and "beautiful" also highlights another area that links masochism to the discussion of active tolerance: the idea that the affirmation of pain amounts not to a negation of life but to the very opposite, namely, an affirmation of life. This idea sits uncomfortably within most of Western thought, and it may explain why masochism so often is either disregarded or criticized in contemporary democratic theory. Freud, for example, argues in an early but still influential critique that masochism amounts to a perverse regression in which the death drive turns back "upon the subject's own ego."[57] The later Freud, however, doubts that this is all there is to say about masochism, as evidenced by his suggestion that the death drive might be part of life's struggle with itself, a suggestion that encourages us to treat practices of masochism not as a perverse regression but as part of a more affirmative drive—one that Mr. Severin experiences as life at its fullest. Notwithstanding the desire for self-preservation, there is some support for this conception of masochism in Spinoza's suggestion that suicide is a real possibility once "unobservable *external causes* condition a man's imagination and affect his body in such a way that the latter assumes a different nature contrary to the previously existing one" (EIVp20s; my emphasis). If we recall Spinoza's own discussion of passions and their status as "external causes," we might say that this account of suicide implies an affirmation of sorts. That is, although death as such is undesirable, it might be that dying in a limited sense, letting go of one's past identity, is necessary to bring about a more empowering life—one in which the question of what one becomes, both as a person and as a community, is more important than what already one "is" or "has been."[58] As we saw in Chapter 2, this orientation toward the future implies an "active forgetting," which seems masochistic because it acknowledges the need to endure pain without reducing this endurance to everything that one could ever be or become.[59]

It is insights such as this one that show how masochism, despite suggestions to the contrary, offers new insight into the possibilities for empowerment and pluralization embedded in tolerance's force field. Masochism is particularly helpful in suggesting how the endurance of pain can be perceived affirmatively, even sought out actively, standing forth as a pleasurable power that simultaneously interrupts and augments one's experience of life (such as it is). Moreover, on the model suggested by the characters in *Venus in Furs*, endurance of pain is desirable not because it is a moral duty, or because it is necessary to secure order and stability, but because it empowers a sociopolitical bond that opens up to the incipient world of new beginnings. Something similar may be true with regard to the gravity point that empowers the practice of active tolerance. Rather than seeing tolerance as a "need" that one fulfills reluctantly—perhaps because there is no better alternative—the practice of active tolerance invokes a politically motivated "want" organized around a set of desires and drives similar to the masochistic ones. Not unlike Mr. Severin, active tolerators seek out the strange mix of pleasure and pain that flows from the world of incipiency, exposing their own vulnerability in an attempt to affect and be affected in many ways.

Comic Bodies: The Case of Dave Chappelle

To be sure, it is one thing to seek out pain for its own sake; it is quite another to endure it involuntarily as part of an attempt to mobilize another, more empowering world defined by equality, pluralism, and social mobility. To better appreciate this dimension of the forces needed to empower the practice of active tolerance, I now want to consider the African American comedian Dave Chappelle's racial humor as representative of a sensibility similar to what Spinoza calls *hilaritas*. As is well known, Spinoza wrote very little about *hilaritas*.[60] From what Spinoza did write, however, we might say that *hilaritas*, like most other sensibilities we know of, strives to become a culturally encoded and temperamentally delimited formation, one predisposing finite bodies to endure pain even as they seek to displace its disabling effects. *Hilaritas*, Spinoza says, expresses a combination of pleasure and pain (EIIIp11s) that uplifts bodies, and that, like sugar going into the blood, energizes them. For our purposes, *hilaritas* is particularly interesting because it entails an incongruity by which the hilarious never is what it appears to be, and because it expresses itself through images that paraphrase rather than explicate the context from which they arise.[61] The combination of these two aspects enables *hilaritas* to attract bodies that endure pain, and to create a rallying point around which these bodies are able to forge new and more expansive connections with the world in which they live. To participate in *hilaritas*, we might say, is to participate in a world in which endurance of pain is a transitory yet necessary step toward a politics of empowerment and pluralization.

Of the many skits produced by the short-lived *Chappelle's Show*, the one that develops this active tolerance best might be Chappelle playing "Clifton," a black milkman who serves a squeaky-clean white middle-class family named "Niggar."[62] The shock produced by this voluptuous recitation of the N-word, referencing it without actually saying it, generates a set of tragiccomic situations in which the endurance of pain participates both to challenge existing race relations and to forge new and more expansive connections with the world in which whites and blacks live together. The most obvious aspect of the skit is how it reverses the usual epithets attached to the predicates "white" and "black": the white family served by Chappelle's black milkman is thus lazy, has big lips, eats pork, and, most importantly for the purposes of comedy, does not pay its bills. (Clifton: "I know how forgetful you Niggars are when it comes to payin' the bill.") The reversal of these epithets is countered by a presumptive generosity, which does not equate tolerance of pain with acquiescence but instead sees tolerance as a way of disclosing inequalities in order to reconfigure their place and meaning in society. This active tolerance stands out in the last scene of the skit, where Clifton and his wife meet his white customers' son and his date at the local restaurant. After some confusion about who actually are the Niggars, and after Clifton's wife has objected to what she thinks is an inappropriate use of the N-word, the white son and his date are finally seated at the table. Clifton, standing back at the entrance of the restaurant, still waiting to be seated at his table, reflects on this situation, uttering what might be one of the funniest, most controversial, and politically charged sentences in recent American comedy: "I bet you'll get the finest table a nigger's ever got in this restaurant. Oooh-wee! Oh, Lord; this racism is *killin'* me inside."

Embodying a Spinozan *hilaritas*, this utterance suggests an endurance of pain that both Spinoza and Marcuse would call "partisan," "subversive," "liberating," and "tolerant." Chappelle's skit, you might say, is an exemplar of the gravity point that empowers active tolerance, especially because it illustrates how tolerators who situate their endurance of pain within a sensibility of *hilaritas* can turn structures of inequality and oppression into an occasion for resistance and subversion. Recalling the Freedom Riders before him, invoking an intertextuality that highlights the importance of civil disobedience and nonviolence, Chappelle's skit reinvigorates the struggle against inequality and oppression. First, the skit insists that racism is disempowering for everyone involved (including whites). Second, the skit does not stipulate redemption of pain but instead tries to reframe it in order to augment rather than diminish the power of those suffering. Third, the skit envisions a community of differences where opponents see each other not as enemies but as agonistic friends who meet at what Chappelle calls "the finest table in the restaurant." Despite all its irony, this reference may indeed be the place where Chappelle's *hilaritas* takes us politically as well as normatively. At the finest table, whites and blacks would meet not because they want to erase their differences but because they desire to augment their power, both as individuals and as a community. At this table, racial differences would be acknowledged without seeing their presence or meaning as essential to what one is, was, or could become, whether as an individual or as a community. At this table, painful experiences would be shared and endured for the purposes of empowering new connections across difference. Might this not be the table where the community of active tolerators are seated?

The very possibility of raising this question suggests some important resonances among active tolerance, masochism, and the sensibility of *hilaritas*. If masochism evokes a proactive desire for pain, and if this desire is most empowering when it is oriented to an affirmative world yet to come, then we might say that *hilaritas* is what brings this orientation into a broader perspective, one in which practices of endurance and resilience are mobilized to both recognize the ubiquity of pain and reframe its disabling effects.[63] That is, by energizing finite bodies, disclosing the incongruity embedded in all situations and contexts, including the ones that seem most repressive, *hilaritas* mobilizes the affective power needed to resist various structures of inequality and oppression. Active tolerance does something similar. Like Dave Chappelle's milkman, active tolerators enter into the world of deep pluralism in order to expand their own presence through new connections with other finite beings. Rather than seeking to restrain their presence in the face of conflict and disagreement, letting opponents and other identities "be" in their own world, active tolerators encourage an ongoing engagement and experimentation with the new and the unforeseen. In so doing, they take up the mantle of democratic contestation, practicing what Nietzsche calls "spiritualization of enmity."[64]

The Limits of Active Tolerance: Abu Ghraib, Guantanamo Bay, and the Critique of Torture

The last example I want to consider—the justification of torture during the George W. Bush administration's so-called war on terror—is both the closest to and the furthest removed from the possibility of something like active tolerance. Our previous discussion of Seneca has already suggested how proponents of active tolerance take issue with the politics of torture and how they refuse to condone its use, even if it shows how the power derived from being tolerant can be mobilized to resist and subvert structures of domination and repression.[65] Nevertheless, one might worry that exclusive attention to active tolerance is morally suspect because it does not conceptualize pain as intrinsically wrong, something that historically has led to a politics of the strongest, making minorities and other under-privileged groups more vulnerable than they already are. Acknowledging this possibility, foregrounding the ambiguity that also characterizes the experience of pain, I turn to the example of torture to explore how we can conceptualize the limits of active tolerance, and thus how an interest in the latter can be mobilized against intolerance in a political setting character-ized by inequality and oppression.

As a first step, it is important to recall that an interest in active tolerance, via a sensorial orientation to politics, invokes a critique of pain that, on a number of points, differs from the more known critiques, including the one Elaine Scarry develops in her seminal book *The Body in Pain*. Although a sensorial orientation to politics does not disagree with Scarry's suggestion that torture involves a relationship of domination—a relationship where the "prisoner's pain" is perceived as the opposite of the "torturer's power" and where the inability of the tortured to resist or escape torture is linked to the infliction of pain—a sensorial orientation to politics does take issue with the general drift of Scarry's critique, which is organized around the claim that there is a "simple and absolute incompatibility of pain and the world."[66] Apart from an ontological disagreement about the nature of pain, in particular with regard to the world-making potential of pain itself, a sensorial orientation to politics criticizes this claim because the juxtaposition of pain and world obscures the plurality embedded in both pain and world, and because in this sense it risks foreclosing a conceptualization of the various connections, intensities, and thresholds embedded in tolerance's force field. Another way of saying this is that even though Scarry's focus is torture, and not tolerance, we should be careful not to treat these two issues separately, since our discussion of one will carry over into the discussion of the other. Insofar as this is the case, we must develop a subtler, more comprehensive perspective, one that does not condone torture but nonetheless remains attuned to the endurance and resilience needed to generate a politics of empowerment and pluralization.

I suggest that we draw on these insights to develop a critique of torture that, like the critique of tolerance, proceeds immanently—that is to say, from within the different yet also interrelated life-worlds of the tortured/tolerator and the torturer/tolerated. Noticing how many of the techniques being used today, including waterboarding, originate in technologies that reach as far back as the Roman period, we can develop this approach by historicizing torture so as to better discern the embodied processes that motivate the infliction of pain as well as to disclose how regimes of discourse and sensation are able to sustain this infliction across time and place.[67] Contrary to Scarry, the idea is to approach torture as a world-making practice that differs from the one of tolerance, not because one is painless and the other is not, but because each of them embodies a distinct set of relationships located within a given regime of discourse and sensation. For the purposes of critique, the central question to be asked is therefore not simply or exclusively whether or not torture is justified, but also whether its sense and future resonate with the aims of democracy: What kind of world (or worlds) does torture empower, and to what extent does this empowerment foreclose a pluralization of the range of acceptable differences in society? Although such questioning may not prevent the infliction of pain, it offers a powerful tool when it comes to criticizing the place of torture in a society like ours. Drawing our attention to the meanings and feelings attached to practices of tolerance and torture respectively, the questioning trains the eyes of society to focus not only on the infliction of pain—on how much, and for how long, it hurts—but also on what the infliction does and what it means in a world where it is practiced more or less covertly.

How, then, to criticize the justification of torture during the so-called war on torture? More specifically, how might an interest in active tolerance counter the success American soldiers and prison guards stationed at the Guantanamo Bay detention camp and the Abu Ghraib prison had in effectuating a model of surveillance and interrogation that turned the infliction of pain into a sign of power and sovereignty?[68] The first answer is similar to the one offered by other critiques of torture: a combination of outrage and repulsion followed by a call for the condemnation of state-sponsored torture. But an interest in active tolerance goes further than this. Concerned with the circulation of the images of naked prisoners at the Abu Ghraib prison, as well as with the testimonies from now-released prisoners at Guantanamo Bay and the legal memoranda written by U.S. government attorneys to justify waterboarding and other techniques of torture, the interest in active tolerance implies focusing on how torture functions as a tacit yet constitutive part of a world that *de jure* rejects its use. In the case of the Abu Ghraib prison images, for example, active tolerance insists that the expression of outrage and repulsion cannot be limited to the events at the prison, but must be extended to a critique of how the images were circulated in the news media and how they framed the perception of sovereignty as a power that ordinary citizens observe as being distinct from their own involvement with local government and electoral politics. Moreover, in the case of waterboarding, an interest in active tolerance goes one step further in order to show how the attempt by journalists and pundits to demonstrate the suffocating effects of waterboarding, reenacting it in public, was driven just as much by a male-dominated society's fascination with suffering as by a desire to criticize torture for its disabling effects. And finally, in relation to the memoranda that legitimized the use of "enhanced interrogation techniques" at Guantanamo Bay, active tolerance holds that it is insufficient to invoke the United States's official commitment to the UN Convention Against Torture, which defines torture as the infliction of "severe pain and suffering." Although reference to this definition can be rhetorically powerful, the worry is that it may be less efficacious than we think because it avoids engaging in an open and public discussion of what constitutes "severe" pain. Failing to engage in such a discussion, the critique of torture risks enabling a Janus-faced situation in which one can be against torture while at the same time participating in a regime of discourse and sensation that, under the cover of bureaucracy and legal proceduralism, raises the definition of severe pain to an unprecedented level. A situation like this one seems to have characterized the discussion of torture during the war on terror, as exemplified by then Assistant Attorney General Jay S. Bybee's claim that the infliction of pain on prisoners at the Guantanamo Bay detention camp would have to "be associated with sufficiently serious physical condition or injury such as death, organ failure, or serious impairment of body functions" before it would constitute a breach of the United Nations Convention Against Torture.[69]

It is the bodily and discursive conditions enabling statements like this one that an interest in active tolerance seeks to criticize, offering a richer vocabulary with which to contest and reposition the place of pain in democratic societies. As already noted, the idea is that the critique of torture should be conceived in tandem with the critique of tolerance because both concern how experiences of pain are situated within regimes of discourse and sensation that must be analyzed in the broadest possible terms in order to appreciate whether the worlds they empower are enabling or repressive, democratic or undemocratic. For the purposes of active tolerance, the intersection of these interests is particularly helpful because it suggests how active tolerance can be delimited without invoking a criterion or standard external to pain itself. On the one hand, a sensorially inflected critique of torture enables proponents of active tolerance to argue that the use of torture at Guantanamo Bay and Abu Ghraib was intolerable not because it inflicted pain per se but because it generated a world—a political spectacle—based on hierarchy, humiliation, and domination rather than empowerment, generosity, and pluralization. On the other hand, the critical approach developed here also enables proponents of active tolerance to counter the use and justification of torture by mobilizing another "world," one that privileges a competing vocabulary of pain, probing pain's world-making character, including its power and meaning within and across diverse contexts, thereby making it more difficult for state officials and other advocates of torture to maintain their privileged position within the societies in which they operate. Without this kind of deep contestation, the definition of torture developed by the states themselves may remain standing as the most authoritative one, even when torture's abhorrent and intolerable implications become public.

In all, considering the three examples—masochism, comedy, and torture—demonstrates how an interest in active tolerance situates itself vis-à-vis some of the most prevalent issues in contemporary democratic politics. Common to the consideration of the three examples is the acknowledgment that the endurance of pain is an ineliminable component of democratic politics, and that the challenge is not to juxtapose the endurance of pain to another, more "pleasurable" experience, but to differentiate between kinds of pain so as to better identify the potential and power embedded in the endurance practiced by citizens in a world of deep pluralism. Focusing our attention on the sensorial aspects of tolerance, highlighting the broader force field that moves tolerators in this or that direction, the turn to active tolerance sees the immersion into struggles against inequality and oppression as part of the receptivity needed to conceptualize the potential and power of endurance itself. Although such an approach may expose the practice of active tolerance to the fluctuations of context, and thus may risk undermining the theory's aspirations as a shared reference point across any number of struggles against inequality and oppression, the approach lends itself to the kind of affirmative critique associated with Spinoza's philosophy of immanence and the theory of active tolerance. The approach is one that opens up new possibilities from within established domains of conflict and disagreement; that aims not only to justify but also to motivate new practices of democratic pluralism; and that seeks to energize alternative constellations of thought and action, emphasizing the potentiality of all situations, including those we find the most repressive.

V. THREE PROPOSITIONS FOR THE THEORY OF ACTIVE TOLERANCE

These remarks bring us back to the primary objective of this chapter, which is to establish the theory of active tolerance affirmatively, and to show how a sensorial orientation to politics, inspired by Spinoza's philosophy of immanence, can be put into conversation with Marcuse's critique of tolerance as a political practice that oscillates between an active side and a passive side. From the preceding discussions, we might say that the theory of active tolerance is characterized by three propositions: (1) the power immanent to tolerance is inherently open-ended and can be expressed in both active and passive ways; (2) tolerance is most active when its power is linked to an experience of "pleasurable pain" that affirms the shared condition of vulnerability and dependency; tolerance is least active when the same condition is perceived as a "painful pain" that diminishes the ability to think and act; and (3) tolerance's active side is linked to a gravity point within the general force field of tolerance that both subverts existing constellations of movement and rest *and* enriches the shared desire to affect and be affected in more ways.[70]

As these three propositions make clear, the theory of active tolerance is inspired by, but not completely in agreement with, the critique that Marcuse leveled against proponents of tolerance almost fifty years ago. Acknowledging that tolerance today is predominantly passive because it tends to privilege the refusal to act, the theory of active tolerance changes the critical inflection of Marcuse's arguments by not concluding that the shift between tolerance's active and passive sides is either unidirectional or irreversible. The theory of active tolerance resists such a conclusion because it reifies tolerance's passivity, and because it thereby prevents us from reimagining the practices of endurance and resilience so important for a vibrant politics of empowerment and pluralization. To avoid overlooking the importance of endurance and resilience, the theory of active tolerance proceeds by broadening the relationship between tolerance and power, and by looking more closely at how the sensorial side of politics entails unexplored resources for a critical engagement with historically sedimented policies of inequality and repression. Insofar as this approach reinvigorates the turning point around which tolerance's two sides evolve, the benefits of the theory of active tolerance may be said to outweigh the costs of entering onto a terrain that is inherently dynamic in both form and content. Not only does the theory of active tolerance reformulate the main insight embedded in Marcuse's 1965 critique—that tolerance has both a passive side *and* an active side—it also suggests how tolerance may both augment and share power maximally, enabling constituents of different stripes to create new and more expansive connections in a world that is always-always plural in its instantiations. The latter, I submit, is more needed than ever.

CHAPTER 4

Framing Tolerance

What causes pain is that one moves from the disgusting image—and that one comes back to it. That oscillation.

Paul Valéry (year unknown)[1]

...tolerance of the incomplete may mean...that completion, the presentation that is objective and convincing for the senses, may no longer be considered necessary or even sufficient and thus that the proper sign of the complete work has been found elsewhere.

Maurice Merleau-Ponty (1969)[2]

I. TOLERANCE IN A WORLD OF DEEP PLURALISM

On September 30, 2005, the Danish newspaper *Jyllands-Posten* published twelve cartoons of the Prophet Muhammad. Placed under the heading "The face of Muhammad"—and with a subtitle citing "freedom of expression"—the cartoons were commissioned by the newspaper's editor, Fleming Rose, who wanted to challenge what he found to be an unreasonable fear of criticizing Muslims living in Denmark.[3] Rose's efforts led to a diverse set of cartoons. The most notorious was a cartoon of the Prophet Muhammad with a detonated bomb in his turban. Another showed him as a next-door-neighbor circled by a half crescent suggesting a halo and/ or horns. Still another rejected the idea behind the Rose initiative and instead drew the Prophet as a subversive seventh grader at Valby Skole, a school outside Copenhagen known for its many Muslim immigrants. The schoolboy took on the *Jyllands-Posten* journalists by pointing to a sentence written on the blackboard in Farsi: "The *Jyllands-Posten* journalists," it said unapologetically, "are a bunch of reactionary provocateurs."[4]

Recalling previous conflicts such as the Salman Rushdie affair, the French hijab case, and the 2003 Theo van Gogh murder case, statements such as this one anticipated the warlike conflict that followed after the cartoons were published.[5] Whereas Muslims in Denmark and around the world protested the cartoons, claiming that they were harmed by them, others saw the cartoons as a legitimate exercise of the right to free speech.[6] A similar bifurcation characterized reactions in contemporary democratic theory where the initial discussion focused on the limits of free speech but later revolved around two separate positions engaging in a zero-sum game similar to the one that defines the discussion of tolerance in contemporary democratic theory: whereas the first position argued that the publication of the twelve cartoons expressed an arrogance that violated the principle of autonomy applicable to all reasonable citizens (Muslims included), the second saw the first position as part of the problem because it did not acknowledge the lived experience of many Muslims for whom the "the offense of the cartoons was not against a moral interdiction . . . but against a structure of affect . . . that feels wounded."[7] The juxtaposition of these two positions seems particularly counterproductive because neither sought to explore the interplay between reason and affect, and in this sense avoided exploring how insights from one position could enrich insights from the other (and vise-versa). The questions provoked by this blind spot are indeed many. Could it be that the juxtaposition of reason and affect, and— by extension—of autonomy and habitat, invoke an obstacle to the contestation and deliberation that both positions envision as normatively and politically desirable? Could it be that reason and affect are framed in similar ways and therefore must be discussed in conjunction with each other? Could it be that new possibilities for empowerment and pluralization open up if we see affect and reason as linked, and if we expand our appreciation of what tolerance means and can do in a context where the lived experiences of interconnectedness and vulnerability are front and center?

Invoking the three propositions outlined at the end of the previous chapter, the theory of active tolerance encourages us to answer these questions in the affirmative. This is not to say that other, more empowering possibilities always hide beneath the veneer of intractability that defines political conflicts such as the Danish cartoon war. Still, the theory of active tolerance holds that if we set out to explore the broader sensorium in which affect and reason alike play a part, mobilizing the creative potential that subsists within all registers of lived experience, it may be that an alternative approach to democratic politics becomes more likely, one that is less about "deciding" a conflict such as the Danish cartoon war and more about reorienting the conditions of contestation and deliberation so that those affected by them can better appreciate how and why a politics of empowerment and pluralization might be desirable in the first place. In the case of the Danish cartoon war, the first step suggested by the theory of active tolerance is thus to bracket the demand for a "solution," and instead appreciate that constituents on both sides of the conflict can be "right" insofar as each highlights a set of attitudes and practices vital to contemporary democratic politics. Such an appreciation can include sensitivity to pain (which typically calls for more regulation of free speech) as well as the cultivation of a resilient attitude to political and religious differences (which typically calls for less regulation of free speech). The second step, however, is not to become indifferent to the conflict, accepting the two opposing sides such as they are, but rather to expand their internal differences in order to interrupt the forces and desires that create the appearance of a binary opposition between them. The theory of active tolerance pursues this expansion by reorienting how we, as political theorists and as members of various democratic regimes, perceive and engage disagreements in a world of deep pluralism. Rather than accepting or positing just one way of perceiving the Danish cartoon war, the theory of active tolerance turns the absence of universally shared standards for thought and action into a reason for a politics of empowerment and pluralization. The idea is to experience conflicts such as the Danish cartoon war differently in order to mobilize an alternative gravity point in which reasons for exploring mutual differences are expanded rather than contracted. As suggested in Chapter 3, this implies connecting the practice of tolerance with the desire to "affect" and to "be affected" in many ways.

The objective of the present chapter is to further elaborate on this insight. Expanding on the discussion of tolerance's force field, foregrounding the plurality represented by the twelve *Jyllands-Posten* cartoons, the chapter suggests that we supplement Spinoza's analysis of affective being with attention to the politics of framing that makes the gravity point associated with the practice of active tolerance shine forth in the manner suggested by examplars such as Bacon's Diogenes, Chappelle's *hilaritas*, and Nietzsche's spiritualization of enmity. Attention to framing is necessary, I argue, because it is at this level of lived experience that the affective dimensions of pain are encountered as either painful or pleasurable, and thus where the endurance of pain itself is perceived as either an obstacle to or a condition of contestation and deliberation.[8] To better conceptualize the possibilities embedded in this encounter, I suggest that we supplement Spinoza's contributions to the theory of active tolerance with a discussion of what Merleau-Ponty, in the cited epigraph, calls "tolerance of the incomplete."[9] As we shall see, the attention to framing embedded in this dictum is particularly helpful to describe how the theory of active tolerance envisions the framing of affection and reasoning that can reorient tolerators toward an affirmative engagement with the feeling of displacement and vulnerability provoked by the plurality of lived experience. Not only does Merleau-Ponty's "tolerance of the incomplete" draw tolerators closer to the creative potiential embedded in lived experience, it reframes the citizenry's need for order and stability, augmenting the desire to expand the politically marked differences that empower as well as trouble the conditions of contestation and deliberation. These insights, I argue, are crucial for grasping how the theory of active tolerance might interrupt the sense of intractability that defines political conflicts such as the Danish cartoon war.

Section II of this chapter outlines the general context of the Danish cartoon war in order to better appreciate how experiences of pain are framed in contemporary democratic politics. Section III examines the right to free speech, in particular as it has been developed by Thomas M. Scanlon, disclosing a "creative instability" (Scanlon's term) that links the politics of framing to the background conditions of contestation and deliberation. Section IV turns to Merleau-Ponty's analysis of perception, including his idea of "tolerance of the incomplete," and it examines how some but not all framings of pain might help to empower the plurality of lived experience that subsists beneath established modes of seeing and feeling. Section V links receptivity to this plurality of lived experience to what I call "sensorial reasoning," a form of reasoning that draws sustenance from the registers of both affect and reason. I conclude with a discussion of how the theory of active tolerance changes our approach to political conflicts in a world of deep pluralism.

II. HARMFUL CARTOONS?

No matter how contemporary democratic theory construes the relationship between experiences of pain and the demands of the law, we should be careful not to accept Art Spiegelman's astonishment at "how banal and inoffensive the *Jyllands-Posten* cartoons" should seem to anyone living in a Western secular democracy.[10] Such astonishment overlooks the importance of political spectacles to the framing of lived experience—what Jeffrey E. Green has called "ocular democracy."[11] Spiegelman's assessment also obscures the underlying conditions that allowed the twelve *Jyllands-Posten* cartoons to become the object of a global "war" that caused the deaths of about 130 individuals.[12] To grasp the conditions leading to this outcome, we must broaden our perspective and analyze not only whether or not *Jyllands-Posten* was right to publish the twelve cartoons but also how and why the twelve cartoons could seem harmful to some and not to others. As it is the case in most conflicts in contemporary democratic theory, the critical question is one in which the normative issue of what is "right" is intimately linked to the phenomenology of how the same experience or utterance can be perceived in almost binary ways by people living in a pluralistic world linked by economic globalization and new information technology.

A common explanation for the differences in the perception of the twelve *Jyllands-Posten* cartoons has been Islam's prohibition of images.[13] On both sides of the conflict, commentators have read this ban as accounting for the sensibilities of all Muslims who as a group were singularly wounded by the cartoons' depictions of the Prophet, turning the debate into a question of whether a Western democracy like Denmark's should treat the ban as an acceptable limitation of free speech. Although this is an important question to ask, we do well if we first acknowledge how the ban is understood, and indeed practiced, across various interpretations of Islam. Such an approach readily suggests that the ban is not as homogeneous as we might think and that differences occur, first, because the ban belongs to the more general *hadith* through which a chain of transmitters (called *isnad*) communicates texts (called *matm*) that combine the words and deeds of the Prophet or some other religious authority, and second, because the linkages of these words and deeds, once placed in a certain context, engender the possibility of contestation and revision.[14] Thus, although the Qur'an includes the story of Abraham as an iconoclast—Abraham breaks the idols of a city because their depiction of god inspires false worship (Qur'an 21.51–70)—this has not ruled out the use of images in Muslim countries. First, images were used on coins in the second half of the seventh century, on official landmarks, and at important places of worship such as the Dome of the Rock in Jerusalem and the Great Mosque of Damascus.[15] Second, in the exegeses of Ibn Kathīr and Sayyid Qutb, we learn that Abraham's iconoclasm represents not so much a ban on images as a warning against the way in which *some* images subvert the oneness of God through mockery and slander.[16] Third, throughout the Middle East we find a tradition of political satire that uses cartoons as a means of critique and resistance.[17] Even though these uses represent only a fraction of all practices within the Muslim world, they nonetheless suggest an openness that draws Islam's ban on images into a more pluralistic world delimited by processes of politicization and retextualization.[18] These processes are felt both by Muslims for whom the ban's openness gives rise to interpretative anxieties and political disagreements, and by non-Muslims for whom the openness precludes the notion of a stable "other" that can be fixed in relation to one's own identity. Still, because contemporary democratic theorists rarely attend to such experiential variety, these processes of politicization and retextualization do not figure prominently in the discussion of tolerance and free speech. It is largely because of this that the initial responses to *Jyllands-Posten* cartoons may have contributed to, rather than alleviated, the sense of intractability and bifurcation that followed.

If the ban on images alone does not explain why Muslims would see the cartoons as harmful, then what made them seem so? One answer might be the emergence of a populist discourse based on moral binaries, attachment to victimization, and stigmatization of minorities—what we, in a Nietzschean vein, could call a culture of *ressentiment*. A carrier of this culture has been the Danish People's Party (DPP), which for the past fifteen years or so has been the third-largest party represented in the Danish parliament. Founded in 1995 by four dissenters from the far-right Progress Party, the DPP supported during the 2000s shifting right-wing governments, using its parliamentary power to argue that perceived failures in the Danish health care and social security systems stem from an unspoken alliance between socially privileged bureaucrats and Muslim immigrants, linking this analysis to the need for stricter border control, limited membership in the EU, and the protection of "Danish" values symbolized by the flag, the monarchy, the currency, and the constitution.[19] Feeding off an effective media strategy, this advocacy empowered a stigmatizing discourse in which Muslims are perceived to be a threat to the future of Danish culture.[20] Muslims living in Denmark at the time noted this perception, relating it directly to the publication of the twelve cartoons. According to one imam living in Denmark, "It's not the cartoons, it is the way [the Prophet] is being presented. . . . The pictures are saying that Muslims are terrorists, because he is a Muslim and he has a bomb in his head."[21]

Although the Danish cartoon war touched on more than what is sketched here, comments such as these show not only why the same cartoons could be perceived in radically different ways but also how the framing of harmful speech is important for the background conditions of contestation and deliberation. The background conditions are never uniform in nature, something that was especially evident in the Danish cartoon war: whereas a majority of Muslims saw the harm provoked by the *Jyllands-Posten* cartoons as a reason for regulating speech through law, the opposite could be said of constituents committed to values promoted by especially the DPP.[22] The co-presence of these contested, multiple perspectives, none of which directly or unequivocally challenges values of tolerance and free speech, reiterates that the normative question of *who* should tolerate *what* is intimately linked to the politics of framing. The question, you might say, is not *if* democratic politics distributes the burdens of suffering unequally (it does), but rather how and with what consequences for the background conditions of contestation and deliberation. How do we, as theorists and as members of democratic regimes, come to perceive some but not other expressions as injurious, and how do divergent perceptions of the same expression affect our identification with the democratic process as such? These questions refer to what Judith Butler, in a not altogether unrelated context, calls the differences between meaning and nonmeaning ("intelligibility") and actor and nonactor ("recognizability")—differences that Butler argues are crucial to how we understand and engage contemporary democratic politics.[23] As noted earlier, attention to the difference between meaning and nonmeaning, actor and nonactor, is what is called for as well by the sensorial orientation to politics underpinning the theory of active tolerance.[24]

III. FREE SPEECH AND CREATIVE INSTABILITY

Attention to the framing of democracy's background conditions is, of course, hardly a novel suggestion. Indeed, if we look at it historically, we readily see that political theorists have examined the issue through a rich and diverse discourse, which invokes a number of conceptual distinctions to ensure a steady commitment to tolerance and free speech, focusing on the object (self-regarding vs. other-regarding), the character (physical vs. emotional), and the intensity (trivial vs. nontrivial) of the harms provoked by this or that speech act.[25] Embedded in various legal procedures and cultural mores of most Western democracies, these distinctions have served as the basis for making judgments about injurious speech and, moreover, have become second nature to a Millian framework of democracy, one that posits free speech as a means for reaching a higher level of truth as well as for nourishing a resiliency that can enable citizens to tolerate a plurality of opinions and ways of life. In recent years, however, contemporary democratic theorists have moved away from this framework in the interest of developing another justification of free speech that either ignores the question of harm or insists that it should be considered independently of the legal and normative questions raised by tolerance and the right to free speech.[26] As we saw in Chapter 1, contemporary democratic theorists have justified this argument with reference to an increased pluralism—what Rawls calls "the fact of pluralism"—which followers of Rawls argue precludes a shared notion of harm, and which therefore necessitates a different framework inspired by a neo-Kantian intellectualist orientation to politics. Troubled by conflicts over the meaning of injurious speech, contemporary democratic theorists have thus sought to bracket the politics of framing in the interest of retaining the universal appeal of tolerance and free speech.

One way to interrupt this trend in contemporary democratic theory is to take a clue from the discussion in Chapters 1 and 2, and explore whether there are blind spots and counterpoints that, once disclosed, might encourage the intellectualist tradition to go beyond its stated ambitions and intentions. Consider here Thomas M. Scanlon's seminal work on tolerance and the right to free speech. According to Scanlon, the increased pluralism in today's democratic societies requires that we base our judgments about harmful speech on a quasi-transcendental principle untainted by the experience of pain itself.[27] The principle favored by Scanlon is personal autonomy, which Scanlon argues should be defined as the ability to be "sovereign in deciding what to believe and in weighing competing reasons for action."[28] Appealing to this definition will, according to Scanlon, allow contemporary democratic theory to both justify the right to free speech—simply put, free speech is requisite for the ability to decide for oneself—and decide the right's limits in relation to expressions that citizens might perceive as harmful. To be more specific: though some cases of harmful speech should be considered intolerable because they lead to injury, panic, ridicule, and defamation, all of which either weaken an autonomous person's ability to weigh competing evidence or repress his or her ability to contest the judgment of others, a host of other expressions remain permissible even though they arise from individuals having false beliefs, or from believing that some acts can be worth performing despite their harmful consequences. The latter creates a fairly broad tolerance for objectionable or even injurious expressions. As Scanlon puts it, "the harm of coming to have false beliefs" is not one that an "autonomous man could allow the state to protect him against through restrictions on expression."[29]

The first thing to note about this way of linking tolerance to the right to free speech is that it entails a framing of the experience of pain that citizens must internalize before they can invoke the principle of autonomy as a way to both justify and determine the limits of harmful speech. The instability of this internalization is particularly evident if we note the differences in a case such as the Danish cartoon war, where some citizens saw the principle of autonomy as capturing their life experiences, whereas others experienced it as a means of disregarding their history, faith, or culture. These differences make it less than obvious why we should assume that the principle of autonomy can safeguard the kind of overlapping consensus that older discourses on harmful speech are criticized for not securing.[30] The differences also raise the question whether limiting the moral and political imaginary to a matter of autonomous decision-making might not be a cause of conflict in a country such as Denmark, which, after all, is known just as much for Kierkegaardian irony as for a commitment to autonomy and respect. To raise this question, of course, is not to say that Denmark's public philosophy (such as it is) does not include some conception of autonomy. It is to say that whatever autonomy means, it is arguably different from other iterations of that concept, including the neo-Kantian one favored by Scanlon and others. In Denmark, the principle of autonomy cohabits with Kierkegaard, Grundtvig, and von Trier; in the United States, it is birthed by Rawls in the company of Rorty, Dworkin, and others; and in Germany it is taken over by the Hegelian critique of Kant and by Habermas's neo-Kantianism. Even though all of these traditions invoke autonomy as a common point of reference, they rarely mean the same thing. Autonomy may therefore not be universal in the sense of being the same in all places and at all times; invoking a multiplicity of traditions, it is rather iterative and always, even if paradoxically so, in difference with itself.

Another way of saying this is that the principle of autonomy is no different from other moral principles insofar as it, too, is subject to a framing of lived experience that privileges some but not other claims for intelligibility and recognition, visibility and retribution. Although Scanlon does not acknowledge this aspect explicitly, it remains important to a consideration of what is at stake in his discussion: the ability to decide whether or not harmful speech is tolerable. What I want to suggest is that the ability to make this decision hinges on the framing of the experience of pain, and that the decision therefore can be more contentious than we might think. In the Danish case, for example, we find that whereas most Muslims emphasized the harm caused by a defaming mockery of the Prophet, the majority of Danes focused on the harm caused by flag burnings, death threats, and assaults on embassy buildings, all performed by or associated with the immigrant community. Moreover, to those who sided with *Jyllands-Posten*, the reaction against the cartoons seemed thin-skinned. Common retorts were thus "Why can't they [the Muslims] take a joke?" or "The cartoons are not as injurious as other cartoons in the history of political satire."[31] Those on the other side did not see it that way. With the focus on the harm already done by the cartoons, decisions such as the one by the Danish government not to meet with ambassadors from the Middle East seemed only to deepen the wound. The Grand Mufti of Egypt expressed this view when he answered charges of violence by asking, "Why can't you apologize now that you so evidently have harmed us?"[32]

Statements like these underscore both the attraction and the insufficiency of a conceptualization of tolerance and free speech based on the principle of autonomy. On the one hand, the right to free speech appears to be so open-ended that it can be co-opted by multiple constituents, each of which can formulate its own claim for recognition in a way that seems more or less intelligible to the other side, refusing a neat separation of law and harm, adjusting and co-opting the limits of tolerance and free speech for purposes that are specific to place and time. On the other hand, however, it is also clear that contemporary democratic theorists who link tolerance and free speech to the principle of autonomy assume that the creativity embedded in this co-optation must be limited, and that the best way to do so is by endowing the principle of autonomy with a quasi-transcendental quality that precludes a more fundamental conflict about democracy's background conditions. Important for the purposes of order and stability, the attempt to manage such a conflict is not only experientially but also politically insufficient—a point borne out by the Danish cartoon war, where each side adopted the principle of autonomy for its own purposes, engendering an undecidability that would unsettle most advocates of tolerance and the right to free speech who base their arguments on this principle. To wit: whereas Muslims saw the defamation of the Prophet as a threat to their autonomy, which suffered because of the discrimination implied by equating Islam with terrorism, Danes saw the assaults on embassies as a politics of fear that short-circuited independent consideration of the twelve cartoons. To the extent that both of these interpretations are valid, a conceptualization of tolerance and the right to free speech based on the principle of autonomy may be less decisive than acknowledged by its proponents. Rather than occupying a place "above the fray," the conceptualization instead appears to be limited to one frame in competition with others, encouraging us to acknowledge that the agonistic openness valued by Scanlon and other contemporary democratic theorists as an aspect of a democratic framework of individual rights extends all the way down to the background conditions of contestation and deliberation.[33] Insofar as this is the case, it is no longer possible to ignore the politics of framing. Indeed, without attention to this aspect of democratic politics, it may not be possible to conceptualize the conditions that move citizens toward a greater commitment to tolerance and free speech.

For our purposes, it is interesting to note that it is Scanlon, rather than Habermas or Rawls, who suggests a way to address this blind spot in contemporary democratic theory.[34] Scanlon does so, mostly against his own intentions, when he explains that all individual rights harbor within themselves a "creative instability," which stems from the friction among three interrelated elements that he argues make up the structure of any right: (1) the ends, (2) the means, and (3) the linking empirical beliefs.[35] Whereas the first two elements touch on the normative reasons we give for rights such as the one to free speech, the last—what Scanlon calls empirical beliefs "about the motivation of the relevant actors, about the opportunities to act that are available to them, and about the collective results of the decisions they are likely to make"[36]—stresses the motivations for executing this right, as well as the consequences that follow from this execution. Scanlon further notes that empirical beliefs are subject to change because they rely on context-dependent encounters with the consequences that follow from implementing the right to free expression in this or that way. The upshot is a dialectical process of sorts, one in which empirical beliefs work back on our justification of the right to free speech. As Scanlon rightly observes, attention to changes in empirical beliefs suggests that the right to free speech does not form a "coherent whole" but instead entails "a dynamic quality" and "creativity instability" that "can lead to an almost constant process of revision."[37]

The turn to creative instability holds great promise for a conceptualization of the politics of framing. Almost poetic in nature, the term at first seems to indicate that the principle of autonomy might not be as self-governing as many contemporary democratic theorists, including Scanlon, seem to assume. But there is more to it than that. Contrary to Scanlon's stated intentions, we can also read his felicitous term as indicating that any conception of democratic politics based on the principle of autonomy should be supplemented by a sensibility attuned to the principle's inherent incompleteness and reliance on the embodied circumstances that frame the citizenry's engagement with differing perceptions of the same expression. For the theory of active tolerance, this is a reason to bring pain back in. It is also a reason to foreground the question of worldliness, that is, the question of whether specific experiences empower or isolate, expand or contract, connections across self, other, and world. Mobilizing what Merleau-Ponty calls a "tolerance of the incomplete"—a dictum that, placed alongside Scanlon's "creative instability," emphasizes an openness to the not-yet-seen-or-felt—the theory of active tolerance encourages us to attend to the "dynamic quality" that organizes not only moral and legal norms but also visual experiences, affective bonds, and perceptual differences. The theory of active tolerance does so because the plurality associated with this quality can be mobilized to expand the conditions of contestation and deliberation, and because as such it can contribute to reorient the conversation about harmful speech. Rather than seeing the effects of harmful speech as private in the sense that they are too subjective to be meaningfully shared with others, the theory of active tolerance sees them disclosing the plurality of lived experience such that the desire to engage the world anew is augmented or diminished. Whether it is one or the other is not a question that can be engaged or settled by the principle of autonomy alone; it requires an approach to perceiving political conflict that straddles the many registers of lived experience, attending to how the experience of pain is framed so as to privilege some modes of tolerance and free speech but not others.

This approach to political conflict raises a number of questions regarding the politics of framing. Does plurality of lived experience motivate citizens to think and act in a particular manner? Is the incompleteness that follows from the plurality of lived experience perceived as painful, or can it also be seen as pleasurable? Do the various registers of lived experience shape our appreciation of incompleteness differently, and if so then what frames might empower rather than restrict such appreciation? To address these questions, I now turn to the work of Merleau-Ponty.

IV. PERCEIVING THE INCOMPLETE: MERLEAU-PONTY AND THE POLITICS OF FRAMING

Unlike Scanlon, who begins with the principle of autonomy, Merleau-Ponty begins his inquiry by examining the heteronomy intrinsic to lived experience in general, and to perception in particular.[38] Adding to the insights offered by a sensorial orientation to politics, noticing how each register of lived experience overlaps with the rest, Merleau-Ponty engages perception at its most general—as the experiential interface that both delimits and troubles the distinction between an outer world of endless manifold and an inner world concerned with feeling and consciousness.[39] To illustrate this approach, imagine a person looking at a painting. The first thing this person does is turn the painting into "an unbroken text" fulfilling what Merleau-Ponty calls the "tacit thesis" of picture-perfect images.[40] In order to appreciate the painting's perspective, however, the same person must also develop a sense of depth that is "hidden" to and "simultaneous" with the pursuit of picture-perfect images.[41] Merleau-Ponty emphasizes the juxtaposition of these two elements because he thinks they delimit the reversibility that enables the perceiver and the perceived to slip in and out of each other, and because the two sides of perception thereby show how perception itself is characterized by an incompleteness that oscillates between a bodily attraction to the richness of lived experience and an auto-somatic warning against getting lost or absolved in this richness.[42] Although the latter seems less desirable, especially insofar as it limits how nuanced a person's experience of something like a painting can be, it remains latently present at all times, reminding us that too much incompleteness can undermine the pursuit of picture-perfect images that protects us against a painful feeling of disorientation and vulnerability. What we have, then, are not two but three elements that jointly define perception: a thesis of picture-perfect images that expects the perceived world to appear as an unbroken text; a depth that enables the perceiver and the perceived to slip in and out of each other; and an enriching as well as anxiety-inducing difference, one subject to both affirmation and disavowal.[43]

Before turning to how this account of perception might change our approach to the politics of framing in conflicts such as the Danish cartoon war, we do well to consider how it more generally adds to the theory of active tolerance based on a sensorial orientation to politics. The first insight that follows from Merleau-Ponty's account of perception is that it encourages us to approach tolerance not simply as a choice that individuals can realize in relation to whatever they deem objectionable, but also as part of how the world of lived experience is constituted prior to the very possibility of making such a choice. When Merleau-Ponty juxtaposes depth and surface, linking perception to a "tolerance of the incomplete," he means to highlight how this incompleteness, fraught with its own anxieties about disorientation and vulnerability, troubles the idea of a neat separation of the world into a set of distinct positions, e.g., between a "tolerator" and someone or something "tolerated."[44] Although the relationship between these two positions might never be perfectly symmetrical (something we also saw in the discussion of masochism in Chapter 3), there is an important sense in which both the tolerator and the tolerated stand out against a shared background, mirroring the reversibility that enables the perceiver and the perceived to slip in and out of each other. One reason to attend to this reversibility is that it broadens our appreciation of the context in which tolerance's force field is structured and framed. Another reason is that it relaxes the assumption that the relationship between the tolerator and the tolerated is marked by restraint and withdrawal rather than openness and engagement. Attention to the reversibility between tolerator and tolerated encourages us to consider how they might slip in and out of each other; creating a more complex situation in which the same agent can be both tolerator and tolerated, it highlights how each side of the relationship embodies a degree of power that potentially can affect the other side. The structure of reversibility may thus be crucial to the background conditions needed for a practice of empowerment and pluralization in which tolerator and tolerated engage and augment elements in each other.

The other general insight embedded in Merleau-Ponty's account of perception speaks to our conception of what it means to approach politics sensorially. Rather than privileging one register of lived experience as more autonomous or more decisive than the rest,[45] Merleau-Ponty encourages us to focus on the interplay between the various registers of lived experience, insisting that perception too is a tactile phenomenon that relates not only to images and seeing but also to other registers of lived experience, including how we feel, touch, and think.[46] From Merleau-Ponty's perspective, and more so than in the case of Spinoza's, it is the synesthetic character of lived experience that counts. What matters is not whether one register of lived experience structures everything else; rather, Merleau-Ponty encourages us to focus on the interstices of lived experience—on the many overlaps where multiple registers of lived experience intertwine and where, through context-specific moments of reverberations and resonances, they help to delimit the conditions of meaning and sense for those affected by them. Keeping this front and center is particularly important if the goal is to examine the sensorium of political life and better grasp how the partitioning of the sensible is a political operation open to various degrees of contestation and change.

For our purposes, a broadening of the sensorial orientation to politics is helpful because it enables us to see how the experience of pain so central to the conceptualization of tolerance and free speech might be subject to diverse framings in the context of incompleteness, plurality, and creative instability. As Scanlon did with the right to free expression, so Merleau-Ponty encourages us to emphasize how the experience of pain is not a "coherent whole"; instead, it possesses a "dynamic quality" that pervades every perception of self, other, and world. To this quality, Merleau-Ponty adds an emphasis on intelligibility and recognizability, which in turn paves the way for a pluralistic conception of how the experience of pain can be framed according to a purpose specific to place and time. On the one hand, we can now speak of pain as linked to perception's inability to fulfill its own thesis of picture-perfect images. (This is what the anxiety mentioned above is about.) On the other hand, we can also speak of pain as being framed along a continuum of outcomes, each of which adds to the Spinozan distinction between painful pains and pleasurable pains, suggesting an element of framing that determines what Merleau-Ponty would call pain's "sense or...future."[47] At one end of the continuum, pain is thus the sign, if not the instigator, of an instability that must be replaced by a legally codified world of perceptual stability and fixed identity. At the other end, pain represents the richness that lies in perception's incompleteness and that opens up to a pluralistic world of contestation and difference.[48]

Fraught with its own experience of pain, this world may nonetheless be affirmable because it connects with the value of visual depth and sensorial abundance.

Merleau-Ponty would be the first to admit that whatever follows from the framing of pain at each end of this continuum is not normative in the sense of being valid at all times and in all places. To Merleau-Ponty, however, this admission is not a weakness; it underscores the heteronomy that haunts the organization of both tolerance and free speech, and that encourages us to place the politics of framing alongside the various sensibilities of affection and reasoning that either either expand or contract the condtions of contestation and deliberation in a world of deep pluralism. Taking up the thread from our discussion in the previous three chapters, Merleau-Ponty is particularly interested in a sensibibility that instills an attitude of critical engagement and presumptive generosity, pushing the sensory apparatus to see, feel, and actively unearth the plurality subsisting within any account we can give of actual lived experience. Merleau-Ponty envisions this sensibility as wiring our senses in two interrelated ways, both of which allow us to see how tolerators might orient themselves to the empowering and pluralizing potential embedded in the gravity point favored by the theory of active tolerance. On the one hand, Merleau-Ponty suggests that the sensibility cultivates the critical distance needed to see beyond the appearance of a binary world in which one must either be "for" or "against"—a distance that Merleau-Ponty calls an attitude of the "perhaps," which he conceives as a "formula of doubt as well as faith."[49] On the other hand, Merleau-Ponty also holds that the sensibility should be one that refuses to withdraw from action, instead drawing sustenance from the pleasure that arises from seeing and feeling the world anew, thereby making both tolerator and tolerated more receptive to experimentation, augmenting the desire to affect and be affected in many ways. The combination of these two aspects is captured by Merleau-Ponty dictum "tolerance of the incomplete," which Merleau-Ponty stresses does not amount to inaction, but instead implies a desire to explore the world of images and signs anew. As Merleau-Ponty suggests, to tolerate the incomplete is to resist the notion that "completion...be considered necessary or even sufficient."[50]

To see more concretely how this sensibility of affection and reasoning might change our attention to the framing of of the background conditions of contestation and deliberation, consider the most notorious of the twelve *Jyllands-Posten* cartoons, the one depicting the Prophet Muhammad with a bomb in his turban (the "bomb cartoon"). Cartoons like this one seem especially prone to force a bifurcation of, on the one hand, sensitivity to pain and harm and, on the other hand, the political and moral value of unrestricted speech. Inspired by Merleau-Ponty's account of perception, a sensibility like the one suggested above challenges this bifurcation by inviting us to see the cartoon as a question of perception in which the cartoon is judged neither by pain as a purely subjective experience nor by law as a category unaffected by the broader sensorium of political life, but rather by its call to see things in certain limited terms, not open to perception's inherent instability and richness. Using black-and-white colors, quoting the Islamic creed on an ignited bomb serving as the Prophet's turban, the bomb cartoon thus combines visuals through collapsing Islam, Muslim identity, and terrorism, and as such blocking an exploration of these terms in conjunction with their various effects on Danish culture. Indeed, the cartoon implies that we don't need such exploration, since "we" (i.e., ethnic Danes) already know that Muslims see no value in reciprocating any interest "we" might show in their faith. This assumption makes the bomb cartoon emblematic of how some framings of pain can foreclose an expansion of tolerance and free speech, replacing mutual contestation (which, of course, has its own harms) with the opposite: moral binaries, cultural stereotypes, and clear lines of causality for pain and suffering. A sensibility oriented to a tolerance of the incomplete sees this as a reason to critically engage the bomb cartoon, seeking to interrupt its representation and invocation of the background conditions of deliberation and contestation.

In reply to this orientation to the politics of framing, neo-Kantians such as Scanlon may counter that even if we ought to criticize the bomb cartoon, we risk a slippery slope if we censure the interests that citizens have in calling something to the attention of a wider audience.[51] Without a protection of these interests—tolerated and legally enforced by the right to free speech—Merleau-Ponty's alternative may in fact be used to justify content regulation that undercuts public scrutiny and mutual contestation. Merleau-Ponty would disagree, I think. His willingness to speak against preconceived dogmas, as well as his interest in a speech situation oriented more toward contestation than regulation, suggests that for him too we should not try to restrict content in any predetermined way. But in response to Scanlon and other neo-Kantians, Merleau-Ponty might add that distinguishing among kinds of interests (as Scanlon does), and then using these interests to categorize domains of speech, is itself a framing of the experience of pain, one that not only makes possible the separation of interests but also names certain domains as "interests." From the perspective of Merleau-Ponty, such moves demand critical scrutiny. For him, the issue is less how to limit harmful speech legally, and more how our hidden assumptions frame the interplay between experiences of pain and institutional frameworks. Another way of saying this is that Merleau-Ponty does not see a contradiction between the two demands posed by the twelve *Jyllands-Posten* cartoons, that is, greater sensitivity to the framing of pain *and* a resilient tolerance based on the reluctance to legally regulate the content produced by divergent uses of the right to free speech.

Still, we need to press further ahead if we want to grasp the sensibility that enables a framing of the experience of pain that actively cherishes the plurality of lived experience. One way to do so is to follow Merleau-Ponty's correlation of perception with the more general category of expression, which he defines as a synthesizing mode of empowerment in which the expressed does not exist prior to expression but instead fuses seemingly disparate elements in "a" world.[52] The fusion occurs at the level of the styles that format the background of speech, at the level of the tones and pauses that direct the rhythm of speech, and at the level of the perspectives that outline the standpoint of speech.[53] Merleau-Ponty stresses that these levels do not form a coherent whole; they always add something new to expression. Like perception, expression is thus part of a revisionary process similar to the one Scanlon identifies: "To express oneself is," Merleau-Ponty says, "a paradoxical enterprise, since it presupposes...a fund of kindred expressions, [. ..] and...from this fund the form used should detach itself and remain new enough to arouse attention."[54]

The idea that expression hinges on the ability to "arouse attention" is helpful, as it allows us to further develop the framing of pain in situations where there is no pregiven definition of harmful speech. In these situations, harmful speech stands out—or, as Merleau-Ponty puts it, "arouses attention"—because it offends those subject to it. But as cases like the Danish cartoon war show, how citizens react to this offense depends importantly on the political context that structures their initial reaction. We should therefore also speak of a second way in which the arousal of attention matters—as the gaze that folds the initial experience into the web of meaning and power that sustains free speech (and the legal norms it implies). The upshot is a circular movement in which both the attention created *by* and the attention paid *to* the experience of pain frame practices of tolerance and free speech, placing both in the context of different worlds and futures. Merleau-Ponty foregrounds this plurality by emphasizing the creative instability of not only rights but also lived experience more generally, orienting us toward the perceptual richness postulated by creative instability and highlighted by the contestability that arises from expressions being subject to revision. A sensibility oriented toward a "tolerance of the incomplete" is one that seeks to augment rather than conceal this perceptual richness. Emphasizing the conditions of reversibility and depth, both of which engender a process of creative instability, the sensibility embedded in Merleau-Ponty's work is one that encourages us to perceive the world of deep pluralism differently—that is to say, from the perspective of the marginalized and the not-yet-seen-or-felt—even if it means relaxing our attachments to an identity displaced by experiences of pain and harmful speech. The aim is not to disavow these experiences but to mobilize them in ways that turn the perception of displacement into an empowering acknowledgment of how demands for revenge and retributions limit the possibilities for expanding connections across self, other, and world. If perceptual incompleteness and creative instability are general attributes of expression, might not these elements be foregrounded so that the privilege of contesting and revising power in this or that context can be more equally shared?

Interestingly, a good example of this framing suggested by Merleau-Ponty's dictum "tolerance of the incomplete" can be found in *Jyllands-Posten*'s original series of images, which also featured cartoons attentive to the framing of pain in particular and lived experience in general. One, the "mirror cartoon," stands out because it refuses the underlying premise of *Jyllands-Posten*'s project. The cartoon draws a scene from a police station in which a middle-aged man looks at a police line-up through a one-way mirror. Although all in the line-up wear a turban, none resembles the Prophet. In fact, they all seem to caricature someone else (number "2," for example, is the chairwoman of the DPP). Even so, the man looking through the mirror states that he "does not recognize him." This way of framing the "frame" and "the framer" is highly suggestive. Calling out the ignorance with which most Danes discuss Islam, as well as highlighting the power of the frame that insulates this ignorance from contestation, the mirror cartoon is both a comment on how a majority culture allocates the recognition of harm unequally *and* an attempt to bring out the creative instability embedded in this situation by mirroring it: Is the viewer the middle-aged man in the cartoon? Or not? Free from claims to superiority or impartiality, the mirror cartoon solicits the viewer into its frame, and it may thus be a model for an empowering as well as pluralizing framing of pain, one that affirms rather than conceals perceptual richness, nurturing conditions of mutual contestation and respect for difference.

The mirror cartoon's ability to create an experience of reversibility and depth embodies much of the sensibility that orients tolerators toward a politics of empowerment and pluralization. True enough, of course, it was the "bomb cartoon"—not the "mirror cartoon"—that caught the most attention during the Danish cartoon war, and this was so in large part because of a political context in which Muslims living in Denmark struggled with stigmatization, and where some groups responded by exploiting the uncertainty about how to interpret Islam's prohibition of images. The combination of these forces funneled a perception of all Muslims as undemocratic fundamentalists unable to laugh at themselves, and it fed into the reactive powers associated with what in Chapter 3 I called "painful pains," nourishing an affective connection among the bomb cartoon, the world of hadiths, and the so-called war on terror, thereby leaving the mirror cartoon behind as a minoritarian outlier incapable of challenging majority assumptions regarding the nature of secular politics and democratic pluralism. The sensibility that embodies the theory of active tolerance seeks to resist this outcome by not allowing us to miss the fact that there were twelve *Jyllands-Posten* cartoons, and by insisting that each one, because of the individual styles, contexts, and purposes, frames harmful speech differently from the others. The challenge, then, is to mobilize conditions of contestation and deliberation that can direct the public eye more toward the mirror cartoon and less toward the bomb cartoon, insisting that the latter is too flat and uninteresting to hold the gaze of a society of persons pitched on creative instability, joyful affirmation, and political pluralization. For these persons, the main aim is to create the conditions necessary for turning harmful speech acts into an agonistic exchange, one in which encounters with pain and harm are not so much obstacles to freedom as signs of difference and contestation. In a democracy like Denmark's, one characterized by deep pluralism, social complexity, and political globalization, this may indeed be the best we can hope and work for.

V. SENSORIAL REASONING AND THE PLURALIST STANCE

The ambition of turning harm and other painful encounters into an agonistic exchange among constituents who experience the same speech act in radically different ways raises the question of how the framing that underpins the theory of active tolerance might envision the role of public reason in relation to the background conditions of contestation and deliberation. Considering the weight given to public reason in contemporary democratic theory, one might suspect that much of the appeal of the theory of active tolerance will depend on how it answers this question. One might also suspect that neo-Kantian intellectualists in particular would say that to speak of public reason from the perspective of a sensorial orientation to politics is as close to a performative self-contradiction as one can get. If the aim of a sensorial orientation to politics is to foreground an interest in sentient beings as generative forces that are both structured by and able to exceed their place within social institutions and political regimes—and if this interest is built around an attempt to undermine the mind-body dualism that delimits reason as a disembodied faculty of cognition—then might it not be nearly impossible to speak meaningfully of something like public reason? Although this may seem so, I want to suggest there is a better way to broach the issue, one that goes to the very heart of what it means to be reasonable in the context of political conflicts such as the Danish cartoon war. What matters, I submit, is not whether a sensorial orientation to politics permits us to speak of public reason, but rather how it changes our conception of its role: How might we conceptualize public reason from the perspective of a sensorial orientation to politics, and how might this conceptualization resonate with the framing and sensibility that underpins the theory of active tolerance?

This question is directly linked to Merleau-Ponty's account of perception, and thus one way to answer it begins by looking at the point where the neo-Kantian principle of autonomy ends—with the sensorial forces that motivate political behavior in both its antagonistic and nonantagonistic modes.[55] Bearing in mind Merleau-Ponty's suggestion that we approach perception as the experiential interface between an outer world of endless manifold and an inner world of feeling and consciousness, we might say that these forces reach all the way up (or down) to the level of reason, which therefore must be seen as an embodied experience of deliberative reflection entangled with context-dependent modes of feeling and seeing.[56] Another way of saying this is that although the task of reason is to judge lived experiences, evaluating the appropriateness of various feelings, images, and desires, reason itself is not exclusively about invoking a critical distance between oneself and the contingencies of lived experience; in addition, and more importantly, reason also stands forth as a sensorially inflected way to examine these contingencies, empowering sentient beings to reason and to pass judgments in manner that resonates with the context from which the need for reasoning arises in the first place. Importantly, this means that it no longer is possible to delimit the reasonable according the mind-body dualism privileged by the intellectualist tradition. Rather, we must approach the limits of reason as always-already embedded with an abundance of possibilities that enable the reasonable to consider the same feeling, image, or desire in a plurality of ways. Some times it may indeed be reasonable to comport oneself according to procedures of generality and reciprocity. At other times, however, the reasonable is closer to militant contestation and active agitation aimed at changing our exposure to an expression or utterance that we find particularly objectionable.

It is important to note that although the plurality highlighted here always subsists latently, it does not follow that the kind of reasoning we call "public" can proceed however it wants.[57] This is especially the case since the form and content of all lived experience, public reason included, depend on the regimes of sensation and discourse that partition the sensible and that thereby set the terms for a political issue and its availability for reframing. The justification for taking this approach follows in part from the phenomenological and sensorial accounts of lived experience developed up to now, and in part from the context in which the politics of tolerance and free speech is perceived and engaged. In the case of the Danish cartoon war, for example, we have already seen how the perception of the twelve cartoons as hostile to Muslim immigrants may have been shaped by a certain angst regarding the future of Denmark's democracy. Such angst was, as I noted in Section II of this chapter, especially present in the nationalist camp, and it was supplemented by a transnational fear associated with the so-called war on terror. And yet, the cartoons were never just about this fear; several offered a more pluralistic picture of how ethnic Danes and Muslim immigrants relate to each other. A sensorially inflected approach to public reason emphasizes this plurality as part of considering what public reason can do in a context of conflict and disagreement. Rather than limiting public reason to a specific set of issues, defined independently of the circumstances in which citizens reason with each other, the approach developed here suggests that we expand and accent the multiplicity of forces that define the background conditions of contestation and deliberation.

Considerations such as these are helpful as they enable us to see how a sensorially inspired approach to politics modifies the demands of public reason to better address the challenges associated with conflicts such as the Danish cartoon war. The modification of the demands are borne out directly in relation to the neo-Kantian approach to tolerance and free speech. If context matters as much as Scanlon and other neo-Kantians suggest it does, then it is only natural to expect that the demands of public reason reflect this by empowering the citizenry as a living collective that thinks and acts in multiple ways. This approach to the demands of public reason, which invokes a line of thinking associated with not only Merleau-Ponty but also Spinoza and Nietzsche, lays the groundwork for what we might call sensorial reasoning. As I use the term, *sensorial reasoning* is characterized by three demands, none of which is politically impartial or philosophically incontestable, instead seeking to recognize how regimes of discourse and sensation can inflect a given issue or event in quite contrasting ways. The demands draw on these insights to make a case for a way of reasoning about matters of shared concern that is both self-critical and open to contestation and revision. The demands are (1) to foreground sensorial abundance so as to acknowledge the plurality of all lived experiences ; (2) to motivate judgments of lived experiences immanently so as to ensure that their evaluations and prescriptions for action resonate with the context they aim to regulate and modify; and (3) to affirm moments of creative instability and perceptual richness so as to augment the shared conditions of empowerment and pluralization.

The idea behind these three demands is to inspire a new mode of public reasoning and to suggest that reason itself is at its noblest and indeed most invigorating when it contests and deliberates in the manner that is more focused on empowerment and pluralization than on categorization and consensus. To be sure, a strictly neo-Kantian framework may contest this view and suggest that the three demands are too context-dependent to create a universally binding moral obligation.[58] But what a Kantian framework reads as weakness may actually be a strength. This is especially the case if we want to show how tolerance and free speech can reorient the citizenry, creating the conditions for an expansive politics of empowerment and pluralization that creates a more equal relationship between members of the majority and various minorities (whether defined in religious, social, or sexual terms). If we begin with the heteronomy intrinsic to the sensorium, then we should not expect any regime—not even the most totalitarian one—to be so uniform that one is limited to perceive or experience the same event or speech act in just one fashion. Pluralism, in other words, is already part of the context that regimes of discourse and sensation seek to regulate. As already noted, the main task of a sensorially inflected conception of public reason is to highlight (and even enhance) this pluralism, something that requires a pluralistic approach to civic virtues and finitude, countering resentment with worldliness rather than a quasi-transcendental principle detached from contexts of power and privilege. No longer are we dealing with the restraint associated with the neo-Kantian principle of personal autonomy; instead, we are invoking a more abundant desire of *wanting* to live in a world where everyone has a chance to express beliefs and ideas in a setting of deep pluralism characterized by creative instability and perceptual richness.

Another objection from the perspective of a neo-Kantian approach might be that the demands public reason, as developed in the above, are so concerned with the differences and the abundance intrinsic to lived experience that it fails to acknowledge the basis for democratic politics in general: respect for human equality.[59] Though it is true that a sensorial orientation to politics does not give exclusive attention to the assumption of human equality—an assumption that has failed to materialize itself in most sociopolitical relationships and also tends to institute another inequality between the human and the nonhuman—we should be careful not to conclude that concerns about equality are ruled out as part of a sensorially inflected public reason. Concerns about equality are significant in the sense that a more equal distribution of resources and privileges can augment the possibility for contestation among various constituents, and thus help to create not a perfect symmetry of sociopolitical relations but a deeper appreciation for creative instability and perceptual richness.[60] As suggested by the Danish cartoon war, the absence of social and economic equality limits the ability of pluralists on both sides of a political conflict to reframe the perception of an event or speech art, even if they have the same right to free speech as everyone else, enabling other forces to speak on behalf of constituencies who are either marginalized or stigmatized by a discourse based on Nietzschean *ressentiment*. A sensorially inflected public reason folds resistance to this outcome into its attempt at disclosing the plurality of all lived experiences. Without positing equality as the only assumption relevant for democratic politics, it sees certain forms of equality as a means to mobilize an expansive politics of tolerance and the right to free speech.

One way in which a sensorially inflected public reason pursues this political agenda in conjunction with the broader sensibility that reorients tolerators to a practice of active tolerance is by taking an explicitly proactive stance with regard to pluralism itself. To take such a stance, you might say, is to immerse oneself in the plurality of lived experience as such, highlighting the "one" as well as the "many." Whether one perceives oneself as part of the majority or the minority—whether one proceeds in a register of philosophy or activism—the pluralist stance implies disclosing the many hidden or overlooked possibilities that subsist within all lived experiences, enabling them to shine forth even more powerfully than if one did not take a stance. Merleau-Ponty develops his account of this approach by suggesting that the two sides of perception (the perceiver and the perceived) are part of a nonteleological dialectic in which the "accomplished work is . . . not the work which exists in itself like a thing, but the work which reaches its viewer and invites him to take up the gesture which created it."[61] Applied to contemporary democratic politics, this dialectic implies a pluralistic stance that changes our assumptions about the best way to reason with and even educate constituents who do not share an expansive view of tolerance and free speech—what Akeel Bilgrami recently has emphasized as the need for a "democratization of communities."[62] Merleau-Ponty encourages us to emphasize the importance of this need as well, but he does so by offering a more open-ended starting point for the use of public reason. Rather than beginning with the issue of how we might rank political ideals according to their normative importance, Merleau-Ponty's dialectical approach to how public reason might embody a pluralist stance is one that begins in the midst of lived experience, where perceptions, judgments, and ideals have not yet reached the threshold of conceptual clarity, and where experience itself is so open-ended that it appears as a plurality of possibilities and outcomes. Public reason is here a means of maintaining this experience of plurality, affirming the incompleteness of one's own expressions to allow other expressions to emerge. The idea is to "take up the gesture," and to engage it pluralistically without believing that it ever can or should be completed, or subjected to some lexical ordering.

There are both theoretical and pragmatic reasons for considering this dialectical approach to public reasoning and the sensibility underpinning the theory of active tolerance. Most attractively, the approach replaces the invocation of quasi-transcendental principles such as "autonomy" with an avowedly political approach to reason giving, making it more likely to mobilize demands like the ones suggested above. Pragmatically, the dialectic envisioned by Merleau-Ponty alerts us to the importance of maintaining the inherent plurality in all lived experiences, and to developing ways of seeing and feeling that augment this sense of inherent plurality. In this regard, as I indicated earlier, the Danish cartoon war has some unsung heroes: the subset of cartoonists who turned the invitation to ridicule a religious minority into a reason to challenge their sponsor (i.e., the editors of the newspaper *Jyllands-Posten*). Several of the cartoons made fun of the idea of mocking Mohammad rather than yield to it, and they even explored why one would want to encourage such mockery in the context of nationalism, ignorance, and xenophobia. Taking a pluralistic stance, bracketing the need for a lexical ordering of political ideals, choosing instead to foreground an expansive politics of tolerance and free speech, these cartoonists were among the few who saw the Danish cartoon war as a reason to rethink democratic pluralism rather than insist on its unchanging requirements. That is why, in my view, they ably represent the prospect of a different, more promising vision of democratic politics and its implications for tolerance and free speech in the twenty-first century.

Let me conclude this part of our discussion by briefly noting that the playfulness performed by the subversive cartoonists highlighted above is also how a sensorially inflected public reason tries to counter constituencies who are more attracted to clear lines of separation and picture-perfect images than to creative instability and perceptual richness. "Wanting" and "self-interest" play an important role here, albeit not in the usual sense stipulated by contemporary democratic theory. Rather than appealing to a position of autonomy, one in which interests and wants are detached from the contexts in which they appear, a sensorially inflected public reason opens the play of discourse and sensation, soliciting new inputs so as to augment the feeling of power and desire. Such solicitation may not resolve the paradox of tolerating what one finds morally painful. But it may make it more desirable to affirm its place in a world of deep pluralism.

VI. ACTIVE TOLERANCE AS A LIVING CREED

On the basis of what we have seen in this chapter, we might say that the Danish cartoon war suggests two important lessons applicable to contemporary democratic theory in general and the theory of active tolerance in particular. The first lesson is that political conflicts often entail a plurality that escapes binary representation and thus invites us to explore how marginalized experiences can be mobilized to expand our standard view of democratic politics and related concepts such as tolerance and the right to free speech. Obvious in one sense, this lesson has eluded the majority of interpretations of the Danish cartoon war, which heretofore have been marked by a tendency to either accept the basic principles of Western liberal democracy or emphasize the opposition between ethnic Danes and Muslim immigrants, invoking two "distinctively different conceptions of the subject, religiosity, harm, and semiosis."[63] One could say that this response is a fair representation of the conflict as the parties on both sides have understood it, or one could say that it at best only represents half of what began as twelve distinct depictions of the Prophet Mummand and the place of Islam in a democracy like Denmark's. The latter strategy is preferable because it both recognizes the power of binary oppositions *and* tries to expand our receptivity to the linkages within and across the lived experiences associated with the Danish cartoon war. The tendency to focus on two opposing sides fighting for their right to exist independently of each other can thus be turned to serve an agonistic encounter in which theorizing about democracy is not just a matter of justifying the ideal, but a practice in which stories, images, myths, and faiths blend together and inspire our accounts of how best to promote a democratic society committed to empowerment and pluralization.

The other lesson we learn from the Danish cartoon war is that the politics of framing not only privileges one kind of pain over others; it also privileges some expressions but not other as harmful or injurious in the first place. This lesson in particular encourages us to politicize all attachments—whether painful or not, wounded or not—foregrounding the question of worldliness: that is, the question of whether specific attachments empower or isolate, expand or contract connections across self, other, and world. To speculate on what the outcome would be if we allowed such worldliness to inflect our commitment to tolerance and free speech would be just that: speculation. And yet, if we accept the previous point, and acknowledge that part of democratic theory's mission is to speculate about possible futures, then perhaps we could say that a society committed to creative instability, perceptual richness, and sensorial reasoning would be one in which tolerance and free speech are more open to their own contestations than contemporary democratic theory has allowed heretofore. Active tolerance names here a living creed that tolerators would seek to live by: resist attempts to homogenize conditions of deliberation and contestation, link public reason directly to the sensorially inflected circumstances in which reasoning is said to make a difference, expand the plurality of lived experience whenever possible, cherish the creative instability of individual rights, experiment with the not-yet-seen-or-felt, practice presumptive generosity in case of doubt and uncertainty, and foreground a sensibility based on Merleau-Ponty's dictum "tolerance of the incomplete." As I suggested earlier, a living creed of this kind is not only worthy of our attention; it may also be *the* best we can hope and work for in a world of deep pluralism.

CONCLUSION

DIOGENES AND US

Guided by Francis Bacon's image of Diogenes the Cynic, who appears in the Athenian marketplace to show his tolerance, the vision of democratic politics I have put forth over the course of the last four chapters is one that emphasizes the ubiquity of pain as a mental and physical phenomenon. But why pursue this vision? Why not mobilize the desire for democracy through a vision that foregrounds the joys of living together in a world of deep pluralism? Is it because life, as depicted in Shakespeare's *King Lear*, is a catastrophe that must be suffered before it can be lived? Or is it because pain opens up to a consciousness of mortality that, as Stephen White puts it, is our best bet for cultivating "the slender and fragile bond of humanity"?[1]

Yes and no. One of my motivations for pursuing a vision of democratic politics that emphasizes the ubiquity of pain has certainly been an interest in the social bonds pain evokes, and a desire to address how these bonds are negotiated in the various conflicts that most capture our attention in contemporary democratic politics. The French hijab case, the politics of racial discrimination in the United States, the Danish cartoon war, and the use of torture during the "war on terror": although very different, these conflicts all revolve around experiences of pain that are invoked or witnessed in the public realm, and that have prompted constituents around the world to mobilize in an attempt to endure or overcome them. An important—even urgent—task of contemporary democratic theory is surely to probe and contribute to the public debates about these conflicts, even if it means diving into some of the darkest aspects of social and political life.

But there is also another insight that has motivated the discussion, one that stems from an appreciation of what I take to be a main insight in the history of political thought: namely, that politics entails an experience of becoming in which pain, broadly understood, is front and center. From Sophocles' depiction of Ancient Greek life as inherently tragic, over St. Augustine's concern with human corruption, to the emphasis on fear, alienation, and resentment in thinkers as different as Hobbes, Marx, and Nietzsche, I cannot help but notice how much attention the history of political thought has paid to the ubiquity of pain and the repeated failure to relieve ourselves from its causes. It is true, of course, that many theorists of democracy have tried to resolve this problem, encouraging us to see democracy as the best way to end pain; but the persistence with which painful experiences occur in democratic regimes suggests that treating democracy and pain as opposites might not be the right way to proceed.[2] Perhaps, then, it is better to say that democracy is uniquely entangled with pain because, in the words of Claude Lefort, it leaves the place of power "empty," instituting a "society without any positive determination."[3] In such a society, there are few shared grounds for consolation if any, and thus democracy can be seen as an inherently paradoxical mode of government, one that continuously turns against its own quest for fulfillment in self-government. A good way to imagine democracy's "turning" against itself is as a discrete yet continuous infliction of pain not unlike what Derrida discusses under the heading of autoimmunity.[4] At one level, the infliction of pain occurs as democracy settles the limit between the included and the excluded, between those who belong and those who do not. At another level, the infliction occurs because democracy endows citizens with individual rights that license expressions and utterances that can be hurtful to themselves and to others.

If these are the starting points, then the crucial question in contemporary democratic theory is neither whether pain can be eliminated nor whether it evokes the last vestige of a shared humanity. Rather, the better question is whether there are ways to live with pain that move democracy in the direction of empowerment and pluralization. What motivates citizens to endure the pain of living in a society that continuously turns against itself, and are some circumstances more conducive to this endurance than others? This way of phrasing the question does not assume that pain in and of itself provokes awareness of a shared finitude or mortality that makes citizens more tolerant of each other. As we have seen over the course of the last four chapters, there is certainly reason to think that pain is a ubiquitous phenomenon that interrupts the capaciousness of thought and action. But this predicament is radically open-ended, and it does not automatically translate into the kinds of practices and laws that are needed for a politics of empowerment and pluralization. That is why the work here encourages democratic theory to consider a different orientation to politics, one that in addition to political institutions and individual rights focuses on issues concerning history, framing, sensibility, and circulation, enlisting phenomenological considerations, ontological assumptions, lived experiences, cultural narratives, technological innovations, spiritual exercises, and political commitments.

It is in the context of this approach that Bacon's account of Diogenes appearing in the Athenian marketplace can serve as a helpful exemplar for contemporary democratic theory. Most obvious is how Bacon's account reminds us that the term that historically has captured our thinking about the politicality of pain is *tolerance*—understood as the practice by which members of society come to accept that pain can and should be endured for the purposes of something or someone. But Bacon's account goes one step further because it also encourages us to reanimate this practice by bringing pain back in. Again, the idea here is not to embrace pain uncritically, in the spirit of some heroic machismo, but rather to acknowledge the ubiquitous presence of painful encounters and to become more receptive to their expressions, frames, and outcomes, noticing the extent to which the connection between pain and tolerance is part of a multilayered process that can be more or less world-making, more or less empowering. Bacon's account is particularly interesting in this regard because its depiction of Diogenes entering the marketplace captures the idea that tolerance need not be a practice of restraint and withdrawal (as assumed by most contemporary neo-Kantians) or a practice of repression and superiority (as assumed by most contemporary critical theorists). Troubling these established images of tolerance, Bacon's Diogenes instead shows us that tolerance also can be an empowering practice that enables tolerators to disclose and affirm the plurality of lived experience while at the same time resisting the drive to foreclose creative instability and perceptual richness. As Bacon rightly notes, Diogenes did not always remain in his tub; he also ventured into the open, revealing his own vulnerability in an attempt to change the hearts and minds of other people who belonged as well to the Athenian world with which he so disagreed.[5] The resilience required to do so suggests that tolerance is more powerful than is usually envisioned in contemporary democratic theory.

I take the cultivation of a shared resilience to be another important aspect of a vibrant democratic society committed to a politics of empowerment and pluralization. A helpful way to think about this aspect might be the Spinozan language that Deleuze and Guattari mobilize in their discussion of the differences in speed that separate one assemblage of desires, feelings, and perceptions from another. Thus, if the endurance embedded in the term "tolerance" connotes a slower, less energetic assemblage of bodily experiences, then we might say that "resilience" is the virtue that adds intensity and velocity to this assemblage. One reason such an increase in intensity and velocity is important is that it endows the body politic with the capacity needed to renew its divergent attachments to a shared world organized around public things such as a constitution or a national park.[6] Another reason concerns the resistance and experimentation that Deleuze and Guattari link to their idea of a "body without organs," arguably the most important concept in their critique of the repressive assemblages produced by a capitalist society. "This is how it should be done," Deleuze and Guattari say: "Lodge yourself on a stratum, experiment..., find an advantageous place on it, find potential movements of deterritorialization..., experience them..., try out continuums of intensities segment by segment, [and] have a small plot of new land at all times."[7] Like Diogenes before them, Deleuze and Guattari suggest here a politics of empowerment and pluralization in which resilience plays an important role in mobilizing the body politic. Rather than envisioning a completely fluid state of affairs, Deleuze and Guattari counsel a prudent ethology in which some parts of the body endure slower, less energetic assemblages of desires, feelings, and perceptions, adding intensity and velocity to other parts where the experimentation with new lines of flight seems more urgent.

Intrinsic to this approach is attention to how new lines of flight are co-optable and indeed have been co-opted in some quarters by neoliberals who use a Diogenes-like resilience for purposes that contract rather than expand the politics of empowerment and pluralization. Diogenes himself lived at a time when the quest for self-government, justified under the rubric of "frank speech" (parrhēsia), was regulated by norms about appropriate behavior, stated more or less explicitly in relation to what some commentators call "a social contract of shame."[8] Both of these aspects—the desire for frank speech and the social contract of shame—are important as well to twenty-first-century politics. But their form and content may have been co-opted by a neoliberal regime in which speaking frankly and feeling shameful sometimes are subsumed under the rationality of a system not unlike the one that Jodi Dean calls "communicative capitalism," by which she means a system in which the "use value of a message is less important than its exchange value," leaving communication to function "fetishistically as the disavowal of a more fundamental political disempowerment or castration."[9] This system is not the only one shaping contemporary democratic politics. But when it takes priority, the system becomes particularly challenging for the purposes of active tolerance and experimental resilience because it links shamelessness and frank speech to processes of accumulation and exploitation. Communicative capitalism not only celebrates reality TV stars and celebrities who expose themselves in return for money and attention, feeding into the neoliberal fantasy of economic success for all; it puts the burdens of inequality and uncertainty on the unemployed, who are expected to be "resilient" while they wait for new jobs to be created by the next boom in the global economy.

In addition to highlighting the politicality of pain, this co-optation emphasizes the need for an approach that takes its energy not from neoliberalism's individualism but from a more horizontal frame that I have here called a sensorial orientation to politics. Countering the intellectualism of contemporary democratic theory, a sensorial orientation to politics insists that there is more to lived experience than what is embodied in one frame or one regime—that lived experience, when placed in certain contexts and in certain force fields, exceeds itself in preventing its future meanings from being domesticated exclusively for the purposes of just one idea or agenda. As I have suggested in this book, a sensorial orientation to politics develops this potential with regard to the politics of tolerance by highlighting a critical perspective attentive to pain's divergent and layered potential for world-making; by emphasizing how this potential for world-making subsists within the broader genealogy of democratic pluralism; by suggesting that there are ways to engage democratic politics that are driven by "pleasurable pains" rather than "painful pains"; and by exploring how such an engagement can expand the body politic, augmenting the speeds and moods embedded in political life as such.

A sensorial orientation of this kind does not lend itself to grand proclamations or some big blueprint for political action. Something more modest might do. As we have seen with conflicts such as the Danish cartoon war, more important than a definitive answer to who is right might be a reorientation of the background conditions of contestation and deliberation. Such reorientation works at the interstices of lived experience, which is to say at the places and moments where the various elements of the sensorium rub up against each other, and where the sum of all is greater than the sum of each. Attending to these places and moments requires a practice similar to what has been the topic of this book: an active tolerance that draws on endurance and resilience to empower and pluralize the potentiality embedded in existing discourses, experiences, and traditions.

NOTES

INTRODUCTION

1. Bacon, *Collection of Apophthegms*, no. 192 (emphases in original).
2. The first camp draws mainly on the model of reasonable tolerance associated with the works of Rainer Forst, Jürgen Habermas, and John Rawls. The second camp finds its main expression in the recent work of Wendy Brown. I examine each camp in Chapters 1 and 3 respectively.
3. I take the term *active tolerance* from Herbert Marcuse who, in his essay on "Repressive Tolerance," argues that tolerance once served "a partisan goal, a subversive liberating notion and practice," but later "turned from an active to a passive state, from practice to non-practice" ("Repressive Tolerance," pp. 81, 82). Although I shall return to Marcuse's critique of tolerance in Chapter 3, it is important to note now how my use of the terms *active* and *passive* differs from Marcuse's: whereas Marcuse sees the transition from active to passive as part of an almost irreversible dialectic that has driven tolerance away from its true meaning, I see the transition as an inherently open-ended process filled with remainders that can be mobilized for different purposes in different contexts. To better appreciate this, we need an approach to democratic politics that supplements an interest in social repression with a concern for how embodied forms of life both reproduce and resist subjection to just one power. The latter is part of what I call a "sensorial orientation to politics."
4. The idea that reorientation begins by putting the context to work differently is similar to what James Martel, in the context of the work of Walter Benjamin, calls "textual conspiracy"—i.e., a way of disclosing language's own blind spots and unintended consequences. The difference between the approach taken here and the one taken by Martel is primarily one of emphasis: whereas Martel emphasizes the remainders embedded in linguistic signification, I seek to disclose the remainders embedded in the sensorium of political life, in particular as they relate to the lived experience of pain. For further elaboration of the former approach, see Martel, *Textual Conspiracies*, p. 6.
5. Although it would be unfair to speculate on Bacon's motivation for depicting Diogenes in this maner, we know from sources also known to Bacon that Diogenes was a particularly controversial character: after being thrown out of the city of Sinope on charges of adulterating the coinage, Diogenes moved to Athens, where, according to Diogenes Laertius' account, he "fell in with Antisthenes" whom he "wore...out" by "sheer persistence" (in *Lives of Eminent Philosophers*, vol. 2, book

6, chap. 2, 20–22). The persistency highlighted by Diogenes Laertius is similar to the one suggested by Bacon's aphorism.

6. Interest in Diogenes is not limited to the early modern period, but can be found in texts written both before and after Bacon's aphorism, including Rabelais's *Gargantua and Pantagruel* (see the prologue to the "Third Book of Pantagruel") and Nietzsche's *Human, All too Human* and *The Gay Science*. In contemporary democratic theory, Diogenes is often depicted as a forerunner to a cosmopolitan politics based on the moral principle of respect (Nussbaum, "Patriotism and Cosmopolitanism"), which in turn has served to reinforce the image of his tolerance as "passive" rather than "active." In an interesting departure from this image, Raymond Geuss notes how the shamelessness with which Diogenes appears in the Athenian marketplace involves a tolerance that "probably [has] a rather different structure from the toleration of divergent *opinions* which has been central to much liberal thinking." Geuss expands briefly on this difference by arguing that "[u]sually I am thought to have better or less good grounds for my opinions, but I do not always have 'grounds' in any analogous sense for simple reactions of disgust" (*Public Goods, Private Goods*, pp. 22, 23; emphasis in original). As we shall see, the turn to pain (and the sensorium more general) is one way to get more and better traction on this issue. The upshot is an alternative approach to Diogenes' tolerance, one that focuses less on the need to restrain oneself in public spaces and more on the power embedded in practices of endurance and resilience. I shall return to this approach, and how it might inform contemporary democratic theory, in the Conclusion.

7. The word *tolerance* is derived from the Latin *tolerāntia*, which literally means "endurance of pain." In addition to the *Oxford English Dictionary*'s account of tolerance's etymological roots, see also the discussion of tolerance's etymology in Schlüter and Grötker, "Toleranz."

8. For further discussion of phenomenology, see Section III of this Introduction as well as the discussion of Merleau-Ponty's analyses of perception and language in Chapter 4, Section IV.

9. When I say that pain plays a role on most, if not all, levels of political life, I mean to say that pain participates in shaping a society's perceptions of what it recognizes as acting politically. At the level of moral imperatives, for example, pain often appears as a source of remorse, which draws on guilt and shame to reinforce an individual's desire to follow a codex of laws and norms. A similar role can be detected at the level of political and social institutions, where pain is used as a form of punishment to maintain as well as to renew political legitimacy among a plurality of individuals who deliberate and contest each other.

10. According to 2 Corinthians 1:6: "And whether we be afflicted, it is for your consolation and salvation, which is effectual in the enduring of the same sufferings which we also suffer: or whether we be comforted, it is for your consolation and salvation." For the Stoic conception of tolerance and its link to Spinoza's philosophy of immanence, see Chapter 3, Section II.

11. Consider here respectively the French hijab case and the American battle over same-sex marriage. Both conflicts evolve around experiences of pain, which in turn highlights the importance of considering the sensorium of democratic politics. In Chapter 1, I develop this point in more detail in relation to the French hijab case.

12. On most accounts, the concept of tolerance is organized around five components: plurality, objection, acceptance, power, and limitation (or reasons for intolerance). For

further discussion, see Creppell, *Toleration and Identity*, pp. 3–6; Forst, "Toleration, Justice and Reason," pp. 71–73; Horton, "Liberalism, Multiculturalism and Toleration," pp. 3–4; King, *Toleration*, pp. 44–54; Mendus, *Toleration and the Limits of Liberalism*, pp. 8–9; Newey, *Virtue, Reason, and Toleration*, pp. 18–35.

13. On the idea that objections must be "normatively substantive," see Forst, "Toleration, Justice and Reason," p. 72.

14. Ibid., p. 78 (emphases in original).

15. By an intellectualist orientation to politics, I mean the belief that mind and body are linked but separate entities, and that the best way to justify norms and principles is to proceed, as far as possible, by reason alone. As discussed in Section III of this Introduction, intellectualism has become the most dominant orientation to politics in contemporary democratic theory; here it is juxtaposed to a sensorial orientation to politics in which the mind and the body are parts of the same substance, working in different yet interrelated ways.

16. Williams, "Toleration: An Impossible Virtue?" Another way to characterize impossible tolerance—to which I return in Chapter 1—is to say that contemporary democratic theory has come to an impasse because the engagement with the practice of endurance has been replaced by two opposing demands: on the one hand, a demand to justify tolerance independently of the sensorial forces that underpin the experience of pain; and on the other hand, a demand to reconfigure pain so that the "objectionable" can become "acceptable." The gap between these two demands—between the justification and practice of tolerance—suggests that even though tolerators must be resilient so as to endure the objectionable (and hence painful), it has become impossible to theorize this resiliency because the motivating forces behind the tolerating subject are seen as either too contextual to be normatively binding, or too abstract to have any effect on the context in which the challenges of tolerance arise. Thus the enabling conditions of thought and action are undercut along with the forces that can turn tolerance into a full-bodied practice of empowerment and pluralization.

17. On the difference between "want" and "need" in contemporary democratic politics, see Brown, *States of Injury*, p. 75.

18. For Heidegger's use of *Unheimlichkeit*, see the discussion in *Being and Time*, esp. pp. 232–233 (H188). Special thanks to one of the two anonymous readers of the manuscript for alerting me to Heidegger's own discussion of the existential difficulties in "becoming home in not being at home."

19. Dickinson, "Poem 650."

20. For a similar point in the context of theater and practices of martyrdom, see Carlson, *Performing Bodies in Pain*, pp. 17, 67.

21. Scarry, *The Body in Pain*, p. 4. For Arendt's account of pain as private, see *The Human Condition*, p. 141.

22. See respectively Braidotti, *Transpositions*, p. 152; Asad, *Formations of the Secular*, p. 81; Biro, *The Language of Pain*, p. 20.

23. This is particularly evident when we look at how the same experience of, say, childbirth or religious sacrifice is understood and recognized differently across cultural boundaries, class structures, religious communities, and historical epochs. For an exploration of these differences, see Morris, *The Culture of Pain*, chap. 2.

24. For a discussion of the idea of the "partitioning of the sensible," see Rancière, "Ten Theses on Politics." As I understand the term, the partitioning of the sensible is a way to emphasize the sensorially inflected context in which structures of meaning and power make sense to a given society (democratic or otherwise).

25. On the difference between *mise en sens* and *mise en scène*, see Lefort, "Permanence of the Theological-Political," p. 153.

26. Brown, *States of Injury*, p. 70 (and *passim*).

27. See Connolly, *Pluralism*, pp. 121–127.

28. Spinoza, *Ethics*, part IV, proposition 38. See the discussion in Chapter 3, Section III for a further elaboration of this proposition in relation to the theory of active tolerance.

29. For an overview of the study of the sensorium in the humanities, see the contributions to Howes, ed., *Empire of the Senses*. For specific engagements with a sensorial orientation to politics within the fields of democratic theory, feminist theory, new media theory, and cultural studies, see Ahmed, *Queer Phenomenology*; Berlant, *Cruel Optimism*; Bennett, *Vibrant Matter*; Connolly, *Neuropolitics*; Grosz, *Becoming Undone*; Hansen, *New Philosophy for New Media*; Massumi, *Parables for the Virtual*; and Panagia, *The Political Life of Sensation*.

30. Grosz, *Volatile Bodies*, p. xi.

31. As already noted, I return to this question in Chapter 4, where I discuss how the sensorial orientation to politics might redefine the principles of public reason, advancing the idea of what I call "sensorial reasoning."

32. Foucault, "Governmentality."

33. Butler, *Frames of War*, p. 10.

34. Butler's concern for vulnerability is part of a move to ethics and the dependency humans owe to each other. See especially *Precarious Life*, p. 29.

35. Borrowing the term from the recent work of Grosz, Hasana Sharp names this "renaturalization": "Renaturalization is a strategy to attenuate the antipathy that plagues our psyches and our life in common [. ..] It founds a new appreciation of ourselves as parts of nature, operating according to the same rules as anything else, invariably dependent upon many other things, human and nonhuman." Sharp, *Spinoza and the Politics of Renaturalization*, p. 5.

36. Deleuze and Guattari, *A Thousand Plateaus*, p, 249.

37. Ibid, p. 213.

38. Marcuse, "Repressive Tolerance," p. 81.

CHAPTER 1

1. Member States of the United Nations Educational, Scientific and Cultural Organization, "Declaration of Principles on Tolerance," p. 209.

2. Derrida, "Faith and Knowledge," p. 21. Although there is no evidence of a direct connection between Derrida's essay and the "Declaration of the Principles of Tolerance," the two texts were conceived at almost the exact same time, suggesting an intertextuality in which tolerance is always more than what it appears to be. Derrida's essay was first presented at a 1994 colloquium and then published in French in 1996; UNESCO's declaration was signed in 1995 after a set of meetings with experts and representatives from the organization's 193 member states.

3. For further illustration of how Teaching Tolerance uses the "Declaration of Principles on Tolerance" to justify its activities, see the material posted on the organization's website, www.tolerance.org.

4. The co-chairman of the "The European Council on Tolerance and Reconciliation" is Viatcheslav Moshe Kantor, who also is the president of the "European Jewish Congress." Moshe Kantor's motto is that "tolerance should be strictly limited

since, like a wholesome medicine used in excess, it can become a poison." For more information, see http://www.moshekantor.com/en/.

5. The Sub-Commission on the Protection and Promotion of Human Rights adopted February 6 as an International Day of Zero Tolerance to Female Genital Mutilation after Stella Obasanjo, then first lady of Nigeria, made a similar declaration at a 2003 conference organized by the Inter-African Committee on Traditional Practices Affecting the Health of Women and Children. The Sub-Commission has since ceased to exist and its mandate and responsibilities have been transferred to Human Rights Council.

6. The expression *somatophobia* is Elizabeth Grosz's, who uses it to characterize how Western philosophy, at least since the early modern period, has defined itself in opposition to the body as a lived experience that sustains various conditions of cognition and reason. For further discussion of the term, see Grosz, *Volatile Bodies,* p., 5.

7. The preamble to the "Declaration of Principles on Tolerance" defines the following as acts of intolerance: "violence, terrorism, xenophobia, aggressive nationalism, racism, anti-Semitism, exclusion, marginalization and discrimination directed against national, ethnic, religious and linguistic minorities, refugees, migrant workers, immigrants and vulnerable groups within societies, as well as acts of violence and intimidation committed against individuals exercising their freedom of opinion and expression."

8. Marx, "On the Jewish Question," p. 42 (emphases in original). Whether this version of Locke's liberalism is the most productive, not to mention most accurate, is an issue to which I shall return in Chapter 2. For a compelling interpretation suggesting that there is more to Locke's writings than what is implied by the canonized version of Locke's liberalism, see McClure, *Judging Rights.*

9. "Declaration of Principles on Tolerance," Articles 1.4 and 4.1.

10. Apart from the works by Rawls and Forst, which I discuss below, see also these contributions: Habermas, "Intolerance and Discrimination" ; Nagel, *Equality and Partiality*; Raz, "Autonomy, Toleration and the Harm Principle"; Scanlon, "Difficulty of Tolerance." The reasonable-tolerance model coexists with at least two other models, both of which I examine later in this section of the chapter. For a general introduction to the variety of approaches to the study of tolerance in contemporary democratic theory, see McKinnon, *Toleration.*

11. "Declaration of Principles on Tolerance," Preamble.

12. Forst, "The Limits of Toleration," p. 320.

13. For discussion of the last point, see Krause, *Civil Passions*, esp. chap. 3. Special thanks to one of the manuscript's two anonymous readers for alerting me to this point.

14. As one U.S.-based Muslim woman asks in a blog post, "What about our sisters in France? How did we forget about this crime that occurs on a daily basis? Where is the body of the ummah that feels pain, when one part of it is hurt?" On http://muslimmatters.org/2008/03/14/the-forgotten-hijab-ban-i-just-couldnt-take-it-off-another-time (accessed on February 25, 2012). For recent accounts of the conflict, see Bowen, *Why the French Don't Like Headscarves*; Brown, "Civilization Delusions"; Scott, *The Politics of the Veil*; Winter, *Hijab and the Republic.*

15. Forst, "Toleration, Justice and Reason," p. 74. For Forst's justification of the separation of ethics and morality, see the discussion in the Introduction, Section II.

16. Kant, "Perpetual Peace," in *Kant: Political Writings*, p. 93.
17. According to Charles Taylor, secular multicultural societies must be "willing to weigh the importance of certain forms of uniform treatment against the importance of cultural survival, and opt sometimes in favor of the latter." In "The Politics of Recognition," p. 62.
18. Galeotti, *Toleration as Recognition*, p. 105.
19. "Declaration of Principles on Tolerance," Article 2.1.
20. Taylor, "The Politics of Recognition," p. 25.
21. "Declaration of Principles on Tolerance," Article 1.1.
22. Taylor, "The Politics of Recognition," p. 59 (emphasis in original).
23. For further discussion of this concern, see the Introduction's account of the sensorial orientation to politics in relation to efforts in twentieth-century phenomenology and contemporary poststructural critical theory.
24. "Declaration of Principles on Tolerance," Articles 1.1 and 1.3.
25. Ibid., Article 1.1.
26. For a critical discussion of this thesis, see Brown, *Regulating Aversion*, Chapter 7.
27. See especially 2 Corinthians 1:6.
28. Tolerance, Locke famously argued, is "agreeable to the Gospel of Jesus Christ, and to the genuine reason of mankind." In "A Letter Concerning Toleration," p. 217.
29. See Asad, "Thinking About Religion." This aspect of the superior-tolerance model may explain why, in cases such as the French hijab case, there is a resistance to the idea that tolerance represents the fairest and most just way to resolve the conflict between the French majority and the Muslim minority. The resistance is exacerbated by tolerance's Latin heritage and the problem of translating it into (especially) Arabic, where the word *tolerance* does not exist.
30. Derrida, "Faith and Knowledge," p. 22 (emphases in original).
31. For further elaboration of this term, see Dietz, *Turning Operations*, p. 1 (and *passim*).
32. Bowen, *Why the French Don't Like Headscarves*, pp. 66, 68.
33. Scott, *The Politics of the Veil*, 24. On pain as hysteria, see Morris, *The Culture of Pain*, chap. 5.
34. "Declaration of Principles on Tolerance," Article 1.1.
35. The following discussion assumes an underlying continuity between Rawls's earlier works and his more mature ones. I note the difference between these works only when necessary.
36. Rawls, *A Theory of Justice*, p. 23 (my emphasis).
37. Rawls, "Justice as Fairness." p. 390. Note how Rawls "narrates" the principle of toleration by tying it first to the Reformation, second to democratic constitutionalism, and third to the emergence of capitalism especially in Western Europe and the United States. I shall return to this narration of tolerance's history—and its broader implications for thinking about the politics of tolerance—in Chapter 2, Section II.
38. Rawls, *A Theory of Justice*, p. xi.
39. See Chapter 4, Section V for further discussion of this conception of reason and what I call "sensorial reasoning."
40. Although Rawls has been the subject of numerous critiques, none of them focus explicitly on the tension I highlight here between his account of reason and his ongoing interest in political context and the democratic tradition. If one were to make a list of the many critiques of Rawls in contemporary political theory, it would as a minimum have to include (1) the need to establish the principle

of impartiality as superior to any other principle (Barry, *Justice as Impartiality*, pp. 61–67); (2) the need to include a more elaborate theory of liberal virtues (Macedo, *Liberal Virtues*, pp. 100–105); (3) the need to provide stronger moral reasons for the idea of an overlapping consensus (Matravers and Mendus, "The Reasonableness of Pluralism," pp. 38–52); (4) the need to account for social antagonisms (Mouffe, *The Return of the Political*, pp. 41–59); (5) the need to appreciate identities below the threshold of existing norms and values (Connolly, *Why I Am Not a Secularist*, pp. 63–70); (6) the need to eliminate ontology or epistemology (Rorty, "The Priority of Democracy," pp. 175–196), and (7) the need not to displace politics (Honig, *Political Theory and the Displacement of Politics*, esp. chap. 5).

41. As indicated in the Introduction, Section II, contemporary democratic theorists normally use five conceptual components to define the circumstances of tolerance. In addition to objection, the components are plurality, acceptance, power, and the limits of tolerance.

42. The phrase "normatively substantive" is Rainer Forst's. See his "Toleration, Justice and Reason," p. 72.

43. For a careful and innovative consideration of religious arguments in public deliberations, see Andrew March, "Rethinking Religious Reasons in Public Justifications." The role of religious reasons in public deliberations is also linked to what I call "sensorial reasoning."

44. See King, *Toleration*, p. 47.

45. One answer to this uncertainty might highlight what Rawls calls "the burdens of judgments." However, as I note below, this answer is, at least in the version envisioned by Rawls himself, fraught with its own problems because it too oscillates between affirming and disavowing the sensorium and its implications for reason and public deliberation.

46. Rawls, *A Theory of Justice*, p. 428.

47. Rawls, *Political Liberalism*, pp. 54ff. With the exception of Alejandro, *Limits of Rawlsian Justice*, pp. 97–115, I do not know of any commentator who focuses on the effects of this tension. This is surprising given the importance of shame, humiliation, and guilt throughout the Rawlsian oeuvre. Rawls introduces these terms in the essay "The Sense of Justice," first published in 1963; he solidifies them in *A Theory of Justice*, esp. at pp. 405–434; and he gives them his final confirmation in *Justice as Fairness*, pp. 195–198. Special thanks to Patchen Markell for encouraging me to address this aspect of Rawls' work.

48. To further develop this argument, note also that at the same time as Rawls seeks to define humiliation and shame as "moral feelings," which are juxtaposed to "natural attitudes" that do not "invoke a moral concept and its associated principles" (*A Theory of Justice*, p. 481), he also acknowledges the link between these two categories, allowing us to see how moral feelings too are bound up with the issue of context, whether defined in relation to specific explanations or to a range of affects and perceptions. In an attempt to clarify the moral feeling of shame and its connection to another important moral feeling—guilt—Rawls argues: "Feelings of guilt and shame have different *settings* and are overcome in distinct ways, and these variations *reflect* the defining principles with which they are connected and their peculiar *psychological* bases. Thus, for example, guilt is relieved by reparation and the forgiveness that permits reconciliation; whereas shame is undone by defects made good, by a renewed confidence in the excellence of one's person" (ibid., p. 484; my emphases). What interests me here are the references to "setting," "reflect," and "psychological," terms suggesting that we may not know the

meaning of justice—and, by extension, reason and morality—unless we also consider the sensorial context in which it is situated and practiced.

49. According to Rawls, "since being moved by ends and ideals of excellence implies a liability to humiliation and shame, and an absence of a liability to humiliation and shame implies a lack of such ends and ideals, one can say of humiliation and shame also that they are part of the notion of humanity." *A Theory of Justice*, p. 428. Rawls goes on to explain that because humiliation and shame are part of the notion of humanity, they are also constitutive elements of our sense of justice (and thus of justice itself).

50. Tarnopolsky, *Prudes, Pervert, and Tyrants*, p. 18. Tarnopolsky suggests that, for Rawls, shame is "dangerous" because it "can instill apathy and cynicism" (p. 3). I would say there might be more to it than that, especially if we consider how Rawls posits shame as an essential feature of what it means to act justly.

51. Whether this turn to the inner self is part of a Christian asceticism is beyond the scope of the argument developed here. For Rawls's own religious sensibility, see Rawls, *A Brief Inquiry into the Meaning of Sin and Faith*.

52. Nietzsche, *On the Genealogy of Morality*, p. 99 (emphasis in original).

53. Williams, "Toleration," p. 18.

54. Ibid., p. 25.

55. William Connolly, in *Why I Am Not a Secularist*, suggests that tolerance fails because it does not engender the proper conditions for contestation and pluralization (p. 62). Wendy Brown, in *Regulating Aversion*, goes one step further and argues that tolerance is limited because it offers a strategy for managing the abhorrent—and in the process it provides a code of conduct that reinforces the liberal paradigm of private beliefs, individual rights, and value pluralism. According to Brown, "tolerance anoints the bearer with virtue" and "offers a robe of modest superiority in exchange for yielding" (p. 24). I return to these critiques, and how they relate to the theory of active tolerance, in Chapter 3.

56. Peters, *Courting the Abyss*, p. 146. Locating it within U.S. First Amendment jurisprudence, Peters defines *homeopathic machismo* as a legally codified sensibility defined by the "notion that a tincture of poison will lift us to heights of tolerance and civic-mindedness."

57. Nietzsche, *The Will to Power*, no. 699 (pp. 371–372).

58. Mill, *Utilitarianism*, p. 11.

59. See also the discussion of Heidegger in the Introduction, Section II.

60. Podoksik, "One Concept of Liberty," p. 235. Thanks to Ilya Winham for alerting me to this reference.

61. This interest is collaborated by anthropological studies of religious rituals in which the endurance of pain appears prominently. One of the most discussed is an India ritual called *bagad*, or hook swinging, in which a young man blesses children and crops as he hangs from steel hooks, which are shoved under his skin and muscles on both sides of his back. The most astounding insight produced by studies of this ritual is that although many of us would feel pain if we shoved hooks under our skin, there is no evidence to suggest that the man participating in the ritual is feeling pain; in fact, the symbolic nature of the *bagad* ceremony produces a state of exaltation so prevalent that it changes the basic coordinates of perception and affect. For discussion of the anthropological evidence produced before the ceremony was outlawed in the 1960s, see Morris, *The Culture of Pain*, p. 180.

62. For a description and critique of the specificity theory of pain, see Wall, *Pain*, pp. 18–23; Melzack and Wall, *The Challenge of Pain*, esp. parts I and II.

63. According to new developments in the neurosciences, the Cartesian specificity theory also fails to engage what is called the "half-second delay," which is the average time between the reception of sensory material and conscious interpretation of it. During this half-second, neuroscientists have suggested, parts of the brain associated with the amygdala generate a set of brute responses that enable individual bodies to react to danger even before they become conscious of something dangerous. The half-second delay thus offers a window into the world of sensation that subsists below the threshold of consciousness. Not only does the half-second delay show how the sensorium structures conditions of reason and agency by engaging our senses in a preliminary yet defining way, it also shows how dependent reason is on processes that no one controls outside of a context specific to time and place. For a discussion of the link between the half-second delay and contemporary democratic theory, see Connolly, *Neuropolitics*, p. 83. In Chapter 2, I show how there is more to Descartes' view on pain than what we learn from the specificity theory.

64. On the idea of politics at the "molecular level," see the Introduction, Section III.

65. As Mill puts it in the formulation cited earlier, pain "is always heterogeneous" with pleasure.

66. In his discussion of pain and the view of agency in Western secular thought, Talal Asad makes a similar point. According to Asad, we should avoid assuming pain is always passive, or that which instigates action without being action. Instead, Asad suggests, we should ask first "whether pain is not simply a cause of action, but can also itself be a kind of action." In *Formations of the Secular*, p. 69.

67. Nietzsche, *The Will to Power*, no. 35 (p. 23), 658 (p. 347).

68. I shall return to the details of this continuum in Chapter 3, Section III; for now it suffices to note the general character and possible implications of the two ends of the continuum.

69. Brown, *States of Injury*, p. 70.

70. In Nietzsche's words: "It is *your* fault if no one loves me, it is *your* fault if I've failed in life and also *your* fault if you fail in yours." Quoted in Deleuze, *Nietzsche and Philosophy*, p. 119.

71. For an account that resuscitates Mill's theory of tolerance without engaging his analysis of pain, see Mendus, *Toleration and the Limits of Liberalism*, esp. chap. 3. Nietzsche, in his most explicit discussion of tolerance, aligns the tolerator with a naïve sense of "superiority," which the "scholar" in particular feels because he believes in a "practical indifference to religious matters in the midst of which he has been born and brought up." Unable to displace this upbringing, the tolerant scholar simply "shuns" or "sublimates" religion, failing to tackle the roots of its power. Nietzsche, *Beyond Good and Evil*, p. 72.

72. For a discussion of the shifts suggested by a sensorial orientation to politics, see the Introduction, Section III.

73. For a similar approach to education, see Coles, *Beyond Gated Communities*, esp. chap. 8.

CHAPTER 2

1. Foucault, "Nietzsche, Genealogy, History," p. 93.
2. For Descartes's discussion of how distinct sense perception can align past experiences with sensory input from the present, see his *Treatise on Man*, pp. 55ff.

3. Foucault, "Nietzsche, Genealogy, History," p. 81.

4. For two contemporary views disagreeing about the importance of tolerance for democratic pluralism and yet sharing the same account of tolerance's genealogy, see Brown, *Regulating Aversion*, chap. 2; Habermas, "Religious Tolerance." For accounts that privilege the early modern period, see Besier and Schreiner, "Toleranz"; Creppell, *Toleration and Identity*; Forst, *Toleranz im Konflikt*; Zagorin, *How the Idea of Religious Toleration Came to the West*.

5. For the purpose of this chapter, disavowal (*Verleugnung*) is similar to what Freud, in his analysis of the fetish, identifies as a perception of time that simultaneously acknowledges *and* displaces an unwelcome fact of reality, its attendant conflict recognized, and then put aside. On Freud's concept of disavowal more generally, see Cohen, *States of Denial*, pp. 25–28.

6. Brown, *Regulating Aversion*, p. 14 (emphasis in original).

7. For particularly insightful discussions of "paralipsis" and "witnessing" as techniques of critique, see respectively Wittenberg, *Philosophy, Revision, Critique*, p. 9 (and passim); and Caruth, *Unclaimed Experience*, esp. chap. 2.

8. Stressing the role of the sensorium, this argument is part of a larger trend in contemporary scholarship focusing on how especially liberal theory is more attuned to issues of embodiment than what we unusually think. For three accounts of this trend, see Macedo, *Liberal Virtues*; Krause, *Civil Passions*; and Abbas, *Liberalism and Human Suffering*.

9. In an earlier incarnation of the argument pursued in this chapter, I suggested that the works especially of Kant and Locke encourage the kind of intellectualism and somatophobia that characterize discussions of contemporary tolerance. (See Tønder, "Toleration Without Tolerance.") I still believe this to be the case, but my ambition now is to show how the same works that encourage a somatophobic staging of the sensorium harbor elements that circumvent these phenomena from within intellectualism itself. As already indicated, my wager is that an approach seeking to do precisely this is the most effective way to reorient the discussion of tolerance, making contemporary democratic theory more amenable to a sensorial orientation to politics.

10. Freeden, *Ideologies and Political Theory*, p. 240.

11. von Goethe, *Maxims and Reflections*, p. 116 (no. 875). The maxim cited here was published posthumously. Goethe died in 1832 at the age of eighty-two.

12. Kant, "An Answer to the Question: 'What Is Enlightenment?'" in *Kant: Political Writings*, p. 59.

13. Ibid., p. 58 (emphasis in original). Kant typically uses the term *presumptuous* to describe a situation of overreach and exaggeration in the domains of human knowledge and divine authority. On this, see Jane Bennett's discussion in *The Enchantment of Modernity*, p. 41.

14. For an example of the hermeneutical strategy, see O'Neill, *Constructions of Reason*, esp. chap. 2. For examples of the revisionist strategy, see the works cited below by Forst, Habermas, and Rawls.

15. Forst, *Toleranz im Konflikt*, p. 355.

16. Rawls, "Justice as Fairness," p. 390.

17. Habermas, "Religious Tolerance," p. 6 (emphases in original). On Bayle as a forerunner to the work of Kant, see Forst, "Bayle's Reflexive Theory of Toleration."

18. For a discussion of the link between fetish, disavowal, and screen memory, see Freud, *Three Essays on Sexuality*, p. 20, note 2.

19. This includes challenging the notion of tolerance as a uniquely "modern" or "liberal" practice. For discussions of this challenge, see Bejczy, "Tolerantia," pp. 365–384; Fiala, "Stoic Tolerance," pp. 149–168; Laursen and Nederman, *Difference and Dissent*; and Nederman, *Worlds of Difference*.

20. Freeden, *Ideologies and Political Theory*, p. 240. According to Kant, we must assume "a universal history of the world" that works "in accordance with a plan of nature aimed at a perfect civil union of mankind." Kant admits that this assumption is speculative—a "strange and at first sight absurd proposition"—but insists nonetheless that the idea of a providential history is "useful" for the advancement of morality and freedom. See Kant, "Idea for a Universal History with a Cosmopolitan Purpose," in *Kant: Political Writings*, Ninth Proposition.

21. On Forst's implicit teleology, and how it informs his reading of the history of tolerance, see Jan-Werner Müller's discussion in "Toleration in Contexts," p. 469.

22. Zuckert, *Launching the Liberal Tradition*. For other accounts that attribute the same importance to Locke's work, see Cranston, "John Locke and the Case for Toleration," pp. 82–83; Dunn, "The Claim to Freedom of Conscience"; Forst, *Toleranz im Konflikt*, p. 276; McKinnon, *Toleration*, p. 10; Perez Zagorin, *How the Idea of Religious Toleration Came to the West*, p. 245; Taylor, *Sources of the Self*, p. 159; Tully, *An Approach to Political Philosophy*, p. 48; and Tuckness, *Locke and the Legislative Point of View*, pp. 17–25.

23. Taylor, *Sources of the Self*, p. 146.

24. On the crisis of the European mind, see Israel, *Radical Enlightenment*, pp. 23–29.

25. Freeden, *Ideologies and Political Theory*, p. 240.

26. Directly related to interpretations of Locke in contemporary democratic theory, these norms are expressed in two interrelated ways: (1) a tendency to displace Kant's critique of Locke's empiricism, which Kant says is "inconsequential" because it "[sensualises] all concepts of the understanding." (Kant, *Critique of Pure Reason*, pp. 127, 283.) Liberals committed to the intellectualist imperative in contemporary democratic theory displace this critique by choosing *not* to include Locke's *Essay* in their conceptualization of tolerance, politics, and democratic practice. The displacement may bring Locke closer to the mode of reasonable tolerance, but as we shall see, it forecloses attention to the more protean elements of the doctrine of indifference. (2) Little, if any, attention to changes in the reception of Locke's *Letter Concerning Toleration*. In the 1960s, for example, historians did not make the *Letter* the centerpiece in their accounts of the history of tolerance: Lecler, in *Toleration and the Reformation*, criticized Locke for being "neither as original nor as liberal as defenses [of tolerance] penned by other European writers" (vol. 2, p. 473); and Kamen, in *The Rise of Toleration*, analyzed Locke's argument from the perspective of "Nonconformist thought, with all its narrow-mindedness" (p. 231). Although these claims do not capture tolerance's historical essence, they highlight how much the reception of Locke's *Letter* has changed, emphasizing how important it is to attend to the contingency that characterizes the history of both liberal democracy and tolerance.

27. Foucault, "Nietzsche, Genealogy, History," p. 80. According to Greek mythology, the chimera is a fire-breathing female monster composed of multiple animals, including the lion, the snake, and the goat.

28. Although this view is shared by most critical theorists, among them Wendy Brown and William Connolly, the tendency is to cede the history of tolerance to Rawls, Habermas, Forst, and other liberals in order to show how tolerance's ahistorical character makes it unable to inspire and empower new social movements.

29. This strategy does not mean we should ignore resources outside the ones privileged by contemporary democratic theory. Rather, the strategy suggests that we *first* seek to excavate what has been disavowed, and *then* examine how the content of this excavation relates to thinkers and texts excluded by existing screen memories. The second move is one I discuss in Chapters 3 and 4.

30. Foucault, in his *Introduction to Kant's Anthropology*, suggests that although the *Anthropology* wasn't published until 1798, Kant drafted the book's main ideas and claims before he embarked on the three *Critiques* written and published between 1781 and 1790.

31. Overall, the *Anthropology* serves the dual purpose of (1) describing how man "is" as a finite being determined by forces he does not choose, and (2) clarifying how man nonetheless can become an autonomous and self-governing individual. This doubling of the passive and the active—what Foucault, in his discussion of modern philosophy, calls the "empirico-transcendental doublet"—structures Kant's philosophy to such an extent that one would have to place it at the heart of the intellectualism underpinning discussions of tolerance in contemporary democratic theory. For discussion of the "empirico-transcendental doublet," see Foucault, *The Order of Things*, p. 318.

32. See Kant, *Anthropology*, book II, §60, p. 126.

33. Ibid., book III, §73, p. 149.

34. Ibid., book II, §60, p. 126 (my emphasis).

35. Ibid., book III, §74, p. 150.

36. Compare Kant, *Anthropology*, book II, §60, p. 127 (n3); Nietzsche, *The Will to Power*, no. 698 (p. 371).

37. As I suggested in the Introduction, the theory of active tolerance is most explicitly articulated by a trajectory in the history of political thought that connects the work of Spinoza with the work of Merleau-Ponty. My objective here is to show how the theory of active tolerance intersects with parts of Kant's oeuvre (as well as the ones of Locke and Descartes), and thus to show that the theory may not be as unfamiliar to discussions in contemporary democratic theory as it sometimes can seem.

38. Kant, *Critique of Judgment*, part I, division I, book II, §27, p. 114 [257].

39. Deleuze goes on to suggest that by unhinging time, Kant's sublime reveals what he calls "the thread of time." Deleuze, *Kant's Critical Philosophy*, p. ix.

40. Kant, *Critique of Judgment*, part I, division I, book II, §§23, 28, pp. 98, 120 [244, 261].

41. To be more specific: the active tolerance suggested by Kant's sublime is similar to the one developed by Forst, Habermas, and Rawls insofar as neither gives us the "true" Kant but instead reworks his transcendental philosophy, bringing it closer to what Kant calls the "phenomenal" world. Active tolerance is different, however, because it accents rather than disavows the nonteleological nature of becoming tolerant. Whether it is the question of timing (when does the endurance of pain link up with difference and becoming?), the question of memory (how should a democratic society negotiate the conflict between differing memories of the same pain?), or the question of progress (is there a way to narrate and visualize the link between politics and pain without assuming a linear movement similar to the

one Habermas projects in his account of tolerance's history?), active tolerance is placed in a context characterized by the open-ended forces of history and time.

42. In Chapter 3, I make the case for a political ontology that affirms the sensorium's indeterminacy and uncertainty. Why it is a good idea to cultivate these effects is a question I discuss most explicitly in Chapter 4.

43. Sydenham is especially famous for his preparation of laudanum, which, despite its effectiveness in alleviating pain, was considered controversial in his own time because of its use of opium. For those tempted, here's Sydenham's recipe: "The laudanum tincture which I have mentioned as being given in daily draughts is quite simply prepared in the following manner: sherry wine, one pint; opium, two ounces; saffron, one ounce; a cinnamon stick and a clove, both powdered. Mix and simmer over a vapour bath for two or three days until the tincture has the proper consistency, strain and lay by for use." Quoted in Rey, *The History of Pain*, p. 83.

44. Locke, *Essay Concerning Human Understanding*, book 2, chap. XX, §§1, 2 (p. 229, emphases in original). Commentators such as Kim Ian Parker and Vivasvan Soni argue that this account is prevalent in Locke's philosophy, and they even suggest that it should be placed at the forefront of early modern political thought more generally. Highlighting the influence of the Jansenist theologian Pierre Nicole (1625–1695), an influence that can be traced back to Locke's translation of three essays from Nicole's *Essai de Morale*, published in mid-1678, Parker sees Locke's account of pain as part of a larger argument concerning the drive to civil society: "there is a naturalistic bent to [Locke's philosophy], which seems to suggest that morality is purely mercenary, or motivated solely by a desire for happiness" (*The Biblical Politics of John Locke*, p. 54). Soni takes this view one step further, situating Locke's analysis of pain within a "trial narrative" in which the question of how to alleviate suffering is suspended until the end of time. Traces of this narrative, Soni argues, is evident in the *Second Treatise* where Locke develops an argument in which happiness—i.e., the opposite of pain—is both marginalized and assumed: whereas the *Second Treatise* marginalizes happiness by invoking a social contract that is said to absolve our natural propensity for pain, the *Treatise* also indicates that the transition to civil society is incomplete, and that the problem of pain therefore remains one a civil government can (and should) resolve. For further elaboration of this argument, see Soni, *Mourning Happiness*, pp. 235, 330, 421.

45. Locke, *An Essay Concerning Human Understanding* book 2, chap. XX, §2 (p. 229, emphases in original).

46. As I suggested in Chapter 1, Locke's work is often seen as delimiting the discursive field within which contemporary models of tolerance operate and relate to each other. The reading proposed here does not dispute this role; it seeks to highlight another side of Locke's work, one that might help us reconfigure some of the impasses and double binds that have come to define contemporary tolerance.

47. Although the *Two Tracts* were composed in 1660, they were not published until 1967. For the history behind this delay of publication, see Philip Abrams's introduction to Locke, *Two Tracts of Government*.

48. As is well known, Locke wrote the major part of the *Letter* while in exile in Utrecht, Holland, reiterating elements of another essay from 1667—entitled *An Essay Concerning Toleration*—which Locke refused to have published. One reason for his refusal might have been that the 1667 essay represented a change in Locke's own thinking, which until then had been rather conservative, favoring (as he had done before in the *Two Tracts*) the right of the civil powers to legislate in

matters of religious worshipping. Mindful of what he had learned from the early Earl of Shaftesbury, who defended the Whig Revolution against King Charles II, Locke became convinced that the time was ripe for another kind of government, one that would guarantee the liberty of individuals opposing the religious views of their government. The realization led to the theory of individual rights, limited government, and private property that lies at the heart of Locke's *Second Treatise*. It also led to what a majority of contemporary democratic theorists see as the secular foundation securing the main argument of the first *Letter Concerning Toleration*. For further discussion, see Marshall, *John Locke*.

49. Locke, "Letter Concerning Toleration," p. 229.

50. See, for example, McClure, "Difference, Diversity, and the Limits of Toleration." McClure argues that Locke's doctrine of indifference is evidence of the search for "a cognitive secular ground" (p. 376), which seeks to both acknowledge and unite the individuality of discrete persons, but in so doing it disavows tolerance's political nature, deploying "the mind-body distinction to activate parallel discursive separations between thought and action, divine and civil obligation, religious faith and political obedience" (p. 372). Without questioning the influence of this account in especially contemporary critical theory, I seek here to show how the hegemony of the neo-Kantian framework as the interpretive framework for Locke's work can be undermined from within intellectualism itself.

51. The fact that Locke's practice of indifference addresses both body and mind suggests that their dualistic relationship is less an actual doctrine in early modern philosophy and more a contemporary invention that interpretative concerns in the present have projected back onto Locke and other thinkers in order to secure a certain way of reading the history of political thought. In the next section (IV), I return to this issue, arguing that Descartes's discussion of the relationship between body and mind is less dualistic than most Cartesians argue.

52. In Chapter 3, Section II, I discuss the force field in which these cross-pressures appear, suggesting that tolerance differs from other ways of responding to pain, including the ones associated with the skeptical tradition in the early modern period.

53. Nietzsche, *On the Genealogy of Morality*, p. 38. The link between forgetting, the sensorium, and the kind of countermemory I discussed at the outset of this chapter is even clearer as Nietzsche continues the quote by saying that forgetting is something we "owe [to] the fact that we what we simply live though, experience, take in, no more enters our consciousness during digestion (one could call it spiritual digestion) than does the thousand-fold process which takes place with physical consumption of food, our so-called ingestion" (ibid.).

54. Although Locke justifies the normative demands of his screen memory through theology, the demands can in principle be linked to most domains of human experience, including ethics, aesthetics, politics, and morality.

55. Merleau-Ponty, *The Visible and the Invisible*, p. 142.

56. Ultimately, the desire for orientation and linearity may be why Kant domesticates the openness provoked by the sublime, claiming that reason's ability to recognize its own finitude in the face of sensory overload makes it a superior source of knowledge compared to "any standard of sense." Kant, *Critique of Judgment*, part I, division I, book II, §25, p. 106 [250].

57. In his discussion of how a Nietzschean genealogy of descent entails a "different form of time," Foucault makes a similar point in relation to the possibility of a historical origin: "What is found at the historical beginning of things is not the

inviolable identity of their origin; it is the dissension of other things. It is disparity." See "Nietzsche, Genealogy, History," p. 79.

58. Ibid., p. 80.

59. For Descartes's legacy in contemporary liberalism, see Holmes, "Ordinary Passions."

60. Descartes, *Treatise on Man*, p. 2. The *Treatise on Man* is part of a project Descartes called *Traité du monde*, the second part of which is the *Treatise on Light*. Although Descartes wrote the *Treatise of Man* before 1634, he feared for how the clergy would receive its depiction of the body, and therefore he decided not to have it published in his own lifetime. As a result, the two *Treatises* did not enter into circulation until 1664, when Descartes's literary executor, Claude Clerselier (1614–1684), published a French translation of each treatise posthumously.

61. Descartes, *Treatise on Man*, pp. 19–20.

62. Ibid., p. 22.

63. Another way of saying this is that the claims Descartes makes about embodied experience are less transcendental and linearly constructed than those made by the neo-Kantian framework. Indeed, insofar as Descartes offers an *image* of how the nervous system works, he does not claim to "know" the relationship between mind and body—far from it, since Descartes sought but never had the instruments needed to prove his ideas about the human body and its reliance on animal spirits and the pineal gland. Descartes's advocacy of animal vivisections is perhaps the most stunning, if not brutal, testimony to this failure.

64. As I noted in Chapter 1, Descartes's specificity theory has been a fixture in the literature, framing the debate among philosophers and physicians concerning the various causes and remedies of pain. Moreover, as noted in the previous section of the present chapter, his work on pain served as a steppingstone for the Oxford School of Physiology, which in turn set the stage for Sydenham's experimentation with pain medicine as well as for Locke's discussions of pain in relation to the doctrine and practice of becoming indifferent. A similar influence can be detected in France, where Descartes's writings is said to have inaugurated the turn to what the editors of a recent volume call "the *physicality* of pain" in early modern philosophy. See Dijkhuizen and Enenkel, "Introduction," in *The Sense of Suffering*, p. 5 (emphasis in original). For other discussions of the transition from premodern to modern discourses on pain, see Glucklich, *Sacred Pain*; Halpern, *Suffering, Politics, Power*; Morris, *The Culture of Pain*; Rey, *The History of Pain*; and Vertosick, *Why We Hurt*.

65. Descartes, *Treatise on Man*, p. 34. Although Nietzsche is right to scorn this metaphor, insisting that it "would go ill with me if, when I stumbled, I had to wait for the fact to ring the bell of consciousness" (*The Will to Power*, no. 699), I suspect that the scorn applies more to the Cartesian legacy, and less to Descartes's own analyses of the circular interplay among the four steps outlined by his theory of pain.

66. Descartes, "The Passions of the Soul," in *Philosophical Writings of Descartes*, vol. 1, p. 376.

67. Asad, *Formations of the Secular*, p. 83.

68. One might say the range of possibilities suggested here by Descartes is too narrow to capture the many ways in which pain can become world-making, a point to which we shall return in Chapter 3's engagement with Spinoza.

69. Tolerance, as it is understood by a majority of contemporary democratic theorists, is clearly limited in this regard as it insists on defining pain in debilitating terms,

as an experience of world-shattering that belongs to the inner world of the self, and because it thereby limits the possibility for contestation and resignification, creating the impossibility that Chapter 1 identified as detrimental to practices of agonistic respect and democratic contestation.

70. For a history of phantom limb pain, see Katz and Melzack, "Phantom Limb Pain." For Descartes's influence on modern medicine's study of pain more generally, see Benini and DeLeo, "René Descartes' Physiology of Pain," p. 2119.

71. Descartes, "Principles of Philosophy," in *Philosophical Writings of Descartes*, vol. 1, pp. 283–284. In the same text he elaborates on this account by suggesting that pain is mainly a mental experience "present in the brain" (p. 284).

72. Ramachandran, *Phantoms in the Brain*, p. 51. Ramachandran substantiates his explanation in two ways. First, he points to the fact that some patients report pain in their phantom limb when they or someone else brushes other parts of their body. Second, he shows how it is possible to alter the feeling of phantom pain through visual manipulation (in particular, the usage of a mirror box).

73. Descartes, quoted in Gombay, "Sigmund Descartes?" p. 293.

74. Ibid., p. 310.

75. Wingrove, *Rousseau's Republican Romance*, p. 56. Wingrove develops her analysis of this question in the context of Rousseau's work, but her analysis applies also to the early modern period more generally.

76. I owe the example as well as its significance for historical memory to Cathy Caruth, "After the End: Psychoanalysis in the Ashes of History." It should be noted that the four cavities found by Fiorelli were only the first ones; many more have been excavated since the initial research done by Fiorelli.

77. Foucault, "Nietzsche, Genealogy, History," p. 93.

78. For an outline of this argument, see the Introduction, Section I. I shall return to the argument in Chapter 3, Section II.

CHAPTER 3

1. Marcuse, "Repressive Tolerance," p. 81.

2. Spinoza, *Ethics*, in *Spinoza: Collected Works*, part III, proposition 2, scholium. References to the *Ethics* will hereafter take the form of EIIIp9s to indicate the scholium to proposition nine of part three of the *Ethics*. Other abbreviations include *d* for demonstration, *c* for corollary, *def* for definition, *s* for scholium, *ap* for appendix, *ax* for axiom, *pref* for preface, *def.aff* for definition of affects, and *ex* for explication.

3. On "turning" as necessary to embolden a new sense of orientation and subject formation in contemporary critical theory, see Ahmed, *Queer Phenomenology*, pp. 15–16.

4. The branch of critical theory that Marcuse's critique inspired suggests a number of important insights, most notably that tolerance can efface "the complex cultural realities of gay and religious lives" (Butler, *Frames of War*, p. 143); that tolerance sometimes "buries the social powers constitutive of difference" (Brown, *Regulating Aversion*, p. 26); and that we need to supplement or go beyond tolerance so that democratic theory can inspire "active work on our current identities in order to modify the terms of relations between us and them" (Connolly, *Why I Am Not a Secularist*, p. 62). Although I have learned from these insights, I worry that exclusive attention to them obscures an alternative set of possibilities, some of them embedded in Marcuse's analysis, assuming what appears to be

a self-defeating equivalence between the concern for new practices of democracy and the critique of tolerance as a form of passive acquiescence. By insisting that the modern State use tolerance for repressive purposes, and by implying that the only way to overcome this fact is by either supplementing or transcending tolerance, critical theorists have marked but not countered their intellectualist counterparts' assumption of a zero-sum game in which tolerance and power operate as separate entities linked by the way one appropriates the other. An important ambition of the present chapter is to displace this conception of the relationship between tolerance and power.

5. A selective reading of Spinoza is inevitable in part because, as Hasana Sharp points out, his texts are so nebulous that there has been a Spinoza for nearly all ages and all philosophical orientations (*Spinoza and the Politics of Renaturalization*, p. 1). For a sample of the many Spinozas in contemporary scholarship, compare Damasio, *Looking for Spinoza*; Hart and Negri, *Empire*; Israel, *Radical Enlightenment*; Nadler, *Spinoza's Heresy*; Rosenthal, "Spinoza's Republican Argument for Toleration"; Smith, *Spinoza, Liberalism, and the Question of Jewish Identity*.

6. In addition to its veiled appearance in Spinoza's philosophical texts, the tragic also seems to have defined his personal life, which was characterized by a recurrent tension between a commitment to radical thinking and a prudent tolerance of the limits of the Dutch Republic. For a discussion of the tension (and the tolerance it produced), see Nadler, *Spinoza: A Life*.

7. Although the interest in endurance of pain is clearest in Butler's discussion of "precarity" and "grievability" as a new standard for ethical action, the interest also appears in calls for "agonistic respect" (Honig), "critical responsiveness" (Connolly), "deterritorialization" (Deleuze), "disagreement" (Rancière), and "unconditional hospitality" (Derrida). Common to these practices is a feeling of displacement that must be endured in order to achieve a transformative politics based on empowerment and pluralization.

8. Another way of saying this is that I read Spinoza's philosophy of immanence as participating in what we could call "affirmative critical theory," which is the kind of critical theory that opens up new possibilities by foregrounding a certain set of "onto-stories" that Jane Bennett and Stephen White associate with the turn to "weak ontology" in contemporary democratic theory. For further discussion, see Bennett, *The Enchantment of Modern Life*, pp. 160–165; White, *Sustaining Affirmation*, esp. chap. 1.

9. For the extant literature on the five components and how they together define the "circumstances of tolerance," see Introduction, note 12.

10. The study of force fields is typically associated with Alfred N. Whitehead's concept of nature (see Whitehead, *The Concept of Nature*), and with Gilbert Simondon's notion of "individuation," which is also referred to as "transindividuality" (see Simondon, "Position of the Problem of Ontogenesis,", pp. 4–16). Both Whitehead and Simondon work in the philosophy of science, but their ideas and concepts, which more recently have been taken up by Deleuze, can be traced back to Spinoza's philosophy of immanence.

11. Brown, *Regulating Aversion*, p. 25. Although Brown cites Marcuse only in a footnote (p. 210 n8), it is clear that her analysis extends Marcusean insights regarding state repression and the role tolerance plays in such repression. For similar analyses, see Laclau, "Deconstruction," p. 51; Povinelli, *Cunning of Recognition*, p. 28; Žižek, "Tolerance and the Intolerable."

12. On Spinoza's use of the terms *potentia* and *potestas*, see Negri, *The Savage Anomaly*, p. 190.

13. Like other Stoics, Seneca follows Epictetus' insight that "what upsets people is not things themselves but their judgments about the things" (*Handbook*, no. 5:13) and thus places the concept and practice of tolerance in circumstances that are as broad as the polysemic nature of pain and as specific as the verbs *phoreo* (to carry) and *anexo* (to hold). The combination of "what" and "how" encourages the Stoics to approach tolerance as the restraint of "passion under the guidance of reason," developing a line of thought that Spinoza continues in parts III and IV of the *Ethics*. For a more detailed discussion of Stoic tolerance, see Fiala "Stoic Tolerance."

14. Spinoza's interest in Stoicism—and its influence on his philosophy of immanence—is well established in the literature. See for example Israel, *Contested Enlightenment*; James, "Spinoza the Stoic"; and DeBrabander, *Spinoza and the Stoics*.

15. On Seneca the Elder's discussion of torture, see Pagán, "Teaching Torture in Seneca Controversiae 2.5," pp. 165–182. For our purposes, Seneca's turn to torture is interesting not only because it sheds light on the power derived from being tolerant but because it emphasizes the historical and conceptual connections between tolerance and torture. Since tolerance and torture share a concern for the infliction and endurance of pain, their various histories belong to the same family of issues and problems, making it difficult, perhaps even unproductive, to think of them as separate practices. The challenges provoked by the link between torture and tolerance are highlighted and discussed in more detail in Section IV of the present chapter.

16. "On Ill-Health and Endurance of Suffering," Ep. 67:10.

17. For a general discussion of this point, see the Introduction, Section III.

18. In Spinoza's own words, we should not "confuse God's power with a king's human power or right" (EIIP3s).

19. As is well known, Spinoza uses "God" and "Nature" interchangeably, allowing him to suggest that the laws of Nature are identical with the laws of God. In what follows I substitute *sensorium* for God or Nature to emphasize Spinoza's connection with the more recent line of thought associated with Whitehead, Simondon, and Deleuze.

20. The notion that citizens are free to choose their own conception of the good is especially prominent in Rawls's discussion of what he calls the "two moral powers" of free and equal citizens. According to Rawls, these powers ensure that citizens have "a capacity for a sense of justice and a capacity for a conception of the good." *Political Liberalism*, p. 19.

21. Brown, *Regulating Aversion*, pp. 83, 29. See also the works cited in notes 4 and 11 above.

22. One reason contemporary critical theory does not consider Spinoza's conception of power in relation to power might be its tendency to accept the genealogy of tolerance as defined by thinkers such as Forst, Habermas, and Rawls. Though this acceptance seems unproblematic given the objective of the critique of tolerance, it disavows the plurality embedded in the history of tolerance, insisting on determining the value of being tolerant according to only one model. The upshot is self-defeating, I believe: not only does the critique participate in intellectualism's own disavowals, it forces us to either accept the status quo or reject tolerance altogether.

23. My understanding of the Freedom Riders has been shaped by the PBS documentary *Freedom Riders*, written, produced, and directed by Stanley Nelson (2011). The documentary is based on Arsenault, *Freedom Riders*.

24. Spinoza, in his reconstruction of the Stoic position, augments this insight, arguing that the Stoics got it wrong when they invoked free will as a way to overcome pain and suffering. Using the Stoic metaphor of dog training as his point of reference, Spinoza points out that a man's ability to train animals often fails, creating puzzling cases such as a "hunting-dog" becoming a "house-dog" (and vice-versa; EVpref). If this is true in the case of dogs, something similar must also be true of humans, who surely have a greater capacity for rational reasoning but also experience more sophisticated emotions than nonhuman animals. As Spinoza concludes, "with experience crying against them they [the Stoics] were obliged against their principles to admit that no little practice and zeal are required in order to check and control the emotions" (EVpref). For an excellent discussion of this passage in Spinoza, see Gatens and Lloyd, *Collective Imaginings*, pp. 42–48.

25. Another motivation for Spinoza's approach stems from the tendency, prominent among liberal thinkers in the seventeenth century, to limit tolerance to the domain of religious belief. Spinoza acknowledges the importance of this domain— as evidenced by the discussion of religion in the *Theological-Political Treatise*—but warns us against assuming that religious beliefs are the most representative for analyzing how citizens become tolerant of each other. Spinoza's argument is here that an assumption of this kind fails to criticize the presuppositions of religion, and that it upholds what Spinoza calls a "kingdom within a kingdom" (EIIIpref) in which finite beings are endowed with a free will, and in which mind and body work independently of each other. The desire to displace this dualism is a constitutive part of Spinoza's philosophy of immanence.

26. Spinoza, *Theological Political Treatise*, chap. 20, p. 225. For evidence that this is Spinoza's only use of *tolerāntia*, see Boscherini, *Lexicon Spinozanum*, p. 1063.

27. For the Stoicism that informs this part of Spinoza's work, see Matheron's discussion in "Le moment stoïcien de l'Éthique de Spinoza," pp. 302–316.

28. Apart from outlining tolerance's force field, the powers of certitude and restraint help to distinguish tolerance from relativism and skepticism. Unlike both alternatives, tolerance does not ask us to suspend judgment but encourages us to inhabit our judgments by keeping them open to revision and change. For a historical perspective on the link between tolerance and skepticism, see Levine, *Early Modern Skepticism and the Origins of Toleration*.

29. In one of his more poetic passages, Spinoza develops his sense of the tragic condition of Being even further by suggesting that "external causes" stand out because they put finite beings in a situation similar to someone caught at sea in strong winds: "From this it is clear that we are in many respects at the mercy of external causes and are tossed about like the waves of the sea when driven by contrary winds, unsure of the outcome or of our fate" (EIIIp59s). Section III of this chapter develops Spinoza's sense of the tragic in more detail.

30. Although the Stoic doctrine of *convenientia* connotes "agreement" and "symmetry," Spinoza emphasizes the asymmetry between the world of finite beings and the world of infinite attributes (of which we know only two: thought and extension). Section IV of the present chapter discusses the implications that this asymmetry has for the politics of tolerance.

31. Note here that how Spinoza and Marcuse develop their respective orientations to power differs insofar as Spinoza rejects the dialectic method, replacing the

doctrines of *aufgehoben* and historical truth with a radical immanence where there is no negativity as such and where "negation is to deny something of a thing because it does not pertain to its nature" (Spinoza, "Letter 21," in *Spinoza: Collected Works*, p. 824). Although important in many respects, this difference between Spinoza and Marcuse should not make us forget that both thinkers see critical inquiry as part of a partisan struggle in which changes in the composition of a body, idea, or practice can affect the broader network in which it participates. Both thinkers, that is, invoke a critique that proceeds affirmatively and immanently—from within the field of forces that define the context-dependent relationship between tolerator and tolerated. My concern is that this mode of critique has lost some of its influence and prominence in contemporary critical theory.

32. To reflect Spinoza's use of the term *affectus*, I modify Shirley's translation, substituting "affect" for "emotion."

33. Deleuze and Guattari, *What Is Philosophy?* p. 48.

34. Emphasis on this goal may be why contemporary critical theory is witnessing a rather unhelpful divide between a position that affirms affect theory because of the autonomy embedded in all affects, and a position that rejects affect theory because of this claim, insisting on the importance of psychoanalysis and its account of the unconscious (and the related questions of intentionality, meaning, and subjectivity). For an account of each position, see respectively Massumi, *Parables for the Virtual*, chap. 1; Leys, "The Turn to Affect: A Critique," pp. 434–472. For an account that modifies the tension between these two positions, replying especially to Leys's arguments, see Connolly, "Complexity of Intention," pp. 791–798.

35. One objection to this interpretation might be that it downplays two aspects important to the self-empowering nature of affective life: first, Spinoza's distinction between affections of the body (*corporis affectiones*) and affects themselves (*affectus*), which gives more autonomy to affects than the tragic interpretation admits; second, Spinoza's claim that finite beings are the "partial cause" of their own passions, which also gives finite beings greater control of their thoughts and actions than the tragic interpretation admits. Although both aspects add nuance to the interpretation pursued here, they may not prevent Spinoza's ethico-political vision from having a certain tragic quality: (1) even if finite beings are the "partial cause" of their own thoughts and actions, we still have the problem of explaining what else causes them to think and act. To insist that finite beings are the "partial cause" of their own passions, in other words, does not eliminate the problem of externality, leading us back to the discussion of how finite beings are driven by passions that they don't control. (2) The distinction between affections of the body and the affects themselves gives greater autonomy to the latter, but it does so at the expense of telling us how affects are embodied in this or that situation. Without an account of this embodiment, we may end up with a theory of politics and ethics that is too abstract to mobilize and inspire a new orientation to pain and democratic subjectivity. (3) We may even turn the objection against itself and see it as a way to elaborate on the agentive repertoire that tolerance invokes as it combines the active and the passive into a practice of endurance. If finite beings are the "partial cause" of their thought and actions, then the outcome is neither complete mastery nor pure docility. Finite beings are in that sense always-already subjects of tolerance. Special thanks to Jane Bennett and Hasana Sharp for pressing me to consider the issues raised by the objection.

36. Spinoza, *Political Treatise*, in *Spinoza: Collected Works* (p. 683).

37. Panagia, *The Political Life of Sensation*, p. 2.
38. Unlike pleasure, pain can never become an active emotion, which is why it seems closer to the power of passion than pleasure. As we shall see shortly, the "passionate" character of pain does not preclude it from empowering a wide range of thoughts and actions.
39. Rey, *The History of Pain*, p. 11. Rey lists six words for pain: *penthos* (mourning), *kèdos* (worry or obsession), *achos* (sudden and violent emotion), *odunè* (a sharp shooting pain), *algos* (suffering involving the whole body), and *pèma* (adversity, scourge, and misfortune).
40. The fact that Spinoza interprets "perfection" in terms of power suggests that his perfectionism is radically different from the one that deliberative liberals such as Rainer Forst identify as the main problem in Spinoza's theory of tolerance. See Forst, *Toleranz im Konflikt*, pp. 270–271.
41. An important exception here is Talal Asad's discussion in *Formations of the Secular*.
42. To be sure, Spinoza's privileging of affective being sets his definition of pain apart from its Cartesian counterpart, which, as we saw in Chapter 2, remained influential up to the 1970s. Though both Spinoza and Descartes see pain as the negation of self-caused activity, Spinoza does not equate negation with negativity and instead expands negation from a private experience with no shared language to one of culture, religion, and politics. For the historical context surrounding this difference in definition, see the contributions to Dijkhuizen and Enenkel, *The Sense of Suffering*.
43. The general experience of pain embedded in Spinoza's discussion of passionate life is not unlike Heidegger's notion of *Unheimlichkeit*, which also invokes an experience of displacement and pain, one that Heidegger thinks must be endured existentially. For discussion of this argument, see Introduction, Section II.
44. This vulnerability that the subversion of affects provokes is often overlooked in contemporary Spinoza scholarship, which favors a sharper distinction between the two kinds of passivity expressed by pain and pleasure respectively. (For a version of this argument, see Sévérac, "Passivité et désir d'activité chez Spinoza," pp. 39–54.) As already indicated, my sense is that a sharp distinction between these two kinds of passivity misses what drives Spinoza into a discussion of passion in the first place. Not only is it difficult to separate one kind of passivity from another, insofar as Spinoza posits self-caused agency as the goal of all things, passions will always be the negation of this goal. The upshot is what I am calling a tragic condition of Being.
45. See Chapter 1, Section IV.
46. A contemporary example might be the French hijab case, where both sides relied on something like painful pain to legitimize their position on whether the hijab is unconstitutional (or un-French). As I suggested in Chapter 1, the result has been an acceleration of affects, which in turn has empowered a zero-sum game based on two mirrorlike images of what it means to be tolerant: whereas the French side emphasizes the need to endure the pain of cultural assimilation, the Muslim side defines tolerance in terms of the pain created by a multicultural society in which opposing identities must coexist and live alongside each other. Mirroring one another, the antagonistic relationship between these images might explain the stalemate and entrenched warfare that have defined the French hijab case for more than twenty years.
47. On wounded attachments, see Brown, *States of Injury*, chap. 3.
48. I return to Spinoza's concept of *hilaritas* and its consequences for the politics of active tolerance in the next section of the present chapter.

49. Marcuse, "Repressive Tolerance," p. 81.

50. See also the discussion of the link between masochism and Descartes's inner emotions in Chapter 2, Section V.

51. Wingrove, *Rousseau's Republican Romance*, p. 56. Although the endurance of pain has been debated for as long as we know, the term *masochism* was not coined until 1886 when the Austrian psychiatrist Richard Freiherr von Krafft-Ebing, in *Psychopathia Sexualis*, used it to characterize the sexual behavior of Leopold von Sacher-Masoch. For a genealogy of masochism, see Noyes, *The Mastery of Submission*.

52. Wingrove, *Rousseau's Republican Romance*, p. 37.

53. *Venus in Furs* is part of a cycle of six novels, titled *The Heritage of Cain*, which was supposed to explore the themes of love, property, state, war, work, and death. Sacher-Masoch managed to complete only two of the novels, of which *Venus in Furs* is the better known.

54. Sacher-Masoch, "Venus in Furs," p. 192. References to the novel will hereafter follow in parentheses.

55. Interestingly, the difference between these two kinds of inequality is not entirely dissimilar from Spinoza's justification of democracy as the "most natural form of state," a justification that, like masochism, begins not by assuming a natural state of equality but by noting the contingent yet very real differences in the distribution of power—what Spinoza calls the "natural right of the individual...according to which we conceive it as naturally determined to exist and to act in a definite way" (*Theological Political Treatise*, pp. 179, 173). For an account sympathetic to the link between Spinoza and the theorization of masochism, see Feuer, *Spinoza and the Rise of Liberalism*, p. 85.

56. Another way of saying this is that the "danger" of masochism is not the drive to pain as such but rather the various contexts in which the masochistic contract appears. If masochism fails to resist the inequality invoked by misogyny and male domination, the reason is mainly a desire to limit rather than augment the potential embedded in the masochistic contract.

57. Freud, quoted in Arsić, "The Rhythm of Pain," p. 145. According to Arsić, masochism is the noneconomical endpoint that challenges everything psychoanalysis ever wanted to be: "No matter how Freud tried to analyze it [masochism], it always appeared as a psychic phenomenon without economy, hence unanalyzable" (p. 143).

58. To be sure, there are parts of this suggestion that seem oddly non-Spinozan As Judith Butler has pointed out, Spinoza's *Ethics* entails a vitalism that "leaves no room for the death drive" because the "desire to live well presupposes the desire to live" ("The Desire to Live," pp. 112, 111). Butler's skepticism concerning the conflation of these two desires is appropriate, encouraging us to consider whether the "desire to live *well*" sometimes contradicts the "desire to live."

59. For the idea that tolerance implies active forgetting, see the discussion of Locke in Chapter 2, Section IV.

60. The most extensive treatment of Spinoza's concept of *hilaritas* is Minna Koivuniemi, *Towards Hilaritas*.

61. In the modern philosophy of humor, Spinoza's idea of *hilaritas* is thus closer to the "incongruity theory" developed by Kant and Nietzsche than it is to the "superiority theory" developed by Hobbes and Descartes. For a discussion of these two

theories, see respectively Critchley, *On Humour*; and Skinner, "Hobbes and the Classical Theory of Laughter."

62. The actual N-word is spelled with an *e* in place of the *a*. The skit, called the "Niggar Family," aired on January 28, 2004, as part of episode 2 of season 2 of *Chappelle's Show*. The show was produced by Comedy Partners and was first shown on the American cable television network Comedy Central.

63. On the relationship of tolerance and humor, see also Owen, "Must a Tolerant Person Have a Sense of Humor?"

64. Nietzsche, *Twilight of the Idols*, p. 53.

65. In addition to Seneca's discussion of torture, the best example of this possibility might be the more than twenty-five thousand lines of poetry that a group of prisoners at the Guantanamo Bay detention camp produced secretly on plastic cups and scrap paper. Similar to the resistance identified by Seneca in his discussion of how to endure torture, the poetry shows how torturers can express their suffering while resisting the world-shattering effects of the pain inflicted on them. For further discussion, see Butler, *Frames of War*, pp. 55–62.

66. Scarry, *The Body in Pain*, pp. 37, 50.

67. For a recent history of the techniques used to torture others, see Diehl and Donnolly, *The Big Book of Pain*.

68. For an analysis of how interrogation procedures at the Guantanamo Bay detention camp within Guantanamo Bay Naval Base inspired use of torture at the Abu Ghraib prison in Iraq, see Danner's discussion in *Torture and Truth*, esp. chap. 3.

69. Jay S. Bybee, Office of the Assistant Attorney General, Memorandum for Alberto R. Gonzales, Counsel to the President, Re: Standards of Conduct for Interrogation under 18 U.S.C. §§ 2340–2340A, August 1, 2002, Section I–B. Reprinted in Danner, *Torture and Truth*, p. 120.

70. See also "Spinoza and the Theory of Active Tolerance," where I develop a similar set of propositions as part of the theory of active tolerance. The discussion in this chapter focuses explicitly on the force field of tolerance and the experience of pain embedded in it; the propositions listed here are rephrased in order to reflect the insights generated by this additional focus.

CHAPTER 4

1. Valéry, "Notebooks," cited in Starobinski, "Monsieur Teste Confronting *Pain*," p. 387.

2. Merleau-Ponty, *The Prose of the World*, p. 55.

3. Rose, "Muhammeds Ansigt."

4. The cartoon cited here was drawn by the Danish cartoonist Lars Refn, who, although he did not support the agenda promoted by *Jyllands-Posten*, decided to participate in the project as a form of protest and subversion. As we shall see later in the chapter, part of the challenge posed by the twelve cartoons is precisely this: to maintain the cartoons in their plurality, and not treat them as uniform in their approach to free speech, tolerance, and multiculturalism.

5. For a general description and explanation of the events that followed after the publication of the cartoons, see Klausen, *The Cartoons That Shook the World*. For accounts of the van Gogh case and the Rushdie affair, see respectively Buruma, *Murder in Amsterdam*; and Pipes, *The Rushdie Affair*. For accounts of the French hijab case, see the works cited in Chapter 1, note 14.

6. The initial wave of reactions to the twelve cartoons was collected in a special issue of *International Migration*, which featured the opposing views of Tariq Modood and Randal Hansen. Whereas Modood argued that the cartoons should have been censured (but not censored) because they incited "racial hatred," Hansen and others did not see the cartoons as racial and insisted they were perfectly legal, if not the desirable outcome of "a liberal democratic framework." See respectively Modood, "Obstacles to Multicultural Integration," p. 52; and Hansen, "Danish Cartoon Controversy." p. 16.

7. See respectively Rostbøll, "Autonomy, Respect, and Arrogance," pp. 623–648; and Mahmood, "Religious Reason and Secular Affect" p. 849. I discuss Rostbøll's position in more detail in "Humility, Arrogance and the Limitations of Kantian Autonomy," pp. 378–385.

8. Although I take my inspiration for the discussion of framing from the work of Merleau-Ponty, a kindred approach can also be found in the recent work of Judith Butler, who argues that to probe the issue of framing is not only to interrogate how regimes of sensation and discourse "organize visual experience" but to ask how this organization operates "to produce certain subjects as 'recognizable' persons and to make others decidedly more difficult to recognize." Butler, *Frames of War*, pp. 3, 6.

9. Merleau-Ponty, *The Prose of the World*, p. 55. Although Merleau-Ponty discusses the dictum in relation to the paintings of Paul Cézanne (1839–1906), the context of his discussion makes it clear that it applies to the basic structure of perception, which in turn relies on what Merleau-Ponty calls *schéma corporel* (body schema). For further discussion of the latter, see Gallagher, "Body Image and Body Schema," pp. 541—554; Tiemersma, "'Body-image' and 'Body-schema'," pp. 246–255.

10. Spiegelman, "Drawing Blood," p. 47.

11. Green, *The Eyes of the People*, p. 9. Although Green does not engage directly with the issue of framing and its implication for the perception of lived experience, his work on ocular democracy provides an important backdrop for the argument I am making in this chapter.

12. The loss of life associated with the global manifestations against the publication of the twelve *Jyllands-Posten* cartoons is why I call the conflict the "Danish cartoon war," and not, as is customary in the existing literature, the "Danish cartoon controversy." The places and number of deaths are listed on the website "Cartoon Body Count," http://web.archive.org/web/20060714002701/www.cartoonbody-count.com/ (accessed November 26, 2012).

13. For an overview of the prohibition against images in Islamic culture, see Paret, "Textbelege," pp. 213–225.

14. See Motzki, "Hadith." According to Motzki, the hadiths "are for Muslims an important source of guidance next to the Qur'an. The 'way' (sunna) of their Prophet and of the first generations of Muslims is taken as a model for how Muslims should live in this world in order to lead a happy eternal life in the hereafter."

15. See Grabar, "From the Icon to the Aniconism," pp. 46–53.

16. Mirza, "Abraham as an Iconoclast,", p. 425.

17. See Göçek, "Political Cartoons."

18. On the link between Islam's ban of images and politicization and retextualization, see Flood, "Between Cult and Culture," pp. 641–659.

19. See Dyrberg, "Racisme som en nationalistisk"; and Pedersen, "Driving a Populist Party."

20. According to a report on Denmark from the European Commission against Racism and Intolerance (ECRI), the "general climate has continued to deteriorate

in Denmark, with some politicians and parts of the media constantly projecting a negative image of minority groups in general and Muslims in particular. In this regard, the relevant law on incitement to racial hatred is seldom applied to those who make statements against these groups, thus creating a sense of impunity that contributes to a further worsening of the public climate." ECRI, "Third Report on Denmark," p. 6.

21. Akkari, in Anna Badkhen, "What's Behind the Muslim Cartoon Outrageous." At the time of the interview, Akkari was the spokesman for the European Committee for Honoring the Prophet, which is an organization that represents twenty-seven groups identifying with Islam.

22. The opposing reactions to the twelve cartoons were intensified by a smaller group of Danish Imams who used images not commissioned by *Jyllands-Posten* to mobilize support among Middle Eastern governments. See Ammitzbøll and Vidino, "After the Danish Cartoon Controversy," pp. 3–11.

23. Butler, *Frames of War*, p. 6.

24. On the differences between Butler's approach and a sensorial orientation to politicc, see the discussion in the Introduction, Section III.

25. For an overview of the distinctions and their place in the history of democratic theory, see McKinnon, *Toleration*, chap. 6. For detailed discussions of harm especially in liberal theory, see Cohen, "Freedom of Expression," pp. 207–263; and Harcourt, "The Collapse of the Harm Principle," pp. 1–93.

26. Another way of saying this is that contemporary democratic theorists have reframed free speech similarly to tolerance being reframed from the perspective of an intellectualist orientation to politics.

27. Scanlon's argument is framed as a "revision" of Mill's harm principle, which, as we saw in Chapter 1, relies on a sensorial orientation to politics.

28. Scanlon, "A Theory of Freedom of Expression," p. 15.

29. Ibid., p. 17. In addition to Scanlon's approach, see also Rostbøll, "Autonomy, Respect, and Arrogance in the Danish Cartoon Controversy," esp. p. 624.

30. To be sure, one could say that because it is a transcendental assumption, the principle of autonomy does not depend on its ability to resonate with the context to which it is applied. Kant himself seems to favor this approach: severing the phenomenal and the noumenal realms, Kant insists that if "the will seeks the law that is to determine it *anywhere else* than in the fitness of its own maxims for its own giving of universal law . . . *heteronomy* always results" (Kant, *Groundwork of the Metaphysics of Morals*, p. 47 [4:441]).

31. See respectively Andersen, "They Can't Take a Joke"; and Stjernfelt, "Den dobbelte metonymi," pp. 42–52.

32. Quoted in Thomsen and Hundsbæk, "Stormuftien af Egypten." My translation.

33. To be sure, in a case like the Danish cartoon war, the possibilities for contestation are never distributed evenly. Scanlon highlights this problem when he introduces a consequentialist consideration to adjudicate cases where unlimited free speech has unacceptable consequences (see Scanlon, "Content Regulation Reconsidered," p. 152). The move to consequences is a good one, but in requiring that we attend to actual political contestation, it moves us beyond the reach of Scanlon's principle of personal autonomy. Also a problem is Scanlon's investment in justification, which may blind him to what we might call the "harm of justification"—that is, the harm occurring when a constituency's experience of hurt and injury is turned aside for reasons that do not resonate with the context to which they are applied. In the Danish cartoon war, this problem arose when the Danish government

claimed it was neutral in its indifference to the cartoons, refusing to meet with ambassadors from eleven Muslim countries who had requested a meeting with the prime minister, Anders Fogh Rasmussen. In refusing to meet with the ambassadors, the government was perceived as favoring the Danish majority's conception of harm, thereby augmenting the harm caused by the cartoons' perceived defamation of the Prophet Muhammad.

34. For Habermas's and Rawls's attempts at addressing similar problems, see respectively Habermas, "Struggles for Recognition"; and Rawls, "The Idea of Public Reason Revisited."

35. Scanlon, "Content Regulation Reconsidered," p. 154.

36. Ibid., p. 152.

37. Ibid., p. 154.

38. On Merleau-Ponty's critique of liberal democracy, see Coole, *Merleau-Ponty and Modern Politics*, pp. 42, 52–53. In the following, I am less interested in this critique and more focused on how Merleau-Ponty's analysis of perception might inform our view of pain and the framing thereof.

39. On Merleau-Ponty's concept of perception and its ontological implications, see Barbaras, *The Being of the Phenomenon* pp. 19–22. Barbaras's book traces how Merleau-Ponty moves from a phenomenological analysis, developed in *Phenomenology of Perception*, to an ontological analysis, developed in *The Visible and the Invisible*.

40. Merleau-Ponty, *Phenomenology of Perception*, p. 54.

41. Merleau-Ponty, *The Visible and the Invisible*, p. 219.

42. On the structure of reversibility intrinsic to perception, see Dillon, *Merleau-Ponty's Ontology*, pp. 153ff.

43. For a more detailed discussion of how Merleau-Ponty arrives at this account of perception, see my discussion in "Subsistent Tolerance," esp. at pp. 42–43.

44. Special thanks to Diana Coole and Aletta Norval for encouraging me to consider this point.

45. In the work of Brian Massumi, for example, we find an argument for the "autonomy of affect" that folds Spinozistic insights into a trend in twentieth-century French thought that Martin Jay calls "antiocularcentric" (see *Downcast Eyes*). Decentering the attention to sight in critical theory, Massumi exemplifies this trend by arguing that the register of affect is autonomous because it "escapes confinement in the particular body whose vitality, or potential for interaction, it is" (*Parables for the Virtual*, p. 35). According to Massumi, this autonomy gives us a reason to include feeling as privileged register in contemporary democratic politics and to subordinate all other registers of lived experience to the one of affect. Indeed, although Massumi is careful to note that perception and feeling "cofunction," he rarely discusses how visual experience not only depends on but also works back on affect, delimiting how citizens can engage feelings of sadness, hatred, injury, woundedness, and vulnerability. The failure to embrace this interplay is especially problematic when it comes to questions of tolerance in contemporary democratic politics. We don't have to accept Guy Debord's thesis regarding the "spectacle of society" to see that visual experience has become a key component in contemporary struggles over tolerance. The twelve cartoons of the Prophet Muhammad, the hijab case in France and elsewhere, the organization of vision and experience at the Los Angeles Museum of Tolerance, the photographs of torture victims at the Abu Ghraib prison, the depiction of homosexuality in movies and television series such as *Brokeback Mountain* and *Modern*

Family, the images of the Twin Towers collapsing on September 11, 2001, and American newspapers using monkeys and other visual slurs to label the Barack Obama presidency—all these examples suggest that visual experience delimits a new battleground in the struggle over what tolerance does and should mean. Perception, we might say, frames these struggles, releasing as well as modifying feelings of pain and pleasure (or some combination thereof). We must therefore be careful not to posit one register as the key to all the rest; rather, we must tackle all registers, including perception and affect, as co-constitutive—that is, as separate yet related registers that shape one another's conditions of possibility.

46. As Merleau-Ponty puts it, "The red dress a fortiori holds with all its fibers into the fabric of the visible, and thereby onto a fabric of invisible being. A punctuation in the field of red things, which includes the tiles of the red roofs, the flags of gatekeepers and of the Revolution, certain terrains near Aix or in Madagascar, it is also a punctuation in the field of red garments, which includes, along with the dresses of women, robes of professors, bishops, and advocate generals, and also in the field of adornments and that of uniforms." *The Visible and the Invisible*, p. 132.

47. Merleau-Ponty, *Humanism and Terror*, p. 109. For the Spinozan distinction between painful pain and pleasurable pain, see Chapter 3, Section III.

48. The later Merleau-Ponty develop this argument in terms of what he calls *chair* (flesh) and *écart*, that is, a primordial divergence disclosing the incompleteness of lived experience in all its layered richness. See Merleau-Ponty, *The Visible and the Invisible*, p. 187. For critical engagements with this argument, see Beaulieu, *Gilles Deleuze et la phénomenologie*, pp. 152–160; Irigaray, *An Ethics of Sexual Difference*, pp. 151–184; and Lingis, "Phantom Equator."

49. Merleau-Ponty, "Sartre and Ultrabolshevism," p. 409.

50. Merleau-Ponty, *The Prose of the World*, p. 55.

51. For a version of this objection, see Scanlon, "Freedom of Expression and Categories of Expression," p. 102.

52. Despite Foucault's claim, advanced in his review essay "Theatrum Philosophicum," that Deleuze's 1969 book *The Logic of Sense* is "the most alien book imaginable from [Merleau-Ponty's] *Phenomenology of Perception*," there is here a close link between Merleau-Ponty's interest in the category of expression as a form of empowerment and Deleuze's suggestion that the expressed "*has no existence* outside its expression and yet bears no resemblance to it" (*Expressionism in Philosophy*, p. 333; emphasis in original). In both cases, the organizing idea is that expression is a force of its own undermining the claim to autonomy so important to contemporary democratic theory. Similar to Merleau-Ponty's view of perception, Deleuze conceptualizes affect as a mode of world-making that keeps subverting its own being, a point Deleuze substantiates by showing how each and every affect is felt as a heterologous combination of joy and sadness. The remainders created by this combination connect the discussion of perception pursued in this chapter with the discussion of affect in Chapter 3, Section III.

53. Merleau-Ponty, *Signs*, pp. 183, 187.

54. Merleau-Ponty, *The Prose of the World*, p. 35. Merleau-Ponty also emphasizes the importance of vulnerability as the starting point for the expression and the world into which it enters. As Merleau-Ponty puts it in relation to painting, we must "value more than the moment when the work is *finished* only that moment, precocious or late, when the spectator is reached by the canvas and mysteriously resumes in his own way the meaning of the gesture through which it was made. Skipping the intermediaries, without any other guide than a certain movement

discovered in the line or an almost immaterial trace of the brush, the spectator then rejoins the silent word of the painter, henceforth uttered and accessible." *The Prose of the World*, p. 55 (emphasis in original).

55. See Chapter 2, Section III for a discussion of how Kant approached these forces, in particular in relation to the experience of pain.

56. As I noted in Chapter 1, Section III, this view of public reason is not dissimilar to the more sensorial elements of Rawls's work, especially those parts that have to do with what Rawls calls the "burdens of judgment."

57. One way to distinguish public reason from reason as such is to say that the former concerns matters affecting society as a whole. As I note below, further delimintation of these matters cannot be determined a priori, but must be engaged on a case-by-case basis.

58. Rainer Forst, for example, argues that even though reasons are "first-personal," they must "retain a validity 'independently' of subjective motives," ensuring that they are "reasons 'for everyone.'" *Contexts of Justice* pp. 245, 243. Forst develops his argument through a critique of Thomas Nagel; the inserted quotes are from Nagel's work on questions of reason, conflict, and context.

59. In an engagement with the argument developed here, Christian Rostbøll thus argues that whereas one might "imagine that accentuating the sensorium can promote pluralization," it does not offer sufficient grounds for "respect for human *equality*." See "From the Standpoint of Practical Reason," p. 391 (emphasis in original).

60. See also the discussion in Chapter 3, Section IV regarding the forms of asymmetry associated with the masochistic contract.

61. Merleau-Ponty, *Signs*, p. 51.

62. See Bilgrami, "Secularism," p. 12.

63. Mahmood, "Religious Reason and Secular Affect," p. 859.

CONCLUSION

1. White, *The Ethos of a Late-Modern Citizen*, p. 9. For similar views in contemporary political theory, see Butler, *Precarious Life*, p. 42; Dumm, *Loneliness as a Way of Life*, p. 9.

2. According to Sheldon Wolin, the link between democracy and pain may have been reinforced by the ideological success that liberalism experienced during the early modern period. "Our thesis," Wolin writes, "is...that the anxieties besetting liberal man were rooted in his belief in the ever-present possibility of pain and that this belief, in turn, shaped in an important way his attitudes towards the role of government, the possibilities of political action, the nature of justice, and the function of law and legal penalties" (*Vision and Politics*, p. 292). Although this thesis seems right, it does not preclude the argument pursued here: that it is possible to imagine another orientation to the endurance of pain, one that is more empowering and pluralizing than the one usually associated with the liberal tradition.

3. Lefort, "The Permanence of the Theologico-Political?" p. 160.

4. Derrida describes autoimmunity as "that strange behavior where a living being, in quasi-*suicidal* fashion, 'itself' works to destroy its own protection, to immunize itself *against* its 'own' immunity." In Borradori, *Philosophy in a Time of Terror*, p. 94 (emphases in original).

5. This view of Diogenes is not unlike the one Foucault develops in *The Courage of Truth*, lectures 9–11.
6. On this important point, see Honig, "The Importance of Public Things."
7. Deleuze and Guattari, *A Thousand Plateaus*, p. 161.
8. See especially Halliwell, *Greek Laughter*, p. 217. Halliwell develops the notion of a social contract of shame in relation to Old Comedy and its use of shameful speech (*aischrologia*) for purposes of laughter and insult. According to Halliwell, shameful speech was only permissible in the theater, at private symposia, and during religious festivals. It was not permissible in the agora and elsewhere, where citizens were expected to observe the unwritten rules of decorum and appropriateness. Diogenes's biggest offense might have been his refusal to accept this way of organizing social and political life.
9. Dean, *Democracy and Other Neoliberal Fantasies*, pp. 27, 33.

BIBLIOGRAPHY

Abbas, Asma. *Liberalism and Human Suffering: Materialist Reflections on Politics, Ethics, and Aesthetics*. Houndmills, Basingstoke: Macmillan, 2010.

Ahmed, Sara. *Queer Phenomenology: Orientations, Objects, Others*. Durham, NC: Duke University Press, 2006.

Alejandro, Roberto. *The Limits of Rawlsian Justice*. Baltimore: Johns Hopkins University Press, 1998.

Ammitzbøll, Pernille, and Lorenzo Vidino. "After the Danish Cartoon Controversy." *Middle East Quarterly*, Winter 2007, pp. 3–11.

Andersen, Kurt. "They Can't Take a Joke." *New York Magazine*, February 20, 2006.

Arendt, Hannah. *The Human Condition*. Chicago: University of Chicago Press, 1998.

Arsenault, Raymond. *Freedom Riders: 1961 and the Struggle for Racial Justice*. Oxford: Oxford University Press, 2006.

Arsić, Branka. "The Rhythm of Pain: Freud, Deleuze, Derrida." In *Derrida, Deleuze, Psychoanalysis*, edited by Gabrielle Schwab. New York: Columbia University Press, 2007.

Asad, Talal. *Formations of the Secular: Christianity, Islam, Modernity*. Stanford: Stanford University Press, 2003.

———. "Thinking About Religion, Belief, and Politics." In *The Cambridge Companion to Religious Studies*, edited by Robert A. Orsi. Cambridge: Cambridge University Press, 2011.

Bacon, Francis. *Collection of Apophthegms New and Old*. Whitefish: Kessinger, 1997.

Badkhen, Anna. "What's Behind the Muslim Cartoon Outrageous." *San Francisco Chronicle*, February 11, 2006.

Barbaras, Renaud. *The Being of the Phenomenon: Merleau-Ponty's Ontology*. Trans. Ted Toadvine and Leonard Lawlor. Bloomington: Indiana University Press, 2004.

Barry, Brian. *Justice as Impartiality*. Oxford: Clarendon Press, 1995.

Beaulieu, Alain. *Gilles Deleuze et la phénoménologie*. Paris: Les Editions Sils Maria, 2004.

Bejczy, István. "Tolerantia: A Medieval Concept." *Journal of History of Ideas*, vol. 58, no. 3 (1997), pp. 365–384.

Benini, Arnaldo, and Joyce A. DeLeo. "René Descartes' Physiology of Pain." *Spine*, vol. 24, no. 20 (1999), pp. 2115–2119.

Bennett, Jane. *The Enchantment of Modernity: Attachments, Crossings, and Ethics*. Princeton: Princeton University Press, 2001.

———. *Vibrant Matter: A Political Ecology of Things*. Durham, NC: Duke University Press, 2010.

Berlant, Lauren. *Cruel Optimism*. Durham, NC: Duke University Press, 2011.

Besier, Gerhard, and Klaus Schreiner. "Toleranz." In *Geschichtliche Grundbegriffe: Historisches Lexikon sur politisch-socialen Sprache in Deutschland*, edited by Otto Brunner, Werner Conze and Reinhart Koselleck. Stuttgart: Klett-Cotta, 2004.

Bilgrami, Akeel. "Secularism: Its Content and Context." *Social Science Research Council Working Papers*, October 2011.

Biro, David. *The Language of Pain: Finding Words, Compassion, and Relief.* New York: Norton, 2010.

Borradori, Giovanna. *Philosophy in a Time of Terror: Dialogues with Jürgen Habermas and Jacques Derrida.* Chicago: University of Chicago Press, 2004.

Boscherini, Emilia Giancotti. *Lexicon Spinozanum.* The Hague: Martinus Nijhoff, 1970.

Bowen, John R. *Why the French Don't Like Headscarves: Islam, the State, and Public Space.* Princeton: Princeton University Press, 2007.

Braidotti, Rosi. *Transpositions: On Nomadic Ethics.* Cambridge: Polity Press, 2006.

Brown, Wendy. *States of Injury: Power and Freedom in Late Modernity.* Princeton: Princeton University Press, 1995.

———. *Regulating Aversion: Tolerance in the Age of Identity and Empire.* Princeton: Princeton University Press, 2006.

Buruma, Ian. *Murder in Amsterdam: The Death of Theo van Gogh and the Limits of Tolerance.* New York: Penguin Press, 2006.

Butler, Judith. *Precarious Life: The Powers of Mourning and Violence.* London: Verso, 2004.

———. *Frames of War: When Is Life Grievable?* London: Verso, 2009.

———. "The Desire to Live: Spinoza's Ethics Under Pressure." In *Politics and the Passions, 1500–1850*, edited by Victoria Kahn, Neil Saccamano, and Daniela Coli. Princeton: Princeton University Press, 2006.

Carlson, Marla. *Performing Bodies in Pain: Medieval and Post-Modern Martyrs, Mystics, and Artists.* New York: Palgrave Macmillan, 2010

Caruth, Cathy. *Unclaimed Experience: Trauma, Narrative, History.* Baltimore: Johns Hopkins University Press, 1996.

———. "After the End: Psychoanalysis in the Ashes of History." Paper presented at Northwestern University, February 18, 2011.

Cohen, Joshua. "Freedom of Expression." *Philosophy and Public Affairs*, vol. 22, no 3 (1993), pp. 207–263.

Cohen, Stanley. *States of Denial: Knowing About Atrocities and Suffering.* Cambridge: Polity Press, 2001.

Coles, Romand. *Beyond Gated Communities: Reflections for the Possibility of Democracy.* Minneapolis: University of Minnesota Press, 2005.

Connolly, William E. *Why I Am Not a Secularist.* Minneapolis: University of Minnesota Press, 1999.

———. *Neuropolitics: Thinking, Culture, Speed.* Minneapolis: University of Minnesota Press, 2002.

———. *Pluralism.* Durham, NC: Duke University Press, 2005.

———. "The Complexity of Intention." *Critical Inquiry*, vol. 37, no. 4 (2011), pp. 792–799.

Coole, Diana. *Merleau-Ponty and Modern Politics After Anti-Humanism.* Lanham, MD: Rowman & Littlefield, 2007.

Cranston, Maurice. "John Locke and the Case for Toleration." In *John Locke: A Letter Concerning Toleration in Focus*, edited by Susan Mendus and John Horton. London: Routledge, 1991.

Creppell, Ingrid. *Toleration and Identity: Foundations in Early Modern Thought*. London: Routledge, 2003.

Critchley, Simon. *On Humour*. New York: Routledge, 2002.

Damasio, Antonio. *Looking for Spinoza: Joy, Sorrow, and the Feeling Brain*. Orlando: Harcourt, 2003.

Danner, Mark. *Torture and Truth: America, Abu Ghraib, and the War on Terror*. New York: New York Review of Books, 2004.

Dean, Jodi. *Democracy and Other Neoliberal Fantasies: Communicative Capitalism and Left Politics*. Durham, NC: Duke University Press, 2009.

DeBrabander, Firmin. *Spinoza and the Stoics: Power, Politics, and the Passions*. New York: Zone Books, 2007.

Deleuze, Gilles. *Nietzsche and Philosophy*. Trans. Hugh Tomlinson. New York: Columbia University Press, 1983.

———. *Kant's Critical Philosophy*. Trans. Hugh Tomlinson and Barbara Habberjam. Minneapolis: University of Minnesota Press, 1984.

———. *Expressionism in Philosophy: Spinoza*. Trans. Martin Joughin. New York: Zone Books, 1992.

Deleuze, Gilles, and Félix Guattari. *A Thousand Plateaus: Capitalism and Schizophrenia*. Trans. Brian Massumi. Minneapolis: University of Minnesota Press, 1987.

———. *What Is Philosophy?* Trans. Hugh Tomlinson and Graham Burshell. New York: Columbia University Press, 1994.

Derrida, Jacques. "Faith and Knowledge: The Two Sources of 'Religion' at the Limits of Reason Alone." Trans. Samuel Weber. In *Religion*, edited by Jacques Derrida and Gianni Vattimo. Stanford: Stanford University Press, 1998.

Descartes, René. *The Philosophical Writings of Descartes*. 3 vols. Trans. John Cottingham, Robert Stoothoff, and Dugald Murdoch. Cambridge: Cambridge University Press, 1985.

———. *Treatise of Man*. Trans. Thomas Steele Hall. Amherst, NY: Prometheus Books, 2003.

Dickinson, Emily. "Poem 650." In *The Complete Poems of Emily Dickinson*, edited by Thomas H. Johnson. Boston: Little, Brown, 1955.

Diehl, Daniel, and Mark P. Donnolly. *The Big Book of Pain: Torture & Punishment Through History*. Charleston, SC: History Press, 2009.

Dietz, Mary G. *Turning Operations: Feminism, Arendt, and Politics*. New York: Routledge, 2002.

Dijkhuizen, Jan Frans van, and Karl A. E. Enenkel, eds. *The Sense of Suffering: Constructions of Physical Pain in Early Modern Culture*. Leiden: Brill, 2009.

Dillon, Martin C. *Merleau-Ponty's Ontology*. 2nd ed. Evanston: Northwestern University Press, 1997.

Dumm, Thomas. *Loneliness as a Way of Life*. Cambridge, MA: Harvard University Press, 2008.

Dunn, John. "The Claim to Freedom of Conscience: Freedom of Speech, Freedom of Thought, Freedom of Worship?" In *From Persecution to Toleration: The Glorious Revolution and Religion in England*, edited by Ole Peter Grell et al. Oxford: Clarendon Press, 1991.

Dyrberg, Torben Bech. "Racisme som en nationalistisk og populistisk reaktion på elitedemokrati." In *Diskursteori på arbejde*, edited by Torben Bech Dyrberg, Allan Dreyer Hansen, and Jacob Torfing. Frederiksberg: Roskilde Universitetsforlag/ Samfundslitteratur, 2000.

European Commission Against Racism and Intolerance. "Third Report on Denmark." Strasbourg, May 16, 2006.

Feuer, Lewis Samuel. *Spinoza and the Rise of Liberalism*. Reprint ed. Piscataway, NJ: Transaction, 1987.

Fiala, Andrew. "Stoic Tolerance." *Res Publica*, vol. 9 (2003), pp. 149–168.

Flood, Finbarr Barry. "Between Cult and Culture: Bamiyan, Islamic Iconoclasm, and the Museum." *Art Bulletin*, vol. 84, no. 4 (2002), pp. 641–659.

Forst, Rainer. *Contexts of Justice: Political Philosophy Beyond Liberalism and Communitarianism*. Trans. John M. M. Farrell. Berkeley: University of California Press, 2002.

———. *Toleranz im Konflikt: Geschichte, Gehalt und Gegenwart eines umstrittenen Begriffs*. Frankfurt am Main: Suhrkamp, 2003.

———. "Toleration, Justice and Reason." In *The Culture of Toleration in Diverse Societies*, edited by Catriona McKinnon and Dario Castiglio. New York: Manchester University Press, 2003.

———. "The Limits of Toleration." *Constellations*, vol. 11, no. 3 (2004), pp. 312–325.

———. "Bayle's Reflexive Theory of Toleration." In *Toleration and Its Limits: Nomos XLVIII*, edited by Melissa S. Williams and Jeremy Waldron. New York: New York University Press, 2008.

Foucault, Michel. *The Order of Things: An Archeology of the Human Science*. London: Routledge, 1970.

———. "Theatrum Philosophicum." In *Language, Counter-Memory, Practice*. Ithaca, NY: Cornell University Press, 1977.

———. "Governmentality." In *The Foucault Effect*, edited by Graham Burchell, Colin Gordon and Peter Miller. Chicago: University of Chicago Press, 1991.

———. "Nietzsche, Genealogy, History." In *The Foucault Reader: An Introduction to Foucault's Thought*, edited by Paul Rabinow. New York: Penguin Books, 1991.

———. *Introduction to Kant's Anthropology*. Trans. Roberto Nigro and Kate Briggs. Los Angeles: Semiotext(e), 2008.

———. *The Courage to Truth (The Government of Self and Others II)*.Trans. Graham Burchell. New York, NY: Palgrave Macmillan, 2011.

Freeden, Michael. *Ideologies and Political Theory: A Conceptual Approach*. Oxford: Oxford University Press, 1996.

Freud, Sigmund. *Three Essays on the Theory of Sexuality*. Trans. James Strachey. New York: Basic Books, 2000.

Galeotti, Anna Elisabetta. *Toleration as Recognition*. Cambridge: Cambridge University Press, 2002.

Gallagher, Shaun. "Body Image and Body Schema: A Conceptual Clarification." *Journal of Mind and Behaviour*, vol. 7, no. 4 (1986), pp. 541—554.

Gatens, Moira, and Genevieve Lloyd. *Collective Imaginings: Spinoza, Past and Present*. London: Routledge, 1999.

Geuss, Raymond. *Public Goods, Private Goods*. Princeton: Princeton University Press, 2001.

Glucklich, Ariel. *Sacred Pain: Hurting the Body for the Sake of the Soul*. Oxford: Oxford University Press, 2001.

Göçek, Fatma Müge. "Political Cartoons as a Site of Representation and Resistance in the Middle East." In *Political Cartoons in the Middle East: Cultural Representation in the Middle East*, edited by Fatma Müge Göçek. Princeton: Markus Weiner, 1998.

Goethe, Johann Wolfgang von. *Maxims and Reflections*. Trans. Elisabeth Stopp. London: Penguin Books, 1998.

Gombay, André. "Sigmund Descartes?" *Philosophy*, vol. *83*, no. 3 (2008), pp. 293–310.

Grabar, Oleg. "From the Icon to the Aniconism: Islam and the Image." *Museum International*, vol. *55* (2003), pp. 46–53.

Green, Jeffrey E. *The Eyes of the People: Democracy in an Age of Spectatorship*. Oxford: Oxford University Press, 2010.

Grosz, Elizabeth. *Volatile Bodies: Toward a Corporeal Feminism*. Bloomington, IN: Indiana University Press, 1994.

———. *Becoming Undone: Darwinian Reflections on Life, Politics, and Art*. Durham, NC: Duke University Press, 2011.

Habermas, Jürgen. "Struggles for Recognition in the Democratic State." In *The Inclusion of the Other: Studies in Political Theory*. Cambridge, MA: MIT Press, 1998.

———. "Intolerance and Discrimination." *International Journal of Constitutional Law*, vol. *1*, no. 1 (2003), pp. 2–12.

———. "Religious Tolerance—The Pacemaker for Cultural Rights." *Philosophy*, vol. *79*, No. 1 (2004), pp. 5–18.

Halliwell, Stephen. *Greek Laughter: A Study of Cultural Psychology from Homer to Early Christianity*. Cambridge: Cambridge University Press, 2008.

Halpern, Cynthia. *Suffering, Politics, Power: A Genealogy in Modern Political Theory*. Albany: State University of New York Press, 2002.

Hansen, Mark B. N. *New Philosophy for New Media*. Cambridge, MA: MIT Press, 2004.

Hansen, Randal. "The Danish Cartoon Controversy: A Defense of Liberal Freedom." *International Migration*, vol. *44*, no. 5 (2006), pp. 7–16.

Harcourt, Bernard R. "The Collapse of the Harm Principle." *Journal of Criminal Law and Criminology*, vol. *90*, no. 1 (1999), pp. 1–93.

Hart, Michael, and Antonio Negri. *Empire*. Cambridge, MA: Harvard University Press, 2000.

Heidegger, Martin. *Being and Time*. Trans. John Macquarrie and Edward Robinsen. Oxford: Blackwell, 1962.

Holmes, Stephen. "Ordinary Passions in Descartes and Racine." In *Liberalism Without Illusions: Essays on Liberal Theory and the Political Vision of Judith N. Shklar*, edited by Bernard Yack. Chicago: University of Chicago Press, 1996.

Honig, Bonnie. *Political Theory and the Displacement of Politics*. Ithaca, NY: Cornell University Press, 1993.

———. "The Importance of Public Things." Interview with Joe Gelonesi. On *The Philosopher's Zone*, ABC Radio National, April 21, 2013.

Horton, John. "Liberalism, Multiculturalism and Toleration." In *Liberalism, Multiculturalism, and Toleration*, edited by John Horton. New York: St. Martin's Press, 1993.

Howes, David, ed. *Empire of the Senses: The Sensual Culture Reader*. New York: Berg, 2005.

Irigaray, Luce. *An Ethics of Sexual Difference*. Trans. Carolyn Burke and Gillian C. Gill. Ithaca, NY: Cornell University Press, 1993.

Israel, Jonathan. *Radical Enlightenment: Philosophy and the Making of Modernity 1650–1750*. Oxford: Oxford University Press, 2001.

———. *Contested Enlightenment: Philosophy, Modernity, and the Emancipation of Man 1670–1752*. Oxford: Oxford University Press, 2006.

James, Susan. "Spinoza the Stoic." In *The Rise of Modern Philosophy: The Tension Between the New and Traditional Philosophies from Machiavelli to Leibniz*, edited by Tom Sorell. Oxford: Clarendon Press, 1993.

Jay, Martin. *Downcast Eyes: The Denigration of Vision in Twentieth-Century Thought*. Berkeley: University of California Press, 1994.

Kamen, Henry. *The Rise of Toleration.* Toronto: McGraw-Hill, 1967.

Kant, Immanuel. *Critique of Pure Reason.* Trans. Norman Kemp Smith. London: Macmillan, 1929.

———. *Kant: Political Writings.* 2nd enlarged ed. Trans. H. B. Nisbet. Cambridge: Cambridge University Press, 1970.

———. *Critique of Judgment.* Trans. Werner S. Pluhar. Indianapolis: Hackett, 1987.

———. *Groundwork of the Metaphysics of Morals.* Trans. Mary Gregor. Cambridge: Cambridge University Press, 1997.

———. *Anthropology from a Pragmatic Point of View.* Trans. Robert B. Louden. Cambridge: Cambridge University Press, 2006.

Katz, Joel, and Robert Melzack. "Phantom Limb Pain." In *Handbook of Neuropsychology: Plasticity and Rehabilitation,* edited by J. Grafman and I. H. Robertson. 2nd ed. Amsterdam: Elsevier, 2003.

King, Preston. *Toleration.* New ed. London: Frank Cass, 1998.

Klausen, Jytte. *The Cartoons That Shook the World.* New Haven: Yale University Press, 2009.

Koivuneimi, Minna. *Towards Hilaritas: A Study of the Mind-Body Union, the Passions and the Mastery of the Passions in Descartes and Spinoza.* Uppsala: University of Uppsala, 2008.

Krause, Sharon. *Civil Passions: Moral Sentiments and Democratic Deliberation.* Princeton: Princeton University Press, 2008.

Laclau, Ernesto. "Deconstruction, Pragmatism, Hegemony." In *Deconstruction and Pragmatism,* edited by Chantal Mouffe. London: Routledge, 1996.

Laertius, Diogenes, *Lives of Eminent Philosophers.* 2 vols. Trans. R. D. Hicks. Cambridge: Cambridge University Press, 1925.

Laursen, John Christian, and Cary J. Nederman, eds. *Difference and Dissent: Theories of Toleration in Medieval and Early Modern Europe.* Lanham, MD: Rowman & Littlefield, 1996.

Lecler, Joseph. *Toleration and the Reformation.* Trans. T. L. Westow. New York: Association Press, 1960.

Lefort, Claude. "The Permanence of the Theological-Political." Reprinted in *Political Theologies: Public Religions in a Post-Secular World,* edited by Hent de Vries and Lawrence Sullivan. New York: Fordham University Press, 2006.

Levine, Alan, ed. *Early Modern Skepticism and the Origins of Toleration.* Lanham, MD: Lexington Books, 1999.

Leys, Ruth. "The Turn to Affect: A Critique." *Critical Inquiry,* vol. 37, no. 3 (2011), pp. 434–472.

Lingis, Alphonso. "Phantom Equator." In *Merleau-Ponty, Hermeneutics, and Postmodernism,* edited by Thomas W. Busch and Shaun Gallagher. Albany: State University of New York Press, 1992.

Locke, John. *Two Tracts of Government.* Cambridge: Cambridge University Press, 1967.

———. *An Essay Concerning Human Understanding.* Oxford: Oxford University Press, 1975.

———. "A Letter Concerning Toleration." In *Two Treatises of Government and A Letter Concerning Toleration,* edited by Ian Shapiro. New Haven: Yale University Press, 2003.

Macedo, Stephen. *Liberal Virtues: Citizenship, Virtue, and Community in Liberal Constitutionalism.* Oxford: Clarendon Press, 1990.

Mahmood, Saba. "Religious Reason and Secular Affect: An Incommensurable Divide?" *Critical Inquiry*, vol. 35, no. 4 (2009), pp. 836–862.

March, Andrew. "Religious Reasons in Public Justifications." *American Political Science Review* (forthcoming 2013).

Marcuse, Herbert. "Repressive Tolerance." In *A Critique of Pure Tolerance*, edited by Robert Paul Wolff, Barrington Moore, Jr., and Herbert Marcuse. Boston: Beacon Press, 1965.

Marshall, John. *John Locke: Resistance, Religion, and Responsibility*. Cambridge: Cambridge University Press, 1994.

Martell, James. *Textual Conspiracies: Walter Benjamin, Idolatry, and Political Theory*. Ann Arbor: University of Michigan Press, 2011.

Marx, Karl. "On the Jewish Question." In *The Marx-Engels Reader*, 2nd ed. New York: Norton, 1978.

Massumi, Brian. *Parables for the Virtual: Movement, Affect, Sensation*. Durham, NC: Duke University Press, 2002.

Matheron, Alexandre. "Le moment stoïcien de l'Éthique de Spinoza." In *Le stoïcisme au XVIe et au XVIIe siècle: Le retour des philosophies antiques à l'Âge classique*, edited by Pierre-François Moreau. Paris: Albin Michel, 1999.

Matravers, Matt, and Susan Mendus. "The Reasonableness of Pluralism." In *The Culture of Toleration in Diverse Societies*, edited by Catriona McKinnon and Dario Castiglio. New York: Manchester University Press, 2003.

McClure, Kirstie M. "Difference, Diversity, and the Limits of Toleration." *Political Theory*, vol. 18, no. 3 (August 1990), pp. 361–391.

———. *Judging Rights: Lockean Politics and the Limits of Consent*. Ithaca, NY: Cornell University Press, 1996.

McKinnon, Catriona. *Toleration: A Critical Introduction*. London: Routledge, 2006.

Melzack, Ronald, and Patrick D. Wall. *The Challenge of Pain*. New York: Basic Books, 1983.

Mendus, Susan. *Toleration and the Limits of Liberalism*. London: Macmillan, 1989.

Merleau-Ponty, Maurice. *Phenomenology of Perception*. Trans. Colin Smith. London: Routledge, 1962.

———. *Signs*. Trans. Richard C. McCleary. Evanston: Northwestern University Press, 1964.

———. *The Visible and the Invisible*. Trans. Alphonso Lingis. Evanston: Northwestern University Press, 1968.

———. *The Prose of the World*. Trans. John O'Neill. Evanston: Northwestern University Press, 1973.

———. *Humanism and Terror: The Communist Problem*. Trans. John O'Neill. New Brunswick: Transaction, 2000.

———. "Sartre and Ultrabolshevism." Reprinted in *The Debate Between Sartre and Merleau-Ponty*, edited by Jon Stewart. Evanston: Northwestern University Press, 1998.

Mill, John Stuart. *Utilitarianism*. 2nd ed. Indianapolis: Hackett, 2001.

Mirza, Younus. "Abraham as an Iconoclast: Understanding the Destruction of 'Images' Through Qur'anic Exegesis." *Islam and Christian—Muslim Relations*, vol. 16 (2005), pp. 413–428.

Modood, Tariq. "Obstacles to Multicultural Integration." *International Migration*, vol. 44, no. 5 (2006), pp. 51–62.

Morris, David. *The Culture of Pain*. Berkeley: University of California Press, 1991.

Motzki, Harald. "Hadith." In *Encyclopedia of Islam and the Muslim World*, edited by Richard C. Martin. New York: Thomson Gale, 2004.

Mouffe, Chantal. *The Return of the Political*. London: Verso, 1993.

Müller, Jan-Werner. "Toleration in Contexts: review of Rainer Forst, 'Toleranz im Konflikt: Geschichte, Gehalt und Gegenwart eines umstrittenen Begriffs'." *European Journal of Political Theory*, vol. 4, no. 4 (2005), pp. 467–470.

Nadler, Steven. *Spinoza: A Life*. Cambridge: Cambridge University Press, 1999.

———. *Spinoza's Heresy: Immortality and the Jewish Mind*. Oxford: Clarendon Press, 2001.

Nagel, Thomas. *Equality and Partiality*. Oxford: Oxford University Press, 1991.

Nussbaum, Martha. "Patriotism and Cosmopolitanism." *Boston Review*, vol. 19, no. 5 (1994), pp. 3–16.

Nederman, Cary J. *Worlds of Difference: European Discourses of Toleration c. 1100–c. 1550*. University Park: Pennsylvania State University Press, 2000.

Negri, Antonio. *The Savage Anomaly: The Power of Spinoza's Metaphysics and Politics*. Trans. Michael Hardt. Minneapolis: University of Minnesota Press, 1991.

Nelson, Stanley. *Freedom Riders*. Television premiere, May 16, 2011, on the PBS series *American Experience*. PBS Distribution (DVD), 120 min.

Newey, Glen. *Virtue, Reason, and Toleration: The Place of Toleration in Ethical and Political Philosophy*. Edinburgh: Edinburgh University Press, 1999.

Nietzsche, Friedrich. *The Will to Power*. Trans. Walter Kaufmann and R. J. Hollingdale. New York: Vintage, 1968.

———. *The Gay Science*. Trans. Walter Kaufman. New York: Vintage, 1974.

———. *Twilight of the Idols and the Anti-Christ: Or How to Philosophize with a Hammer*. Trans. R. J. Hollingdale. London: Penguin, 1990.

———. *On the Genealogy of Morality*. Trans. Carol Diethe. Cambridge: Cambridge University Press, 1994.

———. *Beyond Good and Evil: Prelude to a Philosophy of the Future*. Trans. L. A. Magnus. Fairfield, IA: 1st World, 2004.

Noyes, John K. *The Mastery of Submission: Inventions of Masochism*. Ithaca, NY: Cornell University Press, 1997.

O'Neill, Onora. *Constructions of Reason: Explorations of Kant's Practical Philosophy*. Cambridge: Cambridge University Press, 1989.

Owen, David. "Must the Tolerant Person Have a Sense of Humor? On the Structure of Tolerance as a Virtue." *Critical Review of International Social and Political Philosophy*, vol. 14, no. 3 (June 2011), pp. 385–403.

Pagán, Victoria Emma. "Teaching Torture in Seneca Controversiae 2.5." *Classical Journal*, vol. 103, no. 2 (2007), pp. 165–182.

Panagia, Davide. *The Political Life of Sensation*. Durham, NC: Duke University Press, 2009.

Paret, Rudi. "Textbelege zum islamishen Bilderverbot." In *Schriften zum Islam*. Stuttgart: Kohlhammer, 1981.

Parker, Kim Ian. *The Biblical Politics of John Locke*. Waterloo, Ont.: Wilfrid Laurier University Press, 2004.

Pedersen, Karina. "Driving a Populist Party: The Danish People's Party." Working Paper 2006/06, Department of Political Science, University of Copenhagen.

Peters, John Durham. *Courting the Abyss: Free Speech and the Liberal Tradition*. Chicago: Chicago University Press, 2005.

Pipes, Daniel. *The Rushdie Affair: The Novel, the Ayatollah, and the West*. 2nd ed. New York: Transaction, 2003.

Podoksik, Efraim. "One Concept of Liberty: Towards Writing the History of a Political Concept." *Journal of the History of Ideas*, vol. 71, no. 2 (April 2010), pp. 219–240.

Povinelli, Elizabeth. *The Cunning of Recognition: Indigenous Alterities and the Making of Australian Multiculturalism*. Durham, NC: Duke University Press, 2002.

Rabelais, François. *Gargantua and Pantagruel*. Trans. M. A. Screech. London: Penguin, 2006.

Ramachandran, Vilayanur S. *Phantoms in the Brain: Probing the Mysteries of the Human Mind*. New York: Morrow, 1998.

Rancière, Jacques. "Ten Theses on Politics." *Theory & Event*, vol. 5, no. 3 (2001), pp. 17–34.

Rawls, John. "The Sense of Justice." *Philosophical Review*, vol. 72, no. 3 (July 1963), pp. 281–305.

——. *Political Liberalism*. New York: Columbia University Press, 1993.

——. *A Theory of Justice*. Revised ed. Cambridge, MA: Belknap Press of Harvard University Press, 1999.

——. "Justice as Fairness: Political not Metaphysical." Reprinted in *Collected Papers*. Cambridge, MA: Harvard University Press, 1999.

——. *Justice as Fairness: A Restatement* (Cambridge, MA: Harvard University Press, 2001), pp. 195–198.

——. *A Brief Inquiry in the Meaning of Faith and Sin: With: "On My Religion."* Cambridge, MA: Harvard University Press, 2010.

Raz, Joseph. "Autonomy, Toleration and the Harm Principle." In *Justifying Toleration*. Edited by Susan Mendus. Cambridge: Cambridge University Press, 1988.

Rey, Roselyne. *The History of Pain*. Trans. Louise Elliott Wallace, J. A. Cadden, and S. W. Cadden. Cambridge, MA: Harvard University Press, 1993.

Rorty, Richard. "The Priority of Democracy to Philosophy." Reprinted in *Objectivity, Relativism, and Truth: Philosophical Papers, Vol. 1*. Cambridge: Cambridge University Press, 1991.

Rose, Fleming. "Muhammeds Ansigt." *Jyllands-Posten*, September 30, 2005.

Rosenthal, Michael A. "Spinoza's Republican Argument for Toleration." *Journal of Political Philosophy*, vol. 11, no. 3 (2003), pp. 320–337.

Rostbøll, Christian. "Autonomy, Respect, and Arrogance in the Danish Cartoon Controversy." *Political Theory*, vol. 37, no. 5 (2009), pp. 623–648.

——. "From the Standpoint of Practical Reason: A Reply to Tønder." *Political Theory*, vol. 39, no. 4 (2011), pp. 386–393.

Sacher-Masoch, Leopold von. "Venus in Furs." In *Masochism*. Trans. Jean McNeil. New York: Zone Books, 1989.

Scanlon, Thomas M. "The Difficulty of Tolerance." In *Toleration: An Elusive Virtue*, edited by David Heyd. Princeton: Princeton University Press, 1996.

——. "Content Regulation Reconsidered." In *The Difficulty of Tolerance: Essays in Political Philosophy*. Cambridge: Cambridge University Press, 2003.

——. "Freedom of Expression and Categories of Expression." In *The Difficulty of Tolerance: Essays in Political Philosophy*. Cambridge: Cambridge University Press, 2003.

——. "A Theory of Freedom of Expression." In *The Difficulty of Tolerance: Essays in Political Philosophy*. Cambridge: Cambridge University Press, 2003.

Scarry, Elaine. *The Body in Pain: The Making and Unmaking of the World*. Oxford: Oxford University Press, 1985.

Schlüter, G., and R. Grötker, "Toleranz." In *Historisches Wörterbuch der Philosophie*, edited by Joachim Ritter and Karlfried Gründer. Darmstadt: Wissenschaftliche Buchgesellschaft, 1998.

Scott, Joan W. *The Politics of the Veil*. Princeton: Princeton University Press, 2007.

Seneca, Lucius Annaeus. "On Ill-Health and Endurance of Suffering." In *Ad Lucilium Epistulae Morales*. Trans. Richard M. Gummere. Cambridge, MA: Harvard University Press, 1920.

Sévérac, Pascal. "Passivité et désir d'activité chez Spinoza." In *Groupe de Recherches Spinozistes: Travaux et Decoments, No. 7: Spinoza et les affects*, pp. 39–54. Paris: Presses de l'Université de Paris Sorbonne, 1998.

Sharp, Hasana. *Spinoza and the Politics of Renaturalization*. Chicago: University of Chicago Press, 2011.

Simondon, Gilbert. "The Position of the Problem of Ontogenesis." Trans. Gregory Flanders. *Parrhesia*, no. 7 (2009), pp. 4–16.

Skinner, Quentin. "Hobbes and the Classical Theory of Laughter." Reprinted in *Visions of Politics, Vol. 3*. Cambridge: Cambridge University Press, 2002.

Smith, Steven B. *Spinoza, Liberalism, and the Question of the Jewish Identity*. New Haven: Yale University Press, 1997.

Soni, Vivasvan. *Mourning Happiness: Narrative and the Politics of Modernity*. Ithaca, NY: Cornell University Press, 2010.

Spiegelman, Art. "Drawing Blood: Outrageous Cartoons and the Art of Outrage." *Harper's Magazine*, June 2006.

Spinoza, Baruch de. *Theological Political Treatise*. 2nd ed. Trans. Samuel Shirley. Indianapolis: Hackett, 2001.

———. *Spinoza: Collected Works*. Trans. Samuel Shirley. Indianapolis: Hackett, 2002.

Starobinski, Jean. "Monsieur Teste Confronting Pain." In *Fragments for a History of the Human Body: Part 2*, edited by Michel Feher, Ramona Naddaff, and Nadia Tazi. New York: Zone Books, 1989.

Stjernfelt, Frederik. "Den dobbelte metonymi: Muhammed og Fogh—en komparativ analyse." *Kritik*, no. 179 (2006), pp. 42–52.

Tarnopolsky, Christina H. *Prudes, Pervert, and Tyrants: Plato's Gorgias and the Politics of Shame*. Princeton: Princeton University Press, 2010.

Taylor, Charles. *Sources of the Self: The Making of Modern Identity*. Cambridge: Cambridge University Press, 1989.

———. "The Politics of Recognition." In *Multiculturalism and "The Politics of Recognition."* Princeton: Princeton University Press, 1992.

Thomsen, Carsten, and Thomas Hundsbæk. "Stormuftien af Egypten: 'Men er I dumme?'" *Politiken*, February 21, 2006.

Tiemersma, Douwe. "'Body-image' and 'Body-schema' in the Existential Phenomenology of Merleau-Ponty." *Journal of the British Society for Phenomenology*, vol. 13, no. 3 (1982), pp. 246–255.

Tønder, Lars. "Subsistent Tolerance: Merleau-Ponty and the Embodiment of Democratic Pluralism." *Culture & Politics*, vol. 1, no. 1 (2006), pp. 39–52.

———. "Toleration Without Tolerance: Enlightenment and the Image of Reason." In *Political Theologies: Public Religions in a Post-Secular World*, edited by Hent de Vries and Lawrence Sullivan. New York: Fordham University Press, 2006.

———. "Humility, Arrogance and the Limitations of Kantian Autonomy: A Response to Rostbøll," *Political Theory*, vol. 39, no. 3 (2011), pp. 378–385.

———. "Spinoza and the Theory of Active Tolerance," *Political Theory* (forthcoming, 2013).

Tuckness, Alex. *Locke and the Legislative Point of View: Toleration, Contested Principles, and the Law*. Princeton: Princeton University Press, 2002.

Tully, James. *An Approach to Political Philosophy: Locke in Contexts*. Cambridge: Cambridge University Press, 1993.

United Nations Educational, Scientific and Cultural Organization. "Declaration of Principles on Tolerance." Reprinted in *Diogenes*, vol. 44: 176 (1996), pp. 207–213.

Vertosick, Frank T. Jr. *Why We Hurt: The Natural History of Pain*. New York: Harcourt, 2000.

Wall, Patrick. *Pain: The Science of Suffering*. New York: Columbia University Press, 2000.

White, Stephen K. *Sustaining Affirmation: The Strengths of Weak Ontology in Political Theory*. Princeton: Princeton University Press, 2000.

———. *The Ethos of a Late-Modern Citizen*. Cambridge, MA: Harvard University Press, 2009.

Whitehead, Alfred N. *The Concept of Nature*. Cambridge: Cambridge University Press, 1920.

Williams, Bernard. "Toleration: An Impossible Virtue?" In *Toleration: An Elusive Virtue*, edited by David Heyd. Princeton: Princeton University Press, 1996.

Wingrove, Elizabeth Rose. *Rousseau's Republican Romance*. Princeton: Princeton University Press, 2000.

Winter, Bronwyn. *Hijab and the Republic: Uncovering the French Headscarf Debate*. Syracuse, NY: Syracuse University Press, 2008.

Wittenberg, David. *Philosophy, Revision, Critique: Rereading Practices in Heidegger, Nietzsche, and Emerson*. Stanford: Stanford University Press, 2001.

Wolin, Sheldon. *Politics and Vision: Continuity and Innovation in Western Political Thought*. Expanded Version. Princeton: Princeton University Press, 2004.

Zagorin, Perez. *How the Idea of Religious Toleration Came to the West*. Princeton: Princeton University Press, 2003.

Žižek, Slavoj. "Tolerance and the Intolerable: Enjoyment, Ethics and Event." In Glyn Daly, *Conversations with Žižek*. Cambridge, MA: Polity Press, 2004.

Zuckert, Michael. *Launching the Liberal Tradition: On Lockean Political Philosophy*. Lawrence: University Press of Kansas, 2002.

INDEX

Kant, Immanuel 56, 57, 59–61, 149n21
"An Answer to the Question: What Is
Enlightenment?" 57
*Anthropology from a Pragmatic Point of
View* 62–4, 66
Critique of Judgment 64
and Locke 66–7, 70–1
*Observations on the Feeling of the
Beautiful and the Sublime* 64
on pain 62–6
on sublime 12, 47, 64–5, 69, 70–1,
75, 150n42
see also neo-Kantianism

liberalism 5–6, 12, 30, 56, 60, 88, 90; *see
also* Kant, Immanuel; Locke, John;
Mill, John Stewart; Rawls, John
Locke, John
doctrine of indifference 68–9, 70–1,
73, 75, 152n52; see also *adiaphor*
*An Essay Concerning Human
Understanding* 66–7
Letter Concerning Toleration 32, 67–8
Two Tracts on Government 67
Lockean liberalism 26, 30
Lockean tolerance 31, 60, 66–71

March, Andrew 145n43
Marcuse, Herbert 20, 89–90, 96, 100,
106–7, 139n3
on tolerance 79–81, 86, 106; *see also*
tolerance, active and passive
Marx, Karl 26, 135
masochism 21, 44, 75, 96–9, 101, 105,
120; *see also* Sacher-Masoch,
Leopold von
Massumi, Brian 164n45
McClure, Kirstie 152n51
Merleau-Ponty, Maurice 12, 47, 70–1,
119–20, 165n54
account of perception 111, 120–1,
123, 127
and the sensorial orientation to
politics 119–26
tolerance of the incomplete 110–11,
118, 120, 122, 124, 125
see also embodiment; perception;
phenomenology
Mill, John Stewart 27, 44–6, 47, 49
and Nietzsche, Friedrich 47, 49

on pain 44–5, 66, 82, 94
see also harm
mind and body 6, 16–17, 27, 141n15,
153n64, 157n25
dualism of 13, 14, 16, 30, 68, 72,
127
see also body
molecular level of political life 16–17,
46; *see also* Deleuze, Gilles, and
Guattari, Felix
morality vs. ethics 7, 28; *see also* Forst,
Rainer
Muhammad (Prophet) 8, 108, 112,
116–17, 122, 132; *see also* Danish
cartoon war; Denmark, Muslims
in; Islam, prohibition of images in;
Jyllands–Posten cartoons
multiculturalism 2, 12, 29, 31

nature-culture dualism 16, 30, 44–5
neo-Kantianism 7–8, 60–2, 76–7, 115,
126–9
notion of reason 26, 38
see also Kant, Immanuel
Nietzsche, Friedrich 12, 36, 39, 49, 50,
67, 101, 110
The Gay Science 140n6
On the Genealogy of Morality 70
Human, All too Human 140n6
on pain 44–7, 63–4, 66, 82, 94
ressentiment 25, 41, 47, 113, 130
Will to Power 49
nihilism 8, 30
and subjectivism 20, 26, 27, 33, 42,
48, 50
not-being-at-home, *see* Heidegger,
Martin; *Unheimlichkeit*

objection component 7, 38, 48, 82;
see also acceptance component;
circumstances of tolerance
overlapping consensus 28, 31, 38, 55,
115–16; *see also* Rawls, John

pain 4–5, 6–11, 43–9, 62–6, 90–5
affirmation of 55, 97–8
in contemporary democratic
theory 62–3, 73–4
continuum of 47–9, 94–5, 121–2; *see
also* Nietzsche, Friedrich

"On Ill–Health and Endurance of
    Suffering" 84
  see also Stoicism; *tolerāntia*
sensibility 21, 55, 70, 99–101, 118,
    122–6, 136
sensorial orientation to politics 13–18,
    44, 81–2, 102–3, 126–30, 138; *see
    also* embodiment; phenomenology;
    Spinoza, Baruch de
sensorial reasoning 5, 111, 126–32,
    133; *see also* reasoning
sensorium 14–19, 42–5, 27–30,
    33–5, 66, 69, 85; *see also*
    embodiment; perception;
    phenomenology
sentient beings 14–17, 18, 126
sexuality 6, 14, 26, 38, 63
Shakespeare, William 65, 134
shame 39–41, 62, 137; *see also* Rawls,
    John
social contract 18–19, 75, 96, 137
somatophobia 25, 30–1, 33–5, 43, 47
  as a staging of the sensorium 28, 31,
    35, 42, 51, 61
  see also disavowal
Sophocles 88, 135
Spinoza, Baruch de 79–81, 81–3, 85–6,
    88–91, 92–3, 98
  active tolerance 81, 89–90, 110–11
  affect 12, 91–2, 110
  Ethics 80, 91
  force field of tolerance 84–5, 87–8
  see also hilaritas; sensorial orientation
    to politics; tragic condition of
    Being; *tristitia*
Stoicism 6, 12, 21, 46, 89, 96, 157n24;
    see also convenientia; Seneca, Lucius
    Annaeus
sublime 12, 47, 64–5, 69–70, 75; *see also*
    Kant, Immanuel

Taylor, Charles 29–30, 31
temporality 46, 54, 55, 71
things indifferent, see *adiaphor*; Locke,
    John
time, linear progression of 55, 65
tolerance
  active 3–6, 11–12, 19–22, 104–7,
    109–11, 118–19

as endurance of pain 4–8, 11–12,
    20–2, 35, 74–6, 99–100
  force field 82–3, 85, 87–8
  history of 32, 53–4, 60–1
  of the incomplete 1–3, 32–3, 42–3,
    50–1, 99, 115–17; *see also*
    Merleau-Ponty, Maurice
  link with pain 4, 8, 17–18, 65; *see also*
    pain
  meaning of 4, 23, 140n7
  passive 3, 11, 80, 82, 90
  plurality of 70, 80
  power of 87–8, 90
  sensorial character of 79–80, 105
tolerance, models of
  reasonable 20, 26–8, 29, 31, 57
  recognition 29–31; *see also* Taylor,
    Charles
  superior 31–5
tolerāntia 12, 47, 84, 89, 140n7; *see also*
    Diogenes the Cynic; Seneca, Lucius
    Annaeus; Spinoza, Baruch de
tolerator and tolerated 2–4, 11, 19,
    23–5, 31–5, 41, 50, 82–4, 89–90,
    120
torture 6, 21, 38, 81, 84–5, 134,
    156n15
  critique of 102–6; *see also* Scarry,
    Elaine
  justification of 96, 102
tragic condition of Being 88, 91, 93–5,
    157n29; *see also* pain; Spinoza,
    Baruch de
tristitia 91–2; *see also* Spinoza, Baruch de

UNESCO 23–4, 26, 29–30, 32, 34, 51;
    see also Declaration of Principles
    on Tolerance
Unheimlichkeit 9, 10; *see also* Heidegger,
    Martin; pain
United Nations 23–4, 42, 104

war on terror 21, 102, 104, 126, 128,
    134
White, Stephen 155n8
Williams, Bernard 8, 42
Wingrove, Elizabeth 75, 96
wounded attachment 12, 47, 94–5; *see
    also* Brown, Wendy